PATHWAYS

Listening, Speaking, and Critical Thinking

3

Becky Tarver Chase
Kristin L. Johannsen
Keith S. Folse / Series Consultant

Rolling green hills in Washington state, USA.

NATIONAL GEOGRAPHIC LEARNING

HEINLE
CENGAGE Learning

Australia • Brazil • Japan • Korea • Mexico • Singapore • Spain • United Kingdom • United States

Pathways 3
Listening, Speaking, and Critical Thinking
Becky Tarver Chase
Kristin L. Johannsen
Keith S. Folse / Series Consultant

Publisher: Sherrise Roehr

Executive Editor: Laura Le Dréan

Acquisitions Editor: Tom Jefferies

Senior Development Editor: Mary Whittemore

Director of Global Marketing: Ian Martin

Director of U.S. Marketing: Jim McDonough

Marketing Manager: Caitlin Thomas

Marketing Manager: Katie Kelley

Marketing Coordinator: Jide Iruka

Director of Content and Media Production:
  Michael Burggren

Content Project Manager: Daisy Sosa

Manufacturing Manager: Marcia Locke

Manufacturing Buyer: Marybeth Hennebury

Production Intern: Geena Hillman

Cover Design: Page 2 LLC

Cover Image: Terry W. Eggers/CORBIS

Interior Design: Page 2 LLC

Composition: Nesbitt Graphics, Inc.

Library of Congress Control Number: 2011906626

International Student Edition:

ISBN-13: 978-1-111-29730-5

ISBN-10: 1-111-29730-4

U.S. Edition:

ISBN-13: 978-1-111-39865-1

ISBN-10: 1-111-39865-8

National Geographic Learning
20 Channel Center Street
Boston, MA 02210
USA

Cengage Learning is a leading provider of customized learning solutions with office locations around the globe, including Singapore, the United Kingdom, Australia, Mexico, Brazil, and Japan.

Cengage Learning products are represented in Canada by Nelson Education, Ltd.

Visit National Geographic Learning online at **elt.heinle.com**

Visit our corporate website at **www.cengage.com**

Printed in the United States of America
7   18 17 16

The authors and publisher would like to thank the following reviewers:

UNITED STATES **Adrianne Aiko Thompson,** Miami Dade College, Miami, Florida; **Gokhan Alkanat,** Auburn University at Montgomery, Alabama; **Nikki Ashcraft,** Shenandoah University, Virginia; **Karin Avila-John,** University of Dayton, Ohio; **Shirley Baker,** Alliant International University, California; **John Baker,** Oakland Community College, Michigan; **Evina Baquiran Torres,** Zoni Language Centers, New York; **Michelle Bell,** University of South Florida, Florida; **Nancy Boyer,** Golden West College, California; **Carol Brutza,** Gateway Community College, Connecticut; **Sarah Camp,** University of Kentucky, Center for ESL, Kentucky; **Maria Caratini,** Eastfield College, Texas; **Ana Maria Cepero,** Miami Dade College, Florida; **Daniel Chaboya,** Tulsa Community College, Oklahoma; **Patricia Chukwueke,** English Language Institute – UCSD Extension, California; **Julia A. Correia,** Henderson State University, Connecticut; **Suzanne Crisci,** Bunker Hill Community College, Massachusetts; **Katie Crowder,** University of North Texas, Texas; **Lynda Dalgish,** Concordia College, New York; **Jeffrey Diluglio,** Center for English Language and Orientation Programs: Boston University, Massachusetts; **Tim DiMatteo,** Southern New Hampshire University, New Hampshire; **Scott Dirks,** Kaplan International Center at Harvard Square, Massachusetts; **Margo Downey,** Center for English Language and Orientation Programs: Boston University, Massachusetts; **John Drezek,** Richland College, Texas; **Anwar El-Issa,** Antelope Valley College, California; **Anrisa Fannin,** The International Education Center at Diablo Valley College, California; **Jennie Farnell,** University of Connecticut, American Language Program, Connecticut; **Mark Fisher,** Lone Star College, Texas; **Celeste Flowers,** University of Central Arkansas, Arkansas; **John Fox,** English Language Institute, Georgia; **Pradel R. Frank,** Miami Dade College, Florida; **Sally Gearheart,** Santa Rosa Jr. College, California; **Karen Grubbs,** ELS Language Centers, Florida; **Joni Hagigeorges,** Salem State University, Massachusetts; **Valerie Heming,** University of Central Missouri, Missouri; **Mary Hill,** North Shore Community College, Massachusetts; **Harry L. Holden,** North Lake College, Texas; **Ingrid Holm,** University of Massachusetts Amherst, Massachusetts; **Marianne Hsu Santelli,** Middlesex County College, New Jersey; **Katie Hurter,** Lone Star College – North Harris, Texas; **Justin Jernigan,** Georgia Gwinnett College, Georgia; **Barbara A. Jonckheere,** American Language Institute at California State University, Long Beach, California; **Susan Jordan,** Fisher College, Massachusetts; **Maria Kasparova,** Bergen Community College, New Jersey; **Gail Kellersberger,** University of Houston-Downtown, Texas; **Christina Kelso,** Austin Peay State University, Tennessee; **Daryl Kinney,** Los Angeles City College, California; **Leslie Kosel Eckstein,** Hillsborough Community College, Florida; **Beth Kozbial Ernst,** University of Wisconsin-Eau Claire, Wisconsin; **Jennifer Lacroix,** Center for English Language and Orientation Programs: Boston University, Massachusetts; **Stuart Landers,** Missouri State University, Missouri; **Margaret V. Layton,** University of Nevada, Reno Intensive English Language Center, Nevada; **Heidi Lieb,** Bergen Community College, New Jersey; **Kerry Linder,** Language Studies International New York, New York; **Jenifer Lucas-Uygun,** Passaic County Community College, New Jersey; **Alison MacAdams,** Approach International Student Center, Massachusetts; **Craig Machado,** Norwalk Community College, Connecticut; **Andrew J. MacNeill,** Southwestern College, California; **Melanie A. Majeski,** Naugatuck Valley Community College, Connecticut; **Wendy Maloney,** College of DuPage, Illinois; **Chris Mares,** University of Maine – Intensive English Institute, Maine; **Josefina Mark,** Union County College, New Jersey; **Connie Mathews,** Nashville State Community College, Tennessee; **Bette Matthews,** Mid-Pacific Institute, Hawaii; **Marla McDaniels Heath,** Norwalk Community College, Connecticut; **Kimberly McGrath Moreira,** University of Miami, Florida; **Sara McKinnon,** College of Marin, California; **Christine Mekkaoui,** Pittsburg State University, Kansas; **Holly A. Milkowart,** Johnson County Community College, Kansas; **Warren Mosher,** University of Miami, Florida; **Lukas Murphy,** Westchester Community College, New York; **Elena Nehrebecki,** Hudson Community College, New Jersey; **Bjarne Nielsen,** Central Piedmont Community College, North Carolina; **David Nippoldt,** Reedley College, California; **Lucia Parsley,** Virginia Commonwealth University, Virginia; **Wendy Patriquin,** Parkland College, Illinois; **Marion Piccolomini,** Communicate With Ease, LTD, Pennsylvania; **Carolyn Prager,** Spanish-American Institute, New York; **Eileen Prince,** Prince Language Associates Incorporated, Massachusetts; **Sema Pulak,** Texas A & M University, Texas; **James T. Raby,** Clark University, Massachusetts; **Anouchka Rachelson,** Miami-Dade College, Florida; **Lynn Ramage Schaefer,** University of Central Arkansas, Arkansas; **Sherry Rasmussen,** DePaul University, Illinois; **Amy Renehan,** University of Washington, Washington; **Esther Robbins,** Prince George's Community College, Pennsylvania; **Helen Roland,** Miami Dade College, Florida; **Linda Roth,** Vanderbilt University English Language Center, Tennessee; **Janine Rudnick,** El Paso Community College, Texas; **Rita Rutkowski Weber,** University of Wisconsin – Milwaukee, Wisconsin; **Elena Sapp,** INTO Oregon State University, Oregon; **Margaret Shippey,** Miami Dade College, Florida; **Lisa Sieg,** Murray State University, Kentucky; **Alison Stamps,** ESL Center at Mississippi State University, Mississippi; **Peggy Street,** ELS Language Centers, Miami, Florida; **Lydia Streiter,** York College Adult Learning Center, New York; **Nicholas Taggart,** Arkansas State University, Arkansas; **Marcia Takacs,** Coastline Community College, California; **Tamara Teffeteller,** University of California Los Angeles, American Language Center, California; **Rebecca Toner,** English Language Programs, University of Pennsylvania, Pennsylvania; **William G. Trudeau,** Missouri Southern State University, Missouri; **Troy Tucker,** Edison State College, Florida; **Maria Vargas-O'Neel,** Miami Dade College, Florida; **Amerca Vazquez,** Miami Dade College, Florida; **Alison Vinande,** Modesto Junior College, California; **Christie Ward,** Intensive English Language Program, Central Connecticut State University, Connecticut; **Colin S. Ward,** Lone Star College-North Harris, Texas; **Denise L. Warner,** Lansing Community College, Michigan; **Wendy Wish-Bogue,** Valencia Community College, Florida; **Cissy Wong,** Sacramento City College, California; **Kimberly Yoder,** Kent State University, ESL Center, Ohio.

ASIA **Teoh Swee Ai,** Universiti Teknologi Mara, Malaysia; **Nor Azni Abdullah,** Universiti Teknologi Mara, Malaysia; **Thomas E. Bieri,** Nagoya College, Japan; **Paul Bournhonesque,** Seoul National University of Technology, Korea; **Michael C. Cheng,** National Chengchi University, Taiwan; **Fu-Dong Chiou,** National Taiwan University, Taiwan; **Derek Currie,** Korea University, Sejong Institute of Foreign Language Studies, Korea; **Christoph A. Hafner,** City University of Hong Kong, Hong Kong; **Wenhua Hsu,** I-Shou University, Taiwan; **Helen Huntley,** Hanoi University, Vietnam; **Rob Higgens,** Ritsumeikan University, Japan; **Shih Fan Kao,** JinWen University of Science and Technology, Taiwan; **Ikuko Kashiwabara,** Osaka Electro-Communication University, Japan; **Richard S. Lavin,** Prefecturla University of Kumamoto, Japan; **Mike Lay,** American Institute, Cambodia; **Byoung-Kyo Lee,** Yonsei University, Korea; **Lin Li,** Capital Normal University, China; **Hudson Murrell,** Baiko Gakuin University, Japan; **Keiichi Narita,** Niigata University, Japan; **Huynh Thi Ai Nguyen,** Vietnam USA Society, Vietnam; **James Pham,** IDP Phnom Penh, Cambodia; **Duncan Rose,** British Council, Singapore; **Simone Samuels,** The Indonesia Australia Language Foundation Jakarta, Indonesia; **Wang Songmei,** Beijing Institute of Education Faculty, China; **Chien-Wen Jenny Tseng,** National Sun Yat-Sen University, Taiwan; **Hajime Uematsu,** Hirosaki University, Japan

AUSTRALIA **Susan Austin,** University of South Australia; **Joanne Cummins,** Swinburne College; **Pamela Humphreys,** Griffith University

LATIN AMERICA AND THE CARIBBEAN **Ramon Aguilar,** Universidad Tecnológica de Hermosillo, México; **Livia de Araujo Donnini Rodrigues,** University of São Paolo, Brazil; **Cecilia Avila,** Universidad de Xapala, México; **Beth Bartlett,** Centro Cultural Colombo Americano, Cali, Colombia; **Raúl Billini,** Colegio Loyola, Dominican Republic; **Nohora Edith Bryan,** Universidad de La Sabana, Colombia; **Raquel Hernández Cantú,** Instituto Tecnológico de Monterrey, Mexico; **Millie Commander,** Inter American University of Puerto Rico, Puerto Rico; **Edwin Marín-Arroyo,** Instituto Tecnológico de Costa Rica; **Rosario Mena,** Instituto Cultural Dominico-Americano, Dominican Republic; **Elizabeth Ortiz Lozada,** COPEI-COPOL English Institute, Ecuador; **Gilberto Rios Zamora,** Sinaloa State Language Center, Mexico; **Patricia Veciños,** El Instituto Cultural Argentino Norteamericano, Argentina

MIDDLE EAST AND NORTH AFRICA **Tom Farkas,** American University of Cairo, Egypt; **Ghada Hozayen,** Arab Academy for Science, Technology and Maritime Transport, Egypt; **Barbara R. Reimer,** CERTESL, UAE University; **Jodi Lefort,** Sultan Qaboos University

Dedicated to Kristin L. Johannsen, whose love for the world's cultures and concern for the world's environment were an inspiration to family, friends, students, and colleagues.

Scope and Sequence

Unit	Academic Pathways	Vocabulary	Listening Skills
1 **Gender and Society** *Page 1* **Academic Track:** Interdisciplinary	**Lesson A:** Listening to a Lecture Giving a Presentation about a Name **Lesson B:** Listening to a Conversation between Classmates Participating in a Mini-Debate	Understanding meaning from context Using new vocabulary in a survey Using new vocabulary to give reasons	Note-taking Listening for main ideas Listening for details **Pronunciation:** *Can/can't*
2 **Reproducing Life** *Page 21* **Academic Track:** Life Science	**Lesson A:** Listening to a Conversation about a Documentary Discussing Species Conservation **Lesson B:** Listening to a Conversation between Classmates Creating and Presenting a Group Plan	Understanding meaning from context Using new vocabulary to complete an article Understanding suffixes Using a dictionary to learn new words	Listening for main ideas Listening for details **Pronunciation:** Stress patterns before suffixes Emphasis on key words
3 **Human Migration** *Page 41* **Academic Track:** Sociology	**Lesson A:** Listening to a PowerPoint Lecture Discussing Case Studies **Lesson B:** Listening to a Small Group Discussion Giving a Group Presentation	Understanding meaning from context Using a dictionary	Predicting content Listening for main ideas Listening for details **Pronunciation:** Fast speech
4 **Fascinating Planet** *Page 61* **Academic Track:** Earth Science	**Lesson A:** Listening to a Documentary Explaining Causes and Effects **Lesson B:** Listening to an Informal Conversation Doing and Discussing Internet Research	Using context clues Choosing the correct word	Tuning out distractions Taking notes on a documentary **Pronunciation:** Intonation for choices and lists
5 **Making a Living, Making a Difference** *Page 81* **Academic Track:** Economics/Business	**Lesson A:** Listening to a Guest Speaker Making Comparisons **Lesson B:** Listening to a Class Question and Answer Session Giving a Presentation Based on Internet Research	Understanding meaning from context Using new vocabulary in a conversation	Understanding a speaker's purpose Taking notes on a lecture **Pronunciation:** Contractions

Grammar	Speaking Skills	Viewing	Critical Thinking Skills
Indefinite pronouns Indefinite pronouns and pronoun usage	Talking about rules and expectations Using inclusive language Talking about rules and expectations in the past **Student-to-Student:** Greeting a friend after a long time **Presentation Skills:** Preparing notes for speaking	**Video:** *Wodaabe* Note-taking while viewing Viewing for details	Interpreting information from a map Expressing and explaining opinions Relating information to personal experience Using a graphic organizer Arguing an opinion using reasons **Critical Thinking Focus:** Evaluating reasons
Adjective clauses Making suggestions	Explaining a process Making suggestions **Student-to-Student:** Asking for repetition **Presentation Skills:** Using specific details	**Video:** *Turtle Excluder* Understanding main ideas Taking notes while viewing	Identifying information Using new vocabulary in a discussion Organizing ideas for a presentation Analyzing information for relevance Preparing a research study **Critical Thinking Focus:** Judging the relevance of information
Adjectives with *enough, not enough,* and *too* *Enough, not enough, and too* + nouns Using the past continuous tense	Asking for reasons Telling a personal history **Student-to-Student:** Asking sensitive questions **Presentation Skills:** Using visuals	**Video:** *Turkish Germany* Viewing for general concepts Viewing for specific information	Interpreting information on a map Understanding visuals (a line graph) Applying new grammar in discussions Proposing solutions to a problem Assessing information **Critical Thinking Focus:** Analyzing information
The simple past with the past continuous tense *So* + adjective + *that*	Talking about historical events Talking about causes and effects **Student-to-Student:** Responding to suggestions **Presentation Skills:** Making eye contact	**Video:** *The Giant's Causeway* Viewing for numbers Taking notes in a T-chart while viewing	Recognizing vocabulary words Practicing using words and phrases to indicate causes and effects Categorizing information using a T-chart Deducing meaning from context Synthesizing information from the unit **Critical Thinking Focus:** Using graphic organizers
Making comparisons with *as . . . as* Indirect questions	Using numbers and statistics Using indirect questions **Student-to-Student:** Showing interest in what a speaker is saying **Presentation Skills:** Practicing and timing your presentation	**Video:** *The Business of Cranberries* Viewing for general concepts Viewing for specific information	Interpreting information from a chart Demonstrating comprehension of information from a listening Planning a presentation Formulating sentences based on visuals Evaluating different charity organizations **Critical Thinking Focus:** Identifying the speaker's purpose

Scope and Sequence

Unit	Academic Pathways	Vocabulary	Listening Skills
6 A World of Words *Page 101* **Academic Track:** Literature/Humanities	**Lesson A:** Listening to a Lecture Discussing Fairy Tales **Lesson B:** Listening to a Class Discussion Session Giving a Summary	Understanding meaning from context Using new vocabulary to ask and answer questions	Understanding sidetracks Listening for main ideas Listening for details **Pronunciation:** Review of question intonation
7 After Oil *Page 121* **Academic Track:** Interdisciplinary	**Lesson A:** Listening to a Current Affairs Club Meeting Giving an Informal Presentation **Lesson B:** Listening to a Conversation between Students Developing Materials for a Promotional Campaign	Understanding meaning from context Using new vocabulary to complete a conversation	Listening for main ideas Listening for details Making inferences **Pronunciation:** Reduced /h/ in pronouns
8 Traditional and Modern Medicine *Page 141* **Academic Track:** Health and Medicine	**Lesson A:** Listening to a Conversation in a Professor's Office Evaluating Claims about Public Health **Lesson B:** Listening to a Conversation between Friends Preparing and Presenting a Group Summary	Understanding meaning from context Using a dictionary	Asking questions while listening Listening for details Making inferences **Pronunciation:** Linking vowels with /y/ and /w/ sounds
9 The Legacy of Ancient Civilizations *Page 161* **Academic Track:** Anthropology/History	**Lesson A:** Listening to a Lecture Discussing Timelines **Lesson B:** Listening to a Discussion about a Group Project Giving a Group Presentation	Using a dictionary Understanding meaning from context	Using context clues Listening for details **Pronunciation:** Voicing and syllable length
10 Emotions and Personality *Page 181* **Academic Track:** Psychology	**Lesson A:** Listening to a Radio Interview Conducting a Survey **Lesson B:** Listening to an Informal Conversation Assessing the Credibility of a News Article	Understanding meaning from context Using new vocabulary in small-group discussions	Listening for main ideas Listening for details **Pronunciation:** Intonation for thought groups

Independent Student Handbook

Page 201

Grammar	Speaking Skills	Viewing	Critical Thinking Skills
The simple past vs. the present perfect Negative questions	Making sidetracks and returning to a topic Asking negative questions **Student-to-Student:** Staying neutral **Presentation Skills:** Giving a summary	**Video:** *Sleepy Hollow* Viewing for general concepts Viewing for specific information	Interpreting information on a timeline Discussing personal preferences Applying information from notes Analyzing the use of different tenses Tell a partner about a text **Critical Thinking Focus:** Selecting relevant information
Reported speech Changing time expressions in reported speech Future time with adverb clauses	Reporting what someone has said Making judgements about the future **Student-to-Student:** Softening assertions **Presentation Skills:** Using an appropriate volume	**Video:** *Canadian Oil Sands* Relate video to information in unit View for specific information	Understanding visuals Organizing information based on diagrams Analyzing information from a pie chart Arguing a point of view Developing materials for a promotional plan **Critical Thinking Focus:** Considering viewpoint and bias
Real conditionals Quantifiers with specific and general nouns	Discussing health Making suggestions for home remedies **Student-to-Student:** Ending a conversation **Presentation Skills:** Looking up while speaking	**Video:** *Wild Health* Predicting content Relating video content to personal experiences and ideas	Relating content to personal experience Restating information from notes Using new information in a discussion Inferring meaning from a conversation Contrasting two people **Critical Thinking Focus:** Evaluating claims
The past unreal conditional Comparatives: *The –er, the -er*	Discussing timelines Discussing conclusions **Student-to-Student:** Interrupting and holding the floor **Presentation Skills:** Supporting your co-presenters	**Video:** *Lost Temple of the Mayans* Applying prior knowledge to video content Viewing to confirm information	Identifying information in visuals Categorizing new vocabulary Using new grammar and vocabulary Selecting a research topic Organizing a group presentation **Critical Thinking Focus:** Drawing conclusions
The past perfect tense *Used to + verb vs. be used to + noun*	Discussing past events Discussing study habits **Student-to-Student:** Expressing emotions **Presentation Skills:** Role-playing	**Video:** *Sigmund Freud* Viewing for specific information Relating video to information in the unit	Relating content to personal experience Using new vocabulary in a personality test Explaining answers to questions Surveying classmates about their thoughts and feelings Planning a role-play presentation **Critical Thinking Focus:** Assessing the credibility of sources

Each unit consists of two lessons which include the following sections:

Building Vocabulary
Using Vocabulary
Developing Listening Skills
Exploring Spoken English
Speaking (called "Engage" in Lesson B)

An **academic pathway** is clearly labeled for learners, starting with formal listening (e.g., lectures) and moving to a more informal context (e.g., a conversation between students in a study group).

The **"Exploring the Theme"** section provides a visual introduction to the unit and encourages learners to think critically and share ideas about the unit topic.

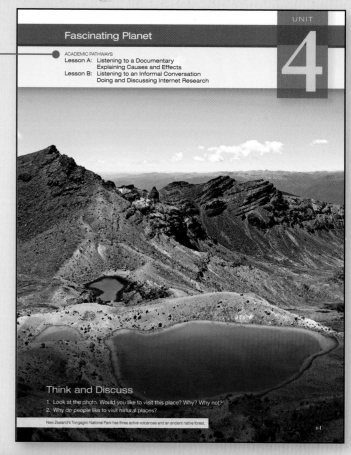

UNIT 4

Fascinating Planet

ACADEMIC PATHWAYS
Lesson A: Listening to a Documentary
Explaining Causes and Effects
Lesson B: Listening to an Informal Conversation
Doing and Discussing Internet Research

Think and Discuss

1. Look at the photo. Would you like to visit this place? Why? Why not?
2. Why do people like to visit natural places?

New Zealand's Tongagiro National Park has three active volcanoes and an ancient native forest.

61

Exploring the Theme:
Fascinating Planet

Look at the photos and read the captions. Then discuss the questions.

1. What do you find interesting or surprising about the information on these pages?
2. What do you think the environment and climate are like in the Tsingy?
3. What are some of the national parks in your country? What makes them special?

Rare Species in the Tsingy

The dry upper parts of the Tsingy are the favorite places for some animals. This dragonfly is cooling itself.

The *Pachypodium* plant does not need much water, so it does well in the highest regions of the Tsingy.

The Tsingy de Bemaraha National Park in Madagascar

The Tsingy de Bemaraha National Park in Madagascar is a very unusual place. Its sharp pointed peaks are made from eroded limestone. The high peaks and low canyons here are home to many unusual species of animals and plants, such as the white Decken's sifaka lemur (shown on the left). Some of the species are so rare that scientists have not yet identified them.

Source: African Natural Heritage

62 | UNIT 4

FASCINATING PLANET | 63

Key academic and high-frequency vocabulary is introduced, practiced, and expanded throughout each unit. Lessons A and B each present and practice 10 terms.

Critical thinking activities are integrated in every unit encouraging continuous engagement in developing academic skills.

A **"Developing Listening Skills"** section follows a before, during, and after approach to give learners the tools necessary to master listening skills for a variety of contexts.

Note-taking activities encourage learners to listen for and consolidate key information, reinforcing the language and allowing learners to think critically about the information they hear.

USING VOCABULARY

D | Discussion. Work with a partner. Discuss the questions.

1. Do you think Jiuzhaigou will stay clean and beautiful with 2 million tourists visiting every year? Why, or why not?
2. What do you think park officials could do to keep the park clean and beautiful?

E | Meaning from Context. Read about glaciers and circle the correct word choice. Then listen and check your answers.

> The lakes in Jiuzhaigou National Park were (formed/dissolved) by glaciers—huge bodies of ice. Today there are glaciers high up in some mountains, but at other times in the earth's history colder temperatures allowed glaciers to exist in much larger areas.
>
> As glaciers grow and move, they push dirt and (stone/rare) along with them. This material, along with the ice itself, is (lack/sharp) enough to (erode/protect) the land where the glaciers move. In this way, hills can become flat land, and flat land can become holes. Later, when temperatures become warmer and the glaciers melt, lakes are the result.
>
> Glacial ice can become water in another way, too. At the bottom edge of a glacier, (cracks/forms) can develop and large pieces of ice can fall into the water below. These pieces of ice then melt and become part of the body of water.

In British Columbia, Canada, a helicopter approaches the bottom edge of a glacier and the lake that it has formed.

F | Discussion. Work with a partner. Discuss the questions.

1. How is climate change affecting the world's glaciers?
2. How do changes to glaciers affect the world in general?

G | Critical Thinking. Form a group with two or three other students and discuss the questions.

1. National parks are rare in some countries and common in others. Which is true in your country?
2. Jiuzhaigou has no lack of tourists. What do you think is the greater benefit of this tourism: the money spent by tourists, or the love and respect for nature tourists feel when they visit the park?
3. The beautiful mountains and lakes in Jiuzhaigou took millions of years to form. How long do you think it would take for human beings to have a major effect on them?
4. Worldwide, there is a limited amount of money and resources for the protection of rare animals such as panda bears. How should people decide which species are worth protecting?

FASCINATING PLANET | 65

LESSON A DEVELOPING LISTENING SKILLS

Before Listening

A | Look at the diagram showing how the Tsingy de Bemaraha was formed. Then write the sentence letters in the correct place on the diagram.

a. More water flows into the caves¹ and enlarges them.
b. Cracks form in the top of the limestone.
c. The tops of some caves collapse, forming larger caves.
d. Rain dissolves the top of the limestone and forms sharp points.
e. Water flows into the cracks and begins to form small caves.
f. The tops of other caves collapse, the water runs out, and deep canyons² are formed.

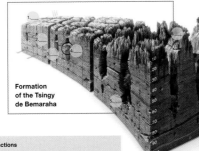
Formation of the Tsingy de Bemaraha

Tuning Out Distractions

In this lesson, you will hear a conversation and part of a television documentary about the Tsingy de Bemaraha. In the real world, there can be distractions while you're trying to listen. A door opens and closes when a student enters a lecture late. A telephone rings during a job interview. Someone talks loudly while you're watching a movie. In each case, your ability to tune out the distraction and concentrate will help you to understand more of what you're listening to.

B | Listen to a conversation in a coffee shop and try to tune out the distractions. Then choose the correct word or phrase to complete each statement below.

1. The woman learned about Tsingy de Bemaraha from a _____.
   a. lecture   b. TV show   c. magazine article
2. The woman's friend asks about the _____ in Tsingy de Bemaraha.
   a. canyons   b. limestone   c. lemurs
3. The woman mentions _____ night.
   a. Tuesday   b. Wednesday   c. Thursday
4. The woman's friend answers the phone when her _____ calls her.
   a. sister   b. daughter   c. mother

¹ A **cave** is a large hole in the side of a cliff or under ground.
² A **canyon** is a long, narrow valley with very steep sides.

66 | UNIT 4

Listening: A Documentary

A | Listen to part of a documentary about the Tsingy de Bemaraha. What distractions do you need to tune out?

_____

B | Note-Taking. Listen again and complete the notes.

- Plants, animals protected in Tsingy because ...   1. _____
                                                     2. _____
- Name means, "place where one cannot _____"
- Walking into Tsingy difficult because ...   1. _____ (above)
                                              2. _____ (below)

Critical Thinking Focus: Using Graphic Organizers

Using graphic organizers, such as flow charts can help you organize important information in a visual way.

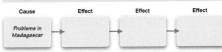
Cause → Effect → Effect → Effect

Problems in Madagascar

C | Using a Graphic Organizer. Listen again and use your notes from exercise **B** to complete the cause and effect flow chart above. (See pages 214-215 of the Independent Student Handbook for more information on using graphic organizers.)

An explorer in one of the deep canyons of the Tsingy de Bemaraha.

After Listening

A | The word because introduces a cause. Read the sentences below and underline the causes. Then circle the effects.

1. The animals in the Tsingy are protected because it's a national park.
2. The peaks in the Tsingy are very sharp because rain has eroded the stone.
3. Because the Tsingy is almost impossible to get to, not many tourists visit it.
4. The caves became larger because the stone that had divided them collapsed.
5. Because there is little money for research, scientists aren't sure how climate change is affecting the Tsingy.

B | Discussion. Compare your sentences with a partner's. Then discuss the question.

1. What do you notice about the placement of the causes and effects in the sentences?

FASCINATING PLANET | 67

Grammar

A | Prior Knowledge. Read each sentence and answer the questions that follow.

1. At two o'clock, Olaf was reading the newspaper.
   How much time does it usually take for a person to read a newspaper?
   What time do you think Olaf started reading? What time did he finish?
2. Teresa fell while we were learning a new dance step.
   Did Teresa fall before, after, or during the dance lesson?

The Simple Past Tense with The Past Continuous Tense

We use the past continuous tense to talk about something that was in progress at a certain time in the past.
   *In the spring of 2007, I **was doing** research in Bolivia.*

To talk about something that happened while another event was in progress in the past, we can use the simple past tense.
   *When I **found** my group, the tour guide **was talking** about glaciers.*

I found
my group   now

The tour guide was talking.

The word *while* often introduces a clause with the past continuous tense.
   *We **saw** several kinds of birds **while** we were **walking** in the national park.*

The word *when* often introduces a clause with the simple past tense.
   ***When** the lights **went out**, Ronald **was giving** his presentation on penguins.*

A group of eco-tourists in Norway listening to birds.

B | Read each situation. With a partner, say two different sentences about each situation using the simple past with the past continuous.

Example: Between six thirty and seven o'clock last night/you and your family/eat dinner.
The telephone/ring/at six forty-one, six forty-eight, and six fifty-five.

> While we were eating dinner, the telephone rang three times.

> The telephone rang every few minutes while we were eating dinner.

1. In September of last year/you/do research in the Tsingy de Bemaraha.
   You discover a new species of frog.
2. Yesterday at five forty-five in the evening/you/get home from work.
   Yesterday from five o'clock to six o'clock at night/your neighbor/paint the front of her house.
3. Debora/see a bear.
   Debora/hike at the national park.
4. The train/arrive/at seven forty-three.
   From seven forty to seven forty-five/Mitch and Jean/buy tickets at the ticket counter.
5. Last night/we/watch TV.
   The dog/start to bark.

Language Function

Talking about Historical Events

We often use the past continuous and the simple past together when talking about historical events that happened while another event (personal or historical) was in progress.
   *I **was playing** soccer with my brother when the first man **landed** on the moon.*

A | Read about the National World Heritage Program. Then look at each date below and discuss with a partner what was happening in your life or in your country at that time.

> **United Nations Educational, Scientific, and Cultural Organization (UNESCO) World Heritage Program**
>
> The World Heritage program was created by UNESCO as a way to conserve places that have cultural or environmental importance for everyone in the world.

1. 1990 – Tsingy de Bemaraha and Tongariro National Park receive World Heritage status.
2. 1992 – Jiuzhaigou National Park receives World Heritage status.
3. 1993 – Tongariro National Park receives World Heritage status under new criterion.
4. 1997 – Lençóis Maranhenses National Park receives World Heritage status.

Los Glaciares National Park in Argentina became a UNESCO World Heritage site in 1981.

The **"Exploring Spoken English"** section allows students to examine and practice specific grammar points and language functions from the unit while enabling them to sharpen their listening and speaking skills.

Lesson A closes with a **full page of "Speaking" activities** including pair and group work activities, increasing learner confidence when communicating in English.

A variety of activity types simulates the academic classroom where multiple skills must be applied simultaneously for success.

SPEAKING

Explaining Causes and Effects

Causes and Effects

To introduce **causes** you can use *due to*, *because of*, and *since*.
   Due to an increase in tourism, more bus drivers are employed.
   Because of the rise in tourism, the company hired more bus drivers.
   Since there are more tourists, more souvenirs are being sold.

Note: A comma is only needed if the explanatory phrase comes first.
   More souvenirs are being sold ***since*** there are more tourists.

To introduce **effects**, you can use *Therefore*, *As a result*, and *so*.
   Tourists walk on the rock formations. ***Therefore***, some formations have been broken and won't be seen by future generations.
   The park charges an admission fee. ***As a result***, it has enough money to build walkways.
   The park is beautiful, ***so*** many people want to see it.

A | With a partner, look at the flow charts that show the advantages and disadvantages of places having World Heritage status. Then follow the steps below.

1. Choose one chart to talk about. Your partner will talk about the other.
2. Take turns explaining your flow chart to your partner. Practice using words and phrases from the chart at the top of the page.

Chart 1: Advantages

| World Heritage status means more people hear about a national park. | → | More visitors go to the national park each year. |
| More people develop a love of natural places. | | More money is spent in and near the park. |

Chart 2: Disadvantages

| More visitors go to places with World Heritage status. | → | The amount of trash and air pollution in the park increases. |
| The national park isn't a beautiful natural place anymore. | ← | Ecosystems can be damaged by human activities. |

B | Switch roles and explain the other chart to your partner.

C | Critical Thinking. Form a group with two or three other students and discuss the questions.

1. Do you think the advantages of World Heritage status outweigh the disadvantages? Why, or why not?
2. Do you know of any cultural or natural attractions that have been helped by tourism? Damaged by tourism?

● A **"Viewing" section** works as a content-bridge between Lesson A and Lesson B and includes two pages of activities based on a fascinating video from National Geographic.

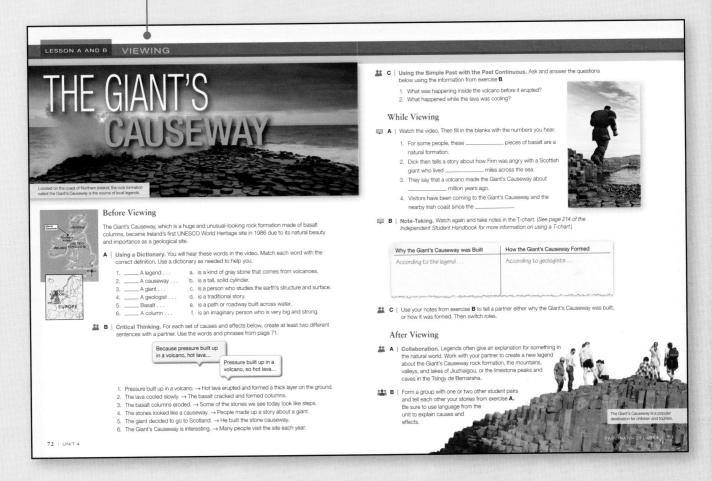

LESSON A AND B   VIEWING

THE GIANT'S CAUSEWAY

Located on the coast of Northern Ireland, the rock formation called the Giant's Causeway is the source of local legends.

Before Viewing

The Giant's Causeway, which is a huge and unusual-looking rock formation made of basalt columns, became Ireland's first UNESCO World Heritage site in 1986 due to its natural beauty and importance as a geological site.

A | **Using a Dictionary.** You will hear these words in the video. Match each word with the correct definition. Use a dictionary as needed to help you.

1. _____ A legend . . .   a. is a kind of gray stone that comes from volcanoes.
2. _____ A causeway . . .   b. is a tall, solid cylinder.
3. _____ A giant . . .   c. is a person who studies the earth's structure and surface.
4. _____ A geologist . . . d. is a traditional story.
5. _____ Basalt . . .   e. is a path or roadway built across water.
6. _____ A column . . .   f. is an imaginary person who is very big and strong.

B | **Critical Thinking.** For each set of causes and effects below, create at least two different sentences with a partner. Use the words and phrases from page 71.

> Because pressure built up in a volcano, hot lava...

> Pressure built up in a volcano, so hot lava...

1. Pressure built up in a volcano. → Hot lava erupted and formed a thick layer on the ground.
2. The lava cooled slowly. → The basalt cracked and formed columns.
3. The basalt columns eroded. → Some of the stones we see today look like steps.
4. The stones looked like a causeway. → People made up a story about a giant.
5. The giant decided to go to Scotland. → He built the stone causeway.
6. The Giant's Causeway is interesting. → Many people visit the site each year.

72 | UNIT 4

C | **Using the Simple Past with the Past Continuous.** Ask and answer the questions below using the information from exercise **B**.

1. What was happening inside the volcano before it erupted?
2. What happened while the lava was cooling?

While Viewing

A | Watch the video. Then fill in the blanks with the numbers you hear.

1. For some people, these _____ pieces of basalt are a natural formation.
2. Dick then tells a story about how Finn was angry with a Scottish giant who lived _____ miles across the sea.
3. They say that a volcano made the Giant's Causeway about _____ million years ago.
4. Visitors have been coming to the Giant's Causeway and the nearby Irish coast since the _____.

B | **Note-Taking.** Watch again and take notes in the T-chart. (See page 214 of the Independent Student Handbook for more information on using a T-chart.)

Why the Giant's Causeway was Built	How the Giant's Causeway Formed
According to the legend . . .	According to geologists . . .

C | Use your notes from exercise **B** to tell a partner either why the Giant's Causeway was built, or how it was formed. Then switch roles.

After Viewing

A | **Collaboration.** Legends often give an explanation for something in the natural world. Work with your partner to create a new legend about the Giant's Causeway rock formation, the mountains, valleys, and lakes of Jiuzhaigou, or the limestone peaks and caves in the Tsingy de Bemaraha.

B | Form a group with one or two other student pairs and tell each other your stories from exercise **A**. Be sure to use language from the unit to explain causes and effects.

The Giant's Causeway is a popular destination for children and tourists.

FASCINATING PLANET | 73

● **A DVD for each level** contains 10 authentic videos from National Geographic specially adapted for English language learners.

HEINLE
CENGAGE Learning

PATHWAYS 3
Listening, Speaking,
and Critical Thinking

ISBN-13: 978-1-111-35042-0
ISBN-10: 1-111-35042-6

DVD
Total Running Time: 30:46

© 2012 Heinle, Cengage Learning. ALL RIGHTS RESERVED.

"Presentation Skills" boxes offer helpful tips and suggestions for successful academic presentations.

An **"Engage" section** challenges learners with an end-of-unit presentation project. Speaking tips are offered for formal and informal group communication, instructing students to interact appropriately in different academic situations.

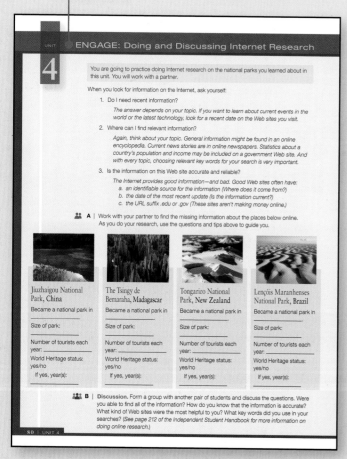

A 19-page **"Independent Student Handbook"** is conveniently located in the back of the book and provides helpful self-study strategies for students to become better independent learners.

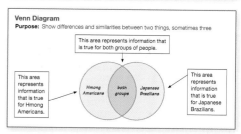

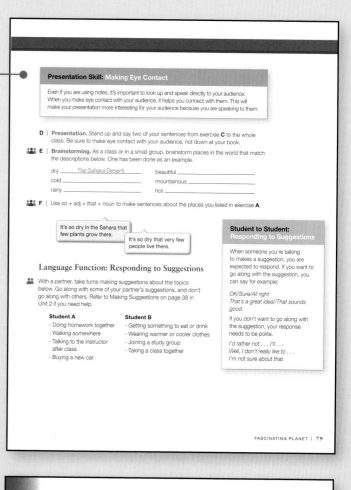

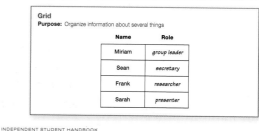

STUDENT AND INSTRUCTOR RESOURCES (for each level)

For the Teacher:

A **Teacher's Guide** is available in an easy-to-use format and includes teacher's notes, expansion activities, and answer keys for activities in the student book.

Perfect for integrating language practice with exciting visuals, **video clips from National Geographic** bring the sights and sounds of our world into the classroom.

The Assessment CD-ROM with **ExamView®** is a test-generating software program with a data bank of ready-made questions designed to allow teachers to assess students quickly and effectively.

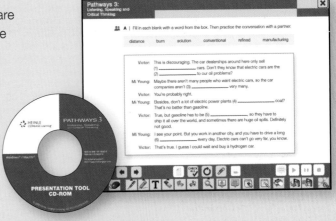

Bringing a new dimension to the language learning classroom, the **Classroom Presentation Tool CD-ROM** makes instruction clearer and learning easier through interactive activities, audio and video clips, and Presentation Worksheets.

For the Student:

The **Student Book** helps students achieve academic success in and outside of the classroom.

Audio CDs contain the audio recordings for the exercises in the student books.

ELT. Powered by MyELT, the **Online Workbook** has both teacher-led and self-study options. It contains 10 National Geographic video clips, supported by interactive, automatically graded activities that practice the skills learned in the student books.

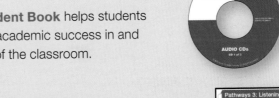

Visit elt.heinle.com/pathways for additional teacher and student resources.

EXPLORE A UNIT   xiii

LISTENING AND TEXT

7: Adapted from, "The King Herself," by Chip Brown: National Geographic Magazine, April 2009, **25:** Adapted from "Every Bird a King," by Tom O'Neill: National Geographic Magazine, September 2009, **29:** Adapted from "Recipe for a Resurrection," by Tom Mueller: National Geographic Magazine, May 2009, **29:** Adapted from "Ox Redux," by Juli Berwald: National Geographic Magazine, July 2010, Conservation Feature, **34:** Adapted from "Love & Lies (Orchids)," by Michael Pollan: National Geographic Magazine, September 2009, **46–47:** Adapted from "The Emptied Prairie," by Charles Bowden: National Geographic Magazine, January 2008, **64–65:** Adapted from "To Paradise, by the Busload: Jiuzhaigou," by Edward Hoagland: National Georgraphic Magazine, March 2009, **69:** Adapted from "Living on a Razor's Edge," by

Neil Shea: National Geographic Magazine, November 2009, **74:** Adapted from, "Between Fire and Ice," by Mel White: National Geographic Magazine, July 2009, **76:** Adapted from, "A Sea of Dunes," by Ronaldo Ribeiro: National Geographic Magazine, July 2010, **86:** Adapted from "India Snake Hunters find Antidote to Joblessness," by Pallava Bagla: National Geographic News, February 2003, **89:** Adapted from "Kudzu Entrepreneurs find Gold in Green Menace," by John Roach: National Geographic News, April 2005, **104:** Adapted from "On the Poet's Trail," by Howard Norman: National Geographic Magazine, February, 2008, **120:** Adapted from "Rare Greek Scroll Found With Egyptian Mummy," by Lara Suziedelis Bogle: National Geographic News October 28, 2002, **124:** Adapted from "Tapped Out," by Paul Roberts: National Geographic Magazine, June 2008, **144:** Adapted from "Nature's RX," by Joel Swerdlow: nationalgeographic.com (Republished from the

pages of National Geographic Magazine), **148:** Adapted from "Olive Oil Fights Heart Disease, Breast Cancer, Studies Say," by Stefan Lovgren: National Geographic News, October 28, 2008, **149:** Adapted from "Feliciano dos Santos Musician and Activist," www.nationalgeographic.com/field/explorers, **165:** Adapted from "Celt Appeal," by Tom O'Neill: National Geographic Magazine, March 2009, **169:** Adapted from "Answers from Angkor," by Richard Stone: National Geographic Magazine, July 2009, **176:** Adapted from "Animals Everlasting," by A. R. Williams: National Geographic Magazine, November 2009, **184:** Adapted from "In Your Face," by James Shreeve: National Geographic Magazine, March 2005, **189:** Adapted from "Hand Washing Wipes away Regrets?," by Rachel Kaufman: National Geographic News, May 6, 2010, **200:** Adapted from "Making Music Boosts Brain's Language Skills," by Victoria Jaggard: National Geographic News, February 20, 2010.

PHOTOS

Cover: Terry W. Eggers/CORBIS, **1:** Ivan Kashinsky/National Geographic **2:** Jimmy Chinn/National Geographic Image Collection, **2:** Cary Wolinsky/National Geographic Image Collection, **3:** Ivan Kashinsky/National Geographic Image Collection, **3:** Randy Olson/National Geographic Image Collection, **3:** AP Photo/Tomas Munita, **3:** Jodi Cobb/National Geographic Image Collection, **3:** Ed Kashi/National Geographic Image Collection, **4:** Pierre Perrin/Sygma/Corbis **4:** Dulwich Picture Gallery, London, UK/The Bridgeman Art Library International, **4:** Moviestore collection Ltd/Alamy, **6:** Kenneth Garrett/National Geographic Image Collection, **8:** Winfield Parks/National Geographic Image Collection, **11:** ColorBlind Images/conica/Getty Images, **12:** Carol Beckwith/National Geographic Image Collection, **13:** Karen Kasmauski/National Geographic Image Collection, **13:** Robert Estall photo agency/Alamy, **14:** Tyrone Turner, **14:** Todd Gipstein/National Geographic Image Collection, **15:** Vstock LLC/Tetra images/Jupiter Images, **16:** GWImages, 2010/Shutterstock.com, **16:** Sean Locke/istockphoto.com, **19:** Monkey Business Images/Shutterstock.com, **20:** Losevsky Pavel/Shutterstock.com, **21:** Matthias Breiter/Minden Pictures, **22–23:** Unterthiner, Stefano/National Geographic Image Collection, **23:** Tom Vezo/Minden Pictures/National Geographic Image Collection, **23:** George Grall/National Geographic Image Collection, **23:** Darlyne A. Murawski/National Geographic Image Collection, **24:** John Eastcott and Yva Momatiuk/National Geographic Image Collection, **24:** John Eastcott and Yva Momatiuk/National Geographic Image Collection, **24:** Yva Momatiuk and John Eastcott/Minden Pictures, **24:** Unterthiner, Stefano/National Geographic Image Collection, **25:** Unterthiner, Stefano/National Geographic Image Collection, **26:** Unterthiner, Stefano/National Geographic Image Collection,

27: Mauricio Handler/National Geographic Image Collection, **27:** Gail Johnson/Shutterstock.com, **28:** Karen Kasmauski/National Geographic Image Collection, **28:** Aristide Economopoulos/Star Ledger/Corbis, **29:** Tim Laman/National Geographic Image Collection, **30:** David Fleetham/Visuals Unlimited, Inc/Visuals Unlimited/Getty Images, **31:** Peter ten Broecke/istockphoto.com, **32:** George Grall/National Geographic/Getty Images, **33:** Robert Sisson/National Geographic Image Collection, **33:** Norbert Wu/ Minden Pictures/National Geographic Image Collection, **34:** Christian Ziegler, **34:** Christian Ziegler/National Geographic Image Collection, **36:** Jonathan Blair/National Geographic Image Collection, **37:** Christian Ziegler/National Geographic Image Collection, **38:** Monkey Business Images/Shutterstock.com, **39:** Dean Bertoncelj/Shutterstock.com, **41:** Theo Westenberger/National Geographic Image Collection, **42:** National Geographic Image Collection, **43:** Reza/National Geographic Image Collection, **43:** Carsten Koall/Visum/The Image Works, **43:** Howell Walker/National Geographic Image Collection, **45:** PANOS PICTURES/National Geographic Image Collection, **46:** Eugene Richards/National Geographic Image Collection, **46:** Andre Jenny/Alamy, **47:** Courtesy of Andrew Filer, **47:** Alaska Stock Images/National Geographic Image Collection, **47:** Eugene Richards/National Geographic Image Collection, **48:** Radu Razvan/Shutterstock.com, **49:** Orange Line Media/Shutterstock.com, **51:** J. Baylor Roberts/National Geographic Image Collection, **51:** Jupiterimages, **51:** Richard Mulonga/ Newscom, **52:** Sean Gallup/Getty Images, **53:** Cotton Coulson/National Geographic Image Collection, **53:** turkishblue, 2010/Shutterstock.com, **55:** Steve Skjold/Alamy, **55:** David Davis Photoproductions/Alamy, **56:** Maggie Steber/National Geographic Image Collection, **56:** Michael Nichols/National Geographic Image

Collection, **59:** Chuck Pefley/Alamy, **60:** The Library of Congress, **60:** Chris Johns/National Geographic Image Collection, **60:** t14/ZUMA Press/Newscom, **61:** Dai Rui/National Geographic Image Collection, **62–63:** Stephen Alvarez/National Geographic Image Collection, **63:** Stephen Alvarez/National Geographic Image Collection, **63:** Stephen Alvarez/National Geographic Image Collection, **64:** Michael S. Yamashita/National Geographic Image Collection, **65:** Taylor S. Kennedy/National Geographic Image Collection, **67:** Stephen Alvarez/National Geographic Image Collection, **68:** KEENPRESS/National Geographic Image Collection, **69:** John Eastcott and Yva Momatiuk/National Geographic Image Collection, **72:** Jim Richardson/National Geographic Image Collection, **73:** Kuttig-Travel/Alamy, **73:** Mark Snyder/American Artists Rep., Inc., **74:** Stuart Franklin/National Geographic Image Collection, **75:** Stuart Franklin/National Geographic Image Collection, **76:** George Steinmetz/National Geographic Image Collection, **77:** George Steinmetz/National Geographic Image Collection, **78:** Paul Nicklen/National Geographic Image Collection, **80:** Michael S. Yamashita/National Geographic Image Collection, **80:** George Steinmetz/National Geographic Image Collection, **80:** Stephen Alvarez/National Geographic Image Collection, **80:** George Steinmetz/National Geographic Image Collection, **82–83:** Chris Rainier/National Geographic Image Collection, **83:** Pete Ryan/National Geographic Image Collection, **83:** Justin Guariglia/National Geographic Image Collection, **84:** Volkmar K. Wentzel/National Geographic Image Collection, **85:** Aaron Huey/National Geographic Image Collection, **86:** Michael & Patricia Fogden/Minden Pictures/Getty Images, **87:** James P. Blair/National Geographic Image Collection, **88:** Melissa Farlow/National Geographic Image Collection,

continued on p.226

Gender and Society

ACADEMIC PATHWAYS

Lesson A: Listening to a Lecture
          Giving a Presentation about a Name
Lesson B: Listening to a Conversation between Classmates
          Participating in a Mini-Debate

Think and Discuss

1. What are these people doing?
2. What surprises you about this picture?
3. Would you enjoy watching this sports event? Explain.

A Sunday sports event in El Alto, Bolivia

1

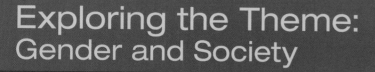

Exploring the Theme: Gender and Society

A | Look at the photos and read the captions. Then discuss the questions.

1. Do you think any of the activities shown should be for men or women only? Explain.
2. Do you think gender (being male or female) is something we are born with or learn? Explain.

B | Look at the map. Then discuss the questions.

1. The map shows popular names for men and women in different countries. (The women's names are listed first.) According to the map, what is a popular woman's name in Brazil? What's a popular man's name in Japan?
2. What are some popular names for men and women in your country?

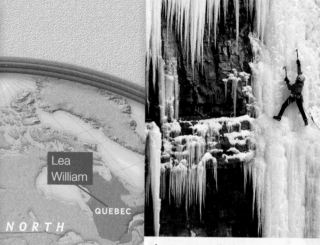

A woman climbs up rock and ice in British Columbia, **Canada**.

Lea
William

QUEBEC

NORTH AMERICA

OHIO

Ava
Jacob

MEXICO

ATLANTIC

Maria Fernanda
Miguel Angel

PACIFIC

OCEAN

OCEAN

SOUTH AMERICA

BRAZIL

A woman works at a steel factory in Pennsylvania, **USA**.

CHILE

Maria
Joao

Constanza
Benjamin

NEW

ZEALAND

Ella
Jack

Lambert Azimuthal Equal-
Area Projection
0 mi   1000
0 km   1000

ANTARCTIC CIRCLE

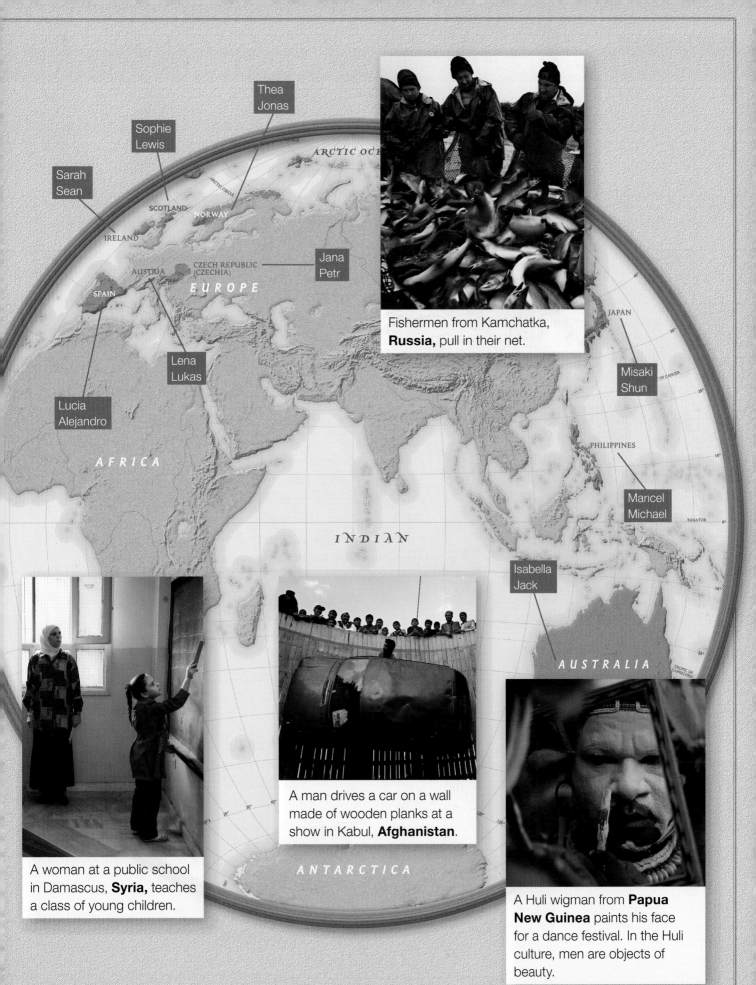

Fishermen from Kamchatka, **Russia,** pull in their net.

A woman at a public school in Damascus, **Syria,** teaches a class of young children.

A man drives a car on a wall made of wooden planks at a show in Kabul, **Afghanistan**.

A Huli wigman from **Papua New Guinea** paints his face for a dance festival. In the Huli culture, men are objects of beauty.

Map labels: Sarah Sean, Sophie Lewis, Thea Jonas, Jana Petr, Lucia Alejandro, Lena Lukas, Misaki Shun, Maricel Michael, Isabella Jack

ARCTIC OCEAN, ARCTIC CIRCLE, SCOTLAND, NORWAY, IRELAND, AUSTRIA, CZECH REPUBLIC (CZECHIA), EUROPE, SPAIN, AFRICA, JAPAN, PHILIPPINES, INDIAN, AUSTRALIA, ANTARCTICA, TROPIC OF CANCER, EQUATOR, TROPIC OF CAPRICORN

A | **Meaning from Context.** Read and listen to the information. Notice the words in blue. These are words you will hear and use in Lesson A.

Kabuki is a traditional form of singing and dancing theater that is still popular in Japan. One unusual characteristic of *kabuki* is that all the roles of women are played by male actors called *onnagata*. These actors spend many years studying women's behavior and activities, such as sewing. Some people say that the actors are more feminine than real women are!

There are many examples of male actors who play roles of the opposite gender, but the reverse doesn't happen very often. *The Year of Living Dangerously* is a famous movie from the 1980s. It's about an Australian journalist who meets a news photographer during a time of terrible violence. Many people didn't notice that the star who played the role of Billy Kwan, the photographer, was actually a woman. Linda Hunt won an Academy Award for her acting in the movie. She gave Billy Kwan many characteristics that people think are masculine, especially courage.

In the time of William Shakespeare, women were generally not allowed to appear on a theater stage. In Shakespeare's plays, female characters like Juliet (in *Romeo and Juliet*) were played by young boys. Some of them became very famous, like Nathan Field in this picture. When their voices changed and they grew older, these actors had to start playing men's roles.

B | Complete each sentence with a word from the box. Use each word only once.

gender	behavior	characteristic	reverse	generally
role	male	female	masculine	feminine

1. _____, names that end in –y are girls' names, but there are exceptions, like *Jeffrey*.

2. In her new movie, Marisa Chang plays the _____ of a spy.

3. My dog's _____ is terrible! He chews on my furniture and takes food off my plate.

4. Only _____ animals can have babies.

5. Patience is an important _____ of a good teacher.

6. Little boys and girls learn a lot about _____ when they start school. They learn the things that boys and girls are supposed to do.

7. In the United States, women wear light colors like pink because they think they look more _____.

8. Usually more men than women are doctors, but in Russia, it's the _____. They have more female doctors there.

9. Some men grow beards because they think it makes them look more _____.

10. All the presidents of my country have been _____, except for our current leader. She was elected in 2010.

C | Read the statements and circle your opinions.

1. **Male** actors can play women's **roles** better than the reverse.   **Agree**   **Not Sure**   **Disagree**
2. If I were an actor/actress, I think I could play a **role** of the opposite **gender**.   **Agree**   **Not Sure**   **Disagree**
3. Children learn a lot of their **behavior** from watching TV.   **Agree**   **Not Sure**   **Disagree**
4. Playing with dolls won't make a little boy **feminine**.   **Agree**   **Not Sure**   **Disagree**
5. Some sports are too **masculine** for women to play.   **Agree**   **Not Sure**   **Disagree**
6. It's important for children to have both **male** and **female** teachers.   **Agree**   **Not Sure**   **Disagree**
7. Girls are **generally** better at math than boys are.   **Agree**   **Not Sure**   **Disagree**
8. Ideas about **gender** have changed in my country.   **Agree**   **Not Sure**   **Disagree**

D | **Discussion.** Compare your answers from the survey with your group. Give reasons and explanations for your opinions.

E | Tell the class about any statements that your group members all had the same opinion about.

Note-Taking

People generally speak more quickly than they write. To take good notes quickly while listening to a lecture, write only the most important ideas.

- Write only the key words.
  all kabuki actors men
- Don't write complete sentences.
  ~~In the~~ time of ~~William~~ Shakespeare, women ~~were generally~~ not allowed ~~to appear~~ on ~~theater~~ stage
- Use abbreviations (short forms) and symbols when possible.
  info information *dr* doctor *w/* with → about

Hatshepsut wearing the traditionally male symbols of a lion's mane and a pharaoh's beard.

A | Cross out the unimportant words in these sentences using the advice from the chart above.

1. In some cultures men and women are expected to follow very strict rules about gender roles.
2. Children learn about gender roles when they watch the behavior of the people around them.

B | Think of abbreviations or symbols to replace these words and phrases.

1. year _____
2. without _____
3. less than _____
4. more than _____

(See pages 206-207 in the Independent Student Handbook for more information on note-taking.)

Before Listening

A | **Prior Knowledge.** Discuss the questions below with a partner.

1. Look at the picture. Who do you think this person was?
2. Do you think it's common or uncommon for a country to have a female president (prime minister, king, etc.)? Which countries can you think of whose leaders are women?

Listening: A Lecture

track 1-3 **A** | **Listening for Main Ideas.** Listen to part of a lecture and read the notes below. Cross out the unimportant words and use symbols and abbreviations if possible.

1. gender socialization ~~is the way~~=how children learn ~~male and female~~ ♂/♀ gender roles

2. children learn their gender roles from their parents, their peers, schools, and their culture

3. parents give children different kinds of compliments; they compliment girls on their appearance, and they compliment boys on their actions.

4. peers make fun of children who are "different"; schools can have separate classes or school uniforms— pants for boys and skirts for girls; our culture also teaches us about gender roles

track 1-3 **B** | Listen again and decide whether your notes in exercise **A** are brief, yet informative enough to help you remember the lecture.

track 1-4 **C** | **Listening for Details.** Listen to the next part of the talk and complete the notes.

- We ask: baby boy or girl? b/c later role in world depends on _____

  But:

1. gender roles today _____

2. some people don't _____

- In ancient Egypt, Hatshepsut became _____ (ca. 150 yrs. aft. Tut)

- While H ruled (_____ yrs.) constructed/repaired _____

  + _____ (wanted to be remembered)

- Early art: H w/_____ characteristics. Later art:

  _____ (reason? maybe easier to keep power w/♂ looks)

LEGACY IN STONE
Hatshepsut erected many monuments along the Nile and in the Sinai but focused on her capital at Thebes, today the ruins of Karnak and Luxor.

After Listening

Critical Thinking. Discuss the questions below with your group.

1. Which of the four ways children learn gender roles do you think is the most powerful? Why?
2. What do you remember about learning gender roles when you were a child?
3. Besides the reason given in the lecture, what are some other possible reasons why Hatshepsut's appearance in artwork changed over time?

Language Function

Talking about Rules and Expectations

We use the following expressions to talk about rules.

*Female students **must** wear dresses.*	*Taxi drivers **must not** overcharge the customers.*
*They **are required to** follow many other rules.*	*Sikhs **are forbidden to** cut their hair.*
*He **has to** arrive before the others.*	*They **aren't allowed to** become soldiers.*

We use the following expressions to talk about expectations.

*Women **are supposed to** take care of the children.*	*Women **aren't supposed to** complain.*
*Men **are expected to** play sports.*	*Men **aren't expected to** do housework.*

These women are members of Bahrain's police force. They handle children's and women's cases.

A | **Critical Thinking.** Look at the picture. Match the columns to form the rules that you think these women must follow.

1. They are required ____
2. They have to ____
3. They are expected to stand up ____
4. They aren't allowed to ____
5. They are not supposed ____

a. when their officer walks in.
b. to wear jewelry.
c. handle men's cases.
d. to wear a uniform.
e. exercise every day.

B | Compare your answers with a partner's. Then discuss the questions below.

1. Which rules do you think would be the most difficult to follow? Why?
2. Do you think the male police officers have to follow the same rules? If not, how do you think the rules for men might be different?

C | Using a Graphic Organizer. Think about what the different rules and expectations are for boys and girls or men and women in your country. Make a T-chart in your notebook like the one below. (*See page 214 of the Independent Student Handbook for information on T-charts.*)

Boys/Men	Girls/Women
have to serve in the military for two years	are expected to take care of the children

D | Use the notes in your T-chart to tell your partner about the different rules and expectations in your country. Take notes as you listen to your partner.

E | Form a group with another pair of students. Talk about the most interesting information you learned from your partner.

Grammar

Indefinite Pronouns

Indefinite pronouns with *some- (someone, somebody, something, somewhere)* refer to an unspecified person, place, or thing.

> Most people marry **someone** who is close to their own age.

Indefinite pronouns with *every- (everyone, everybody, everything, everywhere)* refer to all of a group of people, places, or things.

> He has no clothes to wear. **Everything** in his closet is too small now.

Indefinite pronouns with *no- (no one, nobody, nothing, nowhere)* refer to none of a group of people, places, or things.

> Stella didn't go to the party because **nobody** told her about it.

We use indefinite pronouns with *any- (anyone, anybody, anything, anywhere)* when the person, place, or thing is not important.

> You can choose the restaurant. **Anywhere** is fine with me.

We also use indefinite pronouns with *any-* in negative statements and in questions.

> We didn't go **anywhere** last night. Does **anybody** know what time it is?

Indefinite pronouns take the singular form of the verb.

> Everybody **likes** ice cream. Nothing **is** on the desk.

A | Read the sentences and circle the correct indefinite pronoun.

1. Kevin can't find his keys and he's looked (anywhere/everywhere/somewhere) for them.
2. I'm not really hungry. I don't want (something/nothing/anything) to eat right now.
3. This town is boring. There's (nothing/everything/anything) to do here at night.
4. I'm having a big party and I'm going to invite (nobody/everybody/anybody) in my class.
5. Has Aisha found (everyone/no one/anyone) who can teach her how to drive?

B | Read the sentences and circle the correct verb.

1. Everyone in the company (have/has/is) a specific role.
2. I think someone (are/is/has) at the door. I'll go downstairs and check.
3. (Does/Are/Is) anything bothering you? You look upset.
4. Everybody (is/are/seems) talking about the new movie. I really want to see it.
5. (Is/Does/Do) anybody interested in going hiking with me on Saturday?

C | Read the story below. Then discuss the questions with a partner.

Everybody, Somebody, Anybody, and Nobody

This is a little story about four people named Everybody, Somebody, Anybody, and Nobody. There was an important job to be done, and Everybody was sure that Somebody would do it. Anybody could have done it, but Nobody did it. Somebody got angry about that because it was Everybody's job. Everybody thought that Anybody could do it, but Nobody realized that Everybody wouldn't do it. It ended up that Everybody blamed Somebody when Nobody did what Anybody could have done.

---

1. Do you think the story is funny? Why, or why not?
2. Have you ever experienced a similar situation? Explain.
3. Why do you think the author chose to use indefinite pronouns in this story?

D | Now read the information below. Then with a partner, discuss situations when you think you should use *they* and *their* as indefinite pronouns.

Indefinite Pronouns and Pronoun Usage

Because indefinite pronouns are singular, they should be followed by singular pronouns. However, in casual speech, it's very common to use *they* or *their*. Using *they* and *their* also helps make language inclusive and non-sexist by not leaving out men or women. Using inclusive language is expected in formal academic and business situations.

Somebody left his phone on the chair. (formal usage, but not inclusive, excludes women)
Somebody left his or her phone on the chair. (formal usage, inclusive)
Somebody left their phone on the chair. (informal usage, inclusive)

Giving a Presentation about a Name

A | **Discussion.** Work with a partner. Discuss the questions. Take notes on your partner's answers.

1. When you were a baby, who chose your name? Do you know why they chose that name?
2. Is your name common or uncommon?
3. Were you named after a relative?
4. Does your name have a meaning? If so, what does it mean?
5. Do you think your name is a good name for the opposite gender too, or for only one gender? Explain your reasons.
6. Do you like your name? Why, or why not?

B | **Organizing Ideas.** Prepare to tell the class about your partner's name. Organize your notes from exercise **A** in a chart like the one below.

Name	Notes
Paulina	father chose it, father's name=Paul

Presentation Skills: Preparing Notes for Speaking

Good notes can help you when you speak in front of the class. To be useful, written notes for speaking should be:

- Short—not complete sentences, only words and phrases to help you remember the most important ideas
- Clearly written in LARGE letters
- Written on a card or small piece of paper that's easy to hold

---

C | **Presentation.** Tell the class about your partner's name. Use your notes from exercise **B** to help you.

D | **Discussion.** Discuss the information you found most interesting, unusual, or surprising about the students in your class and their names.

> I think it's interesting that every male member of Alexandre's family is named *Alexandre.* That could be confusing!

Wodaabe

In the Wodaabe culture, special clothes and makeup emphasize male attractiveness, which includes white teeth and the ability to cross one's eyes.

The Wodaabe live in parts of Niger, Nigeria, and surrounding parts of western and central Africa.

Before Viewing

A | Critical Thinking. Discuss the questions with a partner.

1. In your culture, how important is physical beauty for women? What are some of the characteristics of feminine beauty in your culture?
2. In your culture, how important is physical beauty for men? What are some of the characteristics of masculine beauty or handsomeness in your culture?
3. Have you ever seen a beauty contest? What happens at a beauty contest? How are the winners chosen?

 B | Using a Dictionary. Read and listen about a beauty contest in the Wodaabe culture. Use context clues or your dictionary to help you understand the <u>underlined</u> words.

The Wodaabe Geerewol Festival

For most of the year, the Wodaabe are <u>nomadic</u>, moving from place to place to find grass for their cattle. For one week each year, however, it's festival time for the Wodaabe. It's called the *geerewol*, and it's a chance for Wodaabe men to <u>show off</u> for the women.

The *geerewol* is a kind of beauty pageant, and the men who participate wear <u>makeup</u> to emphasize the features that are considered beautiful by the Wodaabe: long noses, strong white teeth, and large eyes, among other characteristics.

The *geerewol* is all about <u>attraction</u>—both physical beauty and <u>charm</u>. While the men dance, the women watch and carefully evaluate the men's <u>appearance</u>. When an available woman finds a man who is <u>irresistible</u> to her, she lets him know with small gestures. With many women watching, the pageant has many winners.

While Viewing

📺 **A | Note-Taking.** Watch the video and take notes in your notebook on your reactions to it.

1. What surprises you?
2. What do you find interesting?
3. What do you have questions about?

📺 **B |** Watch again and take notes on the following details.

1. Purpose of black lipstick: _____
2. Purpose of yellow makeup: _____
3. Who are the judges? _____
4. Who competes in the *geerewol*? _____

This Wodaabe man in Niger is part of a nomadic tribe that trades and herds animals in western Africa.

After Viewing

👥 **Critical Thinking.** Discuss the questions with your group.

1. Why do you think psychologists are interested in the Wodaabe and the *geerewol* festival?
2. What does the video tell you (and not tell you) about gender roles in the Wodaabe tribe?
3. Think about what you learned in Lesson A about gender. Do you think that nature or culture has more to do with our ideas about physical beauty? Explain.

Group of Wodaabe men at festival time

A | **Meaning from Context.** Read and listen to the two articles. Notice the words in blue. These are words you will hear and use in Lesson B.

🎧 track 1-6 Boys and Girls Test Their Geography

Question: Timis County is located in the western part of which European Country?

Eric Yang knew the answer. "Romania!" he said, and became the winner of the National Geographic Geography Bee. Every year, thousands of young people compete in this international contest of geographical knowledge. Three winners from each country go on to the world championship.

For years, however, the contest's organizers have wondered about a question of their own. An equal number of girls and boys enter the contest at the school and regional levels. Why are so many of the national winners boys? In the United States, Eric's home country, only two girls have won the top prize since 1989.

Teams from seventeen countries competed in this year's National Geographic World Championship in Mexico City.

🎧 track 1-7 Canadian Boys Win World Geography Contest

Three boys from Canada have won the National Geographic World Championship in Mexico City, beating 16 other national teams. The second prize went to three boys from the USA, and the third prize to three boys from Poland. All teams also enjoyed several days of sightseeing in Mexico.

As in the past, most contestants were male, and this year two scientists investigated the reasons for this. They concluded that there is in fact a small gender gap in geography, but they couldn't find the cause. Possibly, boys are taught to be more assertive than girls, or they might feel more pressure from their parents. Maybe boys have a better ability to use maps. Or maybe teachers encourage boys more in geography classes.

B | Match each word in **blue** from exercise **A** with its definition.

1. level ___	a. (adj.) the same in number, size, or value
2. equal ___	b. (v.) to arrive at an opinion or judgment
3. investigate ___	c. (adj.) able to give your opinions strongly and clearly
4. conclude ___	d. (n.) a skill that makes it possible to do something
5. gap ___	e. (v.) to look at something carefully, research
6. possibly ___	f. (v.) to give someone the confidence to do or try something
7. assertive ___	g. (adv.) maybe
8. knowledge ___	h. (n.) a point on a certain scale, such as quality or ability
9. ability ___	i. (n.) a space or difference between two things
10. encourage ___	j. (n.) the things you know about

C | **Giving Reasons.** Look back at the second newspaper article and write four possible reasons for the "geography gap" between girls and boys. Then write two more ideas of your own.

Reasons from the article:

1. _____

2. _____

3. _____

4. _____

Your own ideas:

1. _____

2. _____

Critical Thinking Focus: Evaluating Reasons

When you read or hear reasons for something, it's important to ask yourself whether the reasons make sense and are believable based on what you know.

D | **Critical Thinking.** Compare your ideas in exercise **C** with your partner's ideas. What do you think is the best explanation for the **gap**?

E | **Discussion.** Talk about the elementary school subjects below with a partner. Which ones did you have the most **ability** in? Did your teachers and parents **encourage** you in these subjects? Did they pressure you to do well? Do you think there is a gender **gap** in any of these subjects? Explain your reasons.

science	reading and writing
history	foreign languages
art	mathematics
geography	

A firefighter

Before Listening

 Discuss the questions as a class.

1. Which jobs in your country are done mostly by women? mostly by men?
2. Have the jobs that men and women do changed over time?

Listening: A Conversation between Classmates

 track 1-8 **A** | **Listening for Main Ideas.** Listen to the first part of the conversation and answer the questions.

1. What did Dylan do over the summer?

_____

2. What did Mia do over the summer?

_____

3. What class are they taking together?

_____

4. What do you think Dylan will talk about next?

_____

 track 1-9 **B** | Listen to the next part of the conversation and circle the correct answers.

1. Dylan thinks that women firefighters _____.
   a. are a bad idea
   b. are a good idea
   c. don't exist
2. Mia believes that _____.
   a. all men are stronger than all women
   b. some men are stronger than some women
   c. most men are stronger than most women
3. Mia's drawing looks like _____.
   a. graph A
   b. graph B
   c. graph C

A flight attendant

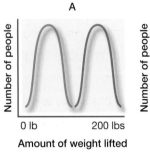

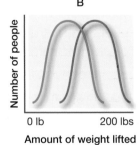

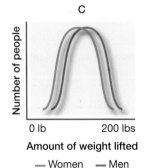

C | **Listening for Details.** Read the statements. Then listen to the last part of the conversation and circle **T** for *true* or **F** for *false*.

track 1-10

1. Mia thinks that women should take jobs away from men.   **T**   **F**
2. Mia's aunt liked working as a flight attendant.   **T**   **F**
3. Dylan thinks being a flight attendant would be interesting.   **T**   **F**
4. Dylan thinks men aren't good flight attendants.   **T**   **F**
5. Mia is angry with Dylan.   **T**   **F**

After Listening

 Collaboration. Complete the activities below with a partner.

1. Talk about the three graphs on the previous page. Can you think of other characteristics of men and women that fit these patterns?
2. Make your own graph about a gender difference, similar to one of the graphs on the previous page. Label the parts.
3. Draw your graph on the board and explain it to the class. Does everyone agree with you?

Pronunciation

Can/Can't

The words *can* and *can't* have very similar pronunciations, but they receive different stress in a sentence. Usually, *can* is not stressed, so the vowel receives a reduced pronunciation. Listen to the difference:

track 1-11

*I **can** speak three languages.*
*We **can't** find our new classroom.*

Paying attention to this difference can help you understand these words better.

 Listen to these sentences from the conversation again and complete them with *can* or *can't*. Then take turns reading them to a partner.

1. But I _____ also see that I disagree with her about a lot of things.
2. A small woman _____ lift more than 20 pounds.
3. And a woman athlete _____ lift 200 pounds.
4. _____ all men lift 200 pounds?
5. I _____ imagine why the airlines didn't want men.
6. Men _____ lift heavier bags for the passengers.

Language Function

Using Inclusive Language

Inclusive language is language that includes both men and women. In speaking and writing academic English, you are expected to use inclusive language as much as you can. Some important points:

1. Don't use words like *man, he, him,* or *his* to refer to all people.
   X *The average student worries about his exam scores.*
   The average student worries about exam scores.

2. Don't use job titles that refer to only one gender.
   X *That book was written for salesmen.*
   That book was written for salespeople.

3. Don't mention gender if it isn't important.
   X *I had a meeting with a lady engineer this morning.*
   I had a meeting with an engineer this morning.

A | Replace the crossed-out job titles with the correct form of one of the titles from the box.

chair	flight attendant	nurse	business executive
firefighter	mail carrier	server	salesperson

1. Many ~~businessmen~~ _____ travel a lot for their work.

2. The ~~mailman~~ _____ usually comes to my house at about ten o'clock.

3. In the hospital, a very kind ~~male nurse~~ _____ took care of me.

4. The ~~chairman~~ _____ asked the people at the meeting to give their suggestions.

5. I think our ~~waitress~~ _____ provided excellent service. Let's leave a big tip.

6. Being a good listener is an important characteristic for a ~~salesman~~ _____ to have.

B | **Discussion.** With a partner, talk about the following sentences. Does each sentence use inclusive language? If not, rewrite it in your notebook using more inclusive language.

1. The hotel rooms have special features for businessmen and businesswomen, such as extra-large desks.
2. A patient should always ask a doctor for his advice before starting an exercise program.
3. Two of the most popular new movies in this country were made by female directors.
4. Early man lived in caves and wore clothes made from animal skins.
5. Mothers should feed their children plenty of fruits and vegetables.

C | **Discussion.** Form a group with two or three other students. Look at the job titles from exercise **A** on page 18. Discuss what skills and characteristics make someone successful at each of these professions. Practice using inclusive language as you discuss your ideas.

> A good server is polite to their customers.

Language Function

Talking about Rules and Expectations in the Past

We use the following expressions to talk about rules in the past.
> Female flight attendants **were required to** be very thin.
> They **had to** stop working when they were 32.
> They **weren't allowed to** keep their jobs if they gained weight.
> They **were forbidden to** get married.
> Female flight attendants **couldn't** get married if they wanted to keep their jobs.

We use the following language to talk about expectations in the past.
> Stewardesses **were supposed to** be attractive.
> They **were expected to** be friendly and polite.

A | Think about men and women in your country 100 years ago. What was different? Complete the sentences with your own ideas.

1. Women were expected to _____.
2. Women were not supposed to _____.
3. Men were not expected to _____.
4. Men were supposed to _____.

B | Discuss your answers from exercise **A** with your partner.

C | Think about some of the rules your parents had for you when you were a child. Discuss the questions with your group.

1. Talk about some of the rules your parents had for you when you were in elementary school.
2. Were the rules the same for your older and younger siblings?
3. Were the rules the same for boys and girls in your family?

> I wasn't allowed to ride my bicycle alone.

You are going to have a mini-debate about where gender differences come from. Your teacher will assign you and your partner one of the opinions below (it might not be your opinion). You and your partner will work together to make an argument that supports your opinion.

Opinion 1: Gender differences come mostly from our biology, not our culture.

Opinion 2: Gender differences come mostly from our culture, not our biology.

A | **Brainstorming.** Brainstorm reasons to support your opinion. Write your ideas in your notebook.

> In some cultures boys and girls are expected to follow different rules.

> In my country parents give their sons and daughters really different kinds of toys.

B | **Collaboration.** Look at the list of reasons from exercise **A**. Decide which three reasons best support your opinion and write them in the outline below. Then think of at least one example to support each of your reasons.

Opinion: _____

Reason 1: _____
Examples: _____
Reason 2: _____
Examples: _____
Reason 3: _____
Examples: _____

C | **Note-Taking.** Form a group with a student pair that discussed the opposite opinion. Present your opinion and your reasons and examples that support it. Listen to the other pair present their opinion and take notes on their reasons and ideas.

> Gender differences come mostly from our biology, because very young boys and girls already like different kinds of toys.

D | **Discussion.** Work with your original partner from exercises **A** and **B**. Look at your notes from exercise **B**. Discuss the reasons and examples the other pair talk about to support their opinion. Think of arguments against their reasons.

E | **Organizing Ideas.** Make notes on your strongest arguments from exercise **D**. Then decide which order you will present them in.

F | **Presentation.** Form a group with the other pair of students again. Take turns presenting your arguments against each other's opinions and reasons.

Reproducing Life

ACADEMIC PATHWAYS

Lesson A: Listening to a Conversation about a Documentary
Discussing Species Conservation

Lesson B: Listening to a Conversation between Classmates
Creating and Presenting a Group Plan

Think and Discuss

1. Young polar bears are called "cubs." What are some other young animals called?
2. Where do these polar bears live? What other kinds of animals do you think live there?

A polar bear mother and her cubs cuddle together for
warmth. These polar bears live in Churchill, Canada.

21

Exploring the Theme:
Reproducing Life

Look at the photos and read the captions. Then discuss the questions.

1. Which species of animal in the photos interests you the most? Why?
2. What types of reproduction are discussed on these pages?
3. How is reproduction a challenge for these penguins?

Three Types of Reproduction

Plants reproduce through a process called **pollination**. Pollination involves the transfer of a powder called pollen from one plant to another. Insects like this bee are important to the pollination process for some plants.

These Amazon molly fish clone (or copy) themselves naturally. Other types of **cloning** can only take place in scientific laboratories.

The quetzal, like all species of birds, **lays eggs**. Young quetzals become independent in just a few weeks.

Case Study: The King Penguins of Possession Island

For the penguins of Possession Island, reproduction can be a challenge. The island is crowded, and each pair of penguins needs its own territory—a small area of land. Penguins lay eggs and have to keep them warm, which is very difficult in this harsh, cold climate. They must also watch out for predators, since other animals might want to eat their eggs or chicks (baby penguins). Penguins live in large groups called colonies. The largest colony on Possession Island contains 100,000 penguins!

track **1-13** **A** | **Meaning from Context.** Look at the photos and read and listen to the captions. Notice the words in blue. These are words you will hear and use in Lesson A.

The King Penguin: Challenges to Reproduction

An elephant seal shares South Georgia Island with a huge **colony** of King Penguins. The penguins have come to the island to reproduce, but space can be a problem. Each penguin must defend its **territory**, a small area less than three feet (one meter) across.

Although adult King Penguins **weigh** around 30 pounds (14 kilograms), they cannot always **defend** their chicks against **predators** such as this skua. In the ocean, seals and other sea animals sometimes eat penguins.

Cold temperatures also challenge penguin **reproduction**. This **adult** penguin keeps its egg warm until its **mate** returns. Adults may swim and eat for two weeks or more before they return and take over the care of the egg.

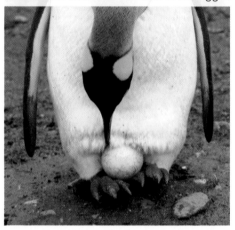

Climate change is creating another **challenge**. Penguin chicks are not independent. They **depend** on their parents for food. Warmer ocean water means less food nearby, so penguin parents are away for longer time periods and more chicks die.

B | Write each word in blue next to its definition.

1. _____ (n.) a person or animal that has finished growing

2. _____ (v.) to have a certain weight

3. _____ (v.) to need (for support)

4. _____ (v.) to take action in order to protect something

5. _____ (n.) animals that eat other animals

6. _____ (n.) a group of animals living together in a certain area

7. _____ (n.) an animal's partner in reproduction

8. _____ (n.) an area of land that belongs to a certain animal

9. _____ (n.) the creation of babies

10. _____ (n.) something difficult that requires effort

A | Read the article and fill in each blank with a word from the box.

colonies	territory	mate	adult

A Land of Kings

It's summer in the southern hemisphere, and time for _____ King Penguins to leave the water and lay their eggs. First, however, each penguin must find a _____.

On Possession Island, there are plenty of penguins to choose from in six different penguin _____. When photographer Stefano Unterthiner visited the largest one, he saw 100,000 penguins. Each one was defending its _____, a small area less than three feet (one meter) across. Said Unterthiner, "The penguins looked very organized, almost like they were in military formation, each guarding its ground."

"Penguins can seem like fish," says photographer Unterthiner, "but here they truly are birds flying in water."

B | Read the statements. Circle **T** for *true* or **F** for *false* using the information from the article.

1. Possession Island is in the northern hemisphere.   **T**   **F**
2. The island's largest penguin colony has 10,000 birds in it.   **T**   **F**
3. Each penguin has a large territory on the island.   **T**   **F**
4. Adult penguins leave the water in the winter.   **T**   **F**
5. Penguins on the island live in six large groups.   **T**   **F**

C | **Critical Thinking.** Write answers to the following questions.

1. Which probably **weighs** more—**adult** penguins or penguin chicks?

   _____

2. What do you think is the greatest **challenge** to penguin **reproduction**?

   _____

3. What are some penguin **predators** you know about? (Is a penguin ever a predator?)

   _____

4. What kinds of **predators** do you think penguins have to **defend** their chicks against?

   _____

5. Do you still **depend** on your parents and other family members for some things?

   _____

D | With a partner, take turns asking and answering the questions in exercise **C.**

Before Listening

track 1-14 **A** | **Meaning from Context.** Read and listen about a new film about penguins. Notice the <u>underlined</u> words.

The Penguins of Possession Island

This is not the only <u>documentary film</u> about penguins this year, but it is one of the year's best. In this beautiful nature documentary, King Penguins come to Possession Island to find mates. Most of the <u>footage</u>[1] shows us penguins on land, but some footage shows us penguins in the water.

There is something in this documentary for everyone—except perhaps for young children. Some <u>scenes</u> of penguin chicks being killed by predators are difficult to watch—even for adults.

I was lucky enough to see *The Penguins of Possession Island* in a movie theater, and everyone in the <u>audience</u> liked the film. Don't miss your chance to see it, even if you have to watch it on TV.

B | Choose the correct ending for each sentence below.

1. *Film* is another word for _____.
   a. movie   b. television
2. A documentary film shows us _____.
   a. a fictional story   b. something from real life
3. Film footage comes from a _____.
   a. camera   b. book
4. The scenes in a film are _____.
   a. small parts of the film   b. the music in the film
5. People in the audience _____.
   a. make a film   b. watch a film

Listening: A Conversation about a Documentary

track 1-15 **A** | **Listening for Main Ideas.** Listen and choose the best answer to the questions.

1. Who do you think the speakers probably are?
   a. They're friends.   b. They're co-workers.   c. They're classmates.
2. What are the speakers doing?
   a. Choosing film footage   b. Adding sound to a film   c. Talking to a photographer

track 1-15 **B** | **Listening for Details.** Listen again. In your notebook, write the answers to the questions.

1. How much footage from Possession Island do the speakers have?
2. What does the man say about the predator birds?
3. Why does the man want to include footage of the photographers?
4. Why doesn't the woman want to include winter scenes?
5. How long will the finished film be?

[1]**Footage** of something is film of it.

After Listening

Critical Thinking Focus: Judging the Relevance of Information

The speakers in the listening passage had a story to tell. In order to do this, they needed to judge and select film footage that was relevant to their story, in other words—footage that was directly connected with their story.

A | Which footage did the speakers choose? Label each idea below **R** (relevant) or **NR** (not relevant).

_____ King Penguins finding their mates

_____ Penguins swimming in the water

_____ Winter on the island

_____ Challenges that the penguins face

_____ Parents feeding chicks

A photographer uses an underwater camera to film this coral reef in Fiji.

B | **Discussion.** Imagine that you and your partner are choosing footage for a new documentary film. You want to show the negative effects of global warming on ocean life.

1. Which footage connects to your story? Label each scene below **R** (relevant) or **NR** (not relevant).

_____ A scientist explaining how global warming causes changes in the ocean

_____ A marine biologist talking about damage to coral reefs due to warmer water

_____ A farmer talking about dry conditions due to climate change

_____ A fish swimming, but finding little food to eat due to warmer water

_____ A beachfront hotel owner who is happy about the longer summer tourist season

_____ A walrus eating food on land that was covered by ice a few years ago

A walrus is a large, fat sea mammal.

C | **Collaboration.** With a partner, plan your own documentary film. Follow the steps below. Take notes in your notebook.

1. Choose a species of animal or plant as your topic.
2. Decide what aspect of the animal or plant's life your documentary will be about (reproduction, eating habits, predators, etc.).
3. Decide what kind of footage you will need for your documentary.

D | **Presentation.** Form a group with another pair of students and talk about your ideas for a documentary. Explain how your film footage is relevant to your story.

track 1-16

Dolly the sheep was the first mammal cloned from an adult cell.

This baby mammoth is a member of an extinct species. Its DNA was preserved by the cold and ice of Siberia.

Pronunciation

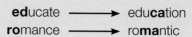

Stress Patterns before Suffixes

When some suffixes are added to words, they change the syllable stress pattern.

educate ⟶ edu**ca**tion
romance ⟶ ro**man**tic

(See page 209 in the Independent Student Handbook for more information on suffixes.)

track 1-17 **A** | Listen to each word and circle the syllable with the strongest stress.

| genetic | technical | reproduction |

B | Underline the suffix in each word from exercise **A.** What do you notice about stress before suffixes in the words from exercise **A**?

C | Practice saying the words in the chart below. Underline the stressed syllables. Notice the stress patterns and write the part of speech of *–ic, -ical,* and *-tion*. Then compare your answers with a partner's.

Suffix: *-ic* Part of Speech: _____	Suffix: *-ical* Part of Speech: _____	Suffix: *-tion* Part of Speech: _____
genetic specific problematic characteristic	ethical practical mechanical psychological	extinction connection conservation reproduction

track 1-18 **D** | Look at the flow chart on page 29 and listen to information about cloning animals. Circle each word in the box when you hear it.

| reproduction | genetic | information | chemicals |

every cell
in the body

Figure 1.1: Cloning from an Adult Cell

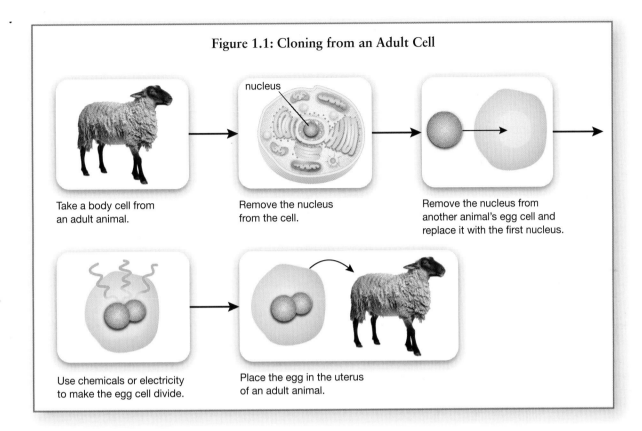

Take a body cell from an adult animal.

nucleus

Remove the nucleus from the cell.

Remove the nucleus from another animal's egg cell and replace it with the first nucleus.

Use chemicals or electricity to make the egg cell divide.

Place the egg in the uterus of an adult animal.

Language Function

Explaining a Process

We use transition words like *then* and *next* when explaining the steps of a process.

  A | Listen to the information about cloning animals again. Take notes on the words and phrases the speaker uses to transition from one step to the next in the process.

 B | Take turns explaining the cloning process to a partner. Use the transition words from exercise **A** and the information from the flow chart.

C | **Discussion.** Form a group with two or three other students and discuss the questions.

1. Cloning could be used to bring animals back from extinction. Should extinct animals such as the mammoth be brought back through cloning?

2. In Europe, the auroch—a very large, extinct form of cattle—could be brought back to help with forest conservation. The aurochs ate beech trees, which are now too numerous in Europe's forests. Should aurochs be brought back to help other tree species survive?

Scottish Highland cattle will be used in efforts to clone aurochs.

Grammar

Adjective Clauses

An adjective clause describes or modifies a noun—just as an adjective does. We can form a complex sentence with an adjective clause from two simple sentences:

I have a sister. My sister works at the airport. = *I have a sister **who** works at the airport.*
noun   adjective clause

In this sentence, the adjective clause describes the noun *sister.*

In subject adjective clauses, the relative pronoun replaces the subject. The subject relative pronouns are: *who, that,* and *which.*
A skua is a type of bird. **A skua** *eats penguins.* = *A skua is a type of bird **that** eats penguins.*

In object adjective clauses, the relative pronoun replaces an object. The object relative pronouns are: *that, which,* and *whom* (or *who* in informal speech).
*I took the class. Professor Riley taught **the class.*** = *I took the class **that** Professor Riley taught.*

Note: When the relative pronoun is an object, it can sometimes be omitted.
I took the class Professor Riley taught.

A | Choose the correct relative pronoun in each sentence below.

1. A cell's nucleus is the part (who/that) contains DNA.
2. Dolly was the first mammal (that/whom) was cloned successfully.
3. It was the first thing (who/that) I learned in Chemistry 101.
4. There are two main predators (that/who) penguins must deal with.
5. Do you know the man (who/which) is wearing the white shirt?
6. We're watching the documentary film (whom/that) our professors made.

B | **Critical Thinking.** Complete each sentence using any appropriate adjective clause.

1. Cloning is a type of reproduction *that does not require a male/happens in a laboratory/etc.* .

2. An island is a piece of land that _____.

3. Stefano Unterthiner is a photographer who _____.

4. I enjoy films that _____.

5. She's the biologist who _____.

C | **Discussion.** Think about the topics below. Then discuss with a partner. Practice using adjective clauses.

1. Interesting facts about your family members or friends
2. Interesting facts you know about animals

> Platypuses are mammals that lay eggs.

Discussing Species Conservation

A | Read the information below.

> Over time, many species of plants and animals have become extinct. This has happened for many different reasons, but nowadays human beings are often the cause of species extinction. In this section, you will discuss species conservation and the causes of extinction.

Panda bears are just one of the earth's endangered species.

B | **Discussion.** Discuss the following question in a small group. How can each of the following lead to species extinction?

- Hunting and fishing
- Logging (cutting down trees)
- Farming
- Global warming and climate change
- An increasing human population

C | **Presentation.** Report some of your group's ideas to the rest of the class.

D | **Critical Thinking.** Discuss the following arguments in favor of species conservation with a partner. Then rank the arguments from 1 (most relevant) to 4 (least relevant).

_____ Some popular endangered animals provide economic benefits (e.g., ecotourism).
_____ The extinction of one plant or animal can affect other plants and animals.
_____ Some species could be beneficial for human health and medicine.
_____ Genetic diversity (a wide variety of living things) makes it possible for plants and animals to evolve and change.

E | **Discussion.** Form a group with two or three other students, and try to agree on the best way to finish each sentence below.

1. We (should/shouldn't) clone species that have become extinct because . . .
2. We (should/shouldn't) spend our time and energy on species conservation because . . .

Student to Student: Asking for Repetition

Use these expressions in informal conversations when you need to ask for repetition.

I'm sorry?
I didn't catch what you said.

What's that?
I missed that.

TURTLE EXCLUDER

Before Viewing

A | **Critical Thinking.** In Lesson A of this unit, you talked about species conservation. In this video, you will learn about a low-tech way to conserve the Kemp's Ridley sea turtle. Before you watch, discuss the questions below with a partner.

1. Nowadays, the Kemp's Ridley sea turtle is seldom eaten by people, yet it has become an endangered species—partly due to fishing in the Gulf of Mexico. Why do you think this is happening?
2. What are some other threats to sea animals besides fishing?

B | **Self-Reflection.** Discuss these questions with a partner. Do you eat fish or seafood? If so, what kind do you like? Does fishing for these species cause any environmental problems?

C | **Using Adjective Clauses.** Work with a partner. Match the sentence beginnings to their endings. Pay attention to the underlined words. Use your dictionary to help you.

1. ___ We usually <u>exclude</u> things that . . .	a. all live in one place.
2. ___ A <u>biologist</u> is someone . . .	b. that live in the sea.
3. ___ A <u>device</u> is something that . . .	c. we don't want.
4. ___ A <u>population</u> is a group of animals that . . .	d. has a special function.
5. ___ <u>Sharks</u>, fish, and <u>shrimp</u> are animals . . .	e. who studies living things.

While Viewing

A | Watch the video. Then answer the questions below.

1. What is the Turtle Excluder?

   _____

2. In your own words, how does the Turtle Excluder work?

   _____

   _____

3. In the U.S., what kind of fishermen must use the Turtle Excluder?

   _____

B | Note-Taking. Watch the video again and fill in the T-chart below.

Disadvantage to Fishermen (according to some fishermen)	Advantage to Fishermen (according to biologists)

A fisherman releases a cascade of shrimp onto the deck of his boat.

Although both men and women fish, *fisherman* is still a very common word. In the future, we may use the word "fisher" instead.

After Viewing

Collaboration. Imagine that you are part of a public relations group. As a group, it's your job to convince fishermen that the Turtle Excluder is good for everyone. Follow the steps below.

1. Brainstorm several benefits of a healthy sea turtle population. Besides the advantages you identified in exercise **B** above, consider the environment, tourism, the future, and any other topics you can think of.

2. Write a letter to send to all the fishermen in the Gulf of Mexico. This letter should make the fishermen feel good about using the Turtle Excluder.

A Turtle Excluder device

track 1-19 **A** | **Meaning from Context.** Read and listen to the information about orchids. Notice the words in blue. These are words you will hear and use in Lesson B.

Orchid Question & Answer

Q: Imagine that you're a flower. Like every other living thing, you want to reproduce. But you can't move! How can you get your DNA to another flower?

A: Offer food. This is a great way to trick birds or insects. They think they're just getting a free meal in the form of nectar, a sweet liquid. However, they're also carrying your pollen—a substance that contains your DNA—to the next flower that they visit.

Q: Nectar is full of calories, so it requires a lot of energy to produce. Is there a less "expensive" way for me to move my pollen around?

A: Absolutely! Many orchids[1] have found fascinating ways to attract insects without offering any food. To do this, they imitate something that the insects want. Here are some ways they do this:

Hummingbird getting food from an orchid

Butterfly on an *Epidendrum* orchid in Panama

> **Shelter:** Even insects need a place to live. Some orchids resemble insect burrows.[2] The insects crawl in, but since it's not really a good place to live, they leave with pollen on their bodies.
>
> **Scents:** Insects are attracted to the smell of food, so orchids produce scents that seem wonderful to bugs, but not always to humans. The *Dracula* orchid attracts tiny insects called gnats by smelling like a dirty diaper!
>
> **Food:** Orchids don't need to offer real food as long as they seem to offer food. The *Epidendrum* orchid resembles milkweed, a favorite food of butterflies. Butterflies visit the plant, but all they obtain is pollen to carry away when they leave.
>
> **Mates:** One of the most common orchid tricks is to offer the promise of a mate. The flower of the *Ophrys* orchid in Italy resembles the wings of a female bee. It even smells like a female bee, so instinct tells every male bee in the area to visit the plant.

B | Use context clues to write each word in blue in the correct box below.

Nouns	Verbs	Adjectives

[1]**Orchids** are flowering plants in the family *orchidaceae*.　　[2]**Burrows** are small holes where insects can live.

A | **Using a Dictionary.** With a partner, fill in each blank with the correct form of a vocabulary word from exercise **B**. Use each word only once, and use your dictionary to help you with words you are not sure about. Then complete each sentence with your own ideas.

1. Please close the window. The smell of the cake is _attracting bees._

2. I'm interested in many subjects at school, but the most _____ subject for me is _____

3. We tried to borrow money from the bank, but we couldn't _____ a loan because _____

4. Many people dislike _____, but bees are _____

5. Don't send them your bank account number! It's a _____. They're really _____

6. I don't like the _____ of that flower. To me, it smells like _____

7. Birds need a safe place for their eggs, so the best kind of _____ for them is _____

8. Baby crocodiles never see their parents. They must use their _____ to _____

9. She doesn't look like her mother at all, but she does _____

10. You need to develop your own artistic style, so don't _____ other artists' _____

B | **Critical Thinking.** Discuss the following questions in a group. Then share some of your ideas with the rest of the class.

1. In your culture, which characteristics help a person to **attract** a mate?

2. People use perfume because the **scent** can be very attractive. What other **tricks** do people use to make themselves more attractive?

3. In the animal world, a mate that can offer food and **shelter** might be very attractive. Is that true in the human world as well?

4. Animals have **instincts**, and these **instincts** cause certain behaviors that help the animals survive. Do human beings also have **instincts**, or do we only think and reason?

Before Listening

Emphasis on Key Words

Some words in a sentence or in a conversation receive more stress or emphasis than other words. Look at the information below. Then complete the activities that follow.

Growing orchids in a greenhouse

track 1-20

Content Words	Content words carry the most meaning in a sentence. They include nouns, verbs, and sometimes other words. *He **told** me he was **finished** with the **assignment.*** *Is that a **cow** in the **road?***
New Information	When a speaker puts extra emphasis, or stress, on new information in a conversation, the listener can follow the ideas more easily. *A: What did the professor tell you?* *B: Nothing, because I talked to the **secretary.*** *A: **Which** secretary?* *B: The secretary in the **botany department.***

A | Read part of a conversation between two university students. Underline the words and phrases that you think will get extra emphasis.

> **Leo:** Hi, Elena. Are you on your way to the greenhouse?
>
> **Elena:** Hi, Leo. Yes, I am.
>
> **Leo:** Good. We can walk there together. Have you been to the greenhouse before?
>
> **Elena:** I have. It's a fascinating place—to me, anyway.
>
> **Leo:** Oh, I totally agree. They have plants from all over the world—even tropical plants.

track 1-21 **B** | Listen and check your predictions from exercise **A.**

Listening: A Conversation between Classmates

A | **Listening for Main Ideas.** Listen to the whole conversation and choose the best answer.

1. What was the last lecture about?
   a. Greenhouses
   b. Orchids
   c. Tropical plants

2. What is special about epiphytes?
   a. They don't need sunlight to grow.
   b. They don't grow in the ground.
   c. They don't have any predators.

A male sand bee is attracted to this Italian orchid's flowers, which resemble a female sand bee.

B | **Listening for Details.** Listen again and answer the questions about epiphytes.

1. How do epiphytes obtain water?

   _____

2. Where do epiphytes grow?

   _____

3. Why do epiphytes grow there?

   _____

4. How are epiphytes able to grow there?

   _____

5. What's the connection between orchids and epiphytes?

   _____

After Listening

Self-Reflection. Discuss the following questions with a partner.

1. Are you comfortable talking with people whom you don't know very well? Explain.
2. The speakers in the listening passage didn't know each other well, but they did have a good conversation. Check the things the speakers had in common to talk about.

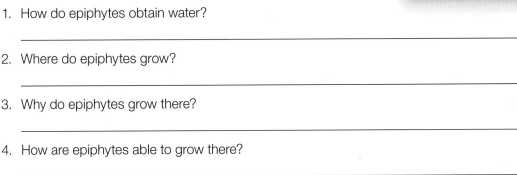

- ❏ Their class schedules
- ❏ A class lecture
- ❏ The greenhouses
- ❏ Knowledge of epiphytes
- ❏ Knowledge of orchids
- ❏ Knowledge of houseplants

3. What do you and your partner have in common? Find a topic and have a friendly conversation for at least two minutes.

Language Function

Making Suggestions

There are several ways to make polite suggestions. You can be less direct or more direct depending on the situation and how strongly you feel about your suggestion.

Less direct	We **could meet** after class to talk about the assignment.
	Why don't you **call** him and find out?
More direct	I **recommend talking** to your professor.
	I **suggest** that you **talk** to your professor.
	Let's get together at the coffee shop this afternoon.

Although we usually use **should** to give advice, it can also be used for suggestions.
Maybe you **should send** *her a text message.*

Grammar Note: The verbs *recommend* and *suggest* are transitive verbs. Their objects can be:

1. nouns	I recommend **hot tea.**
2. gerunds	I suggest **taking** the bus.
3. noun clauses	I recommend **that we do some research online.**

A | Complete the conversation below with a partner. Use the less direct language from the **Making Suggestions** chart.

> **Rasa:** Bob isn't doing well in the class. What do you think we should do?
>
> **Doris:** Maybe we _____ help him with his homework.
>
> **Rasa:** That's a good idea, but the homework usually isn't a group assignment.
>
> **Doris:** True. He's supposed to do it himself.
>
> **Rasa:** _____ ask the instructor to talk to Bob.
>
> **Doris:** Yes, but that's going behind his back. He might not like that.
>
> **Rasa:** Then _____ talk to Bob about it?
> We _____ suggest that he talk to the instructor.
>
> **Doris:** That's probably the best idea.

B | Practice the conversation with your partner. Then switch roles and practice it again.

C | Complete the conversation below with a partner. Use the more direct language from the **Making Suggestions** chart. There may be more than one correct answer.

Miguel:	What's the matter? You look worried.
Pierre:	It's my oldest son. He finished high school, and now he spends all his time watching TV.
Miguel:	I _____ telling him to get a job. He needs to earn his own money.
Pierre:	That's true, but I really want him to get more education.
Miguel:	Then I _____ that you go and visit some universities with him. He might like that.
Pierre:	Sure, he'd like that, but then what?
Miguel:	_____ introduce him to some of the professional people that we know.
Pierre:	That's a good idea. They could tell my son about their careers.
Miguel:	Exactly. And he might find something that he wants to do.

 D | Practice the conversation with your partner. Then switch roles and practice it again.

 E | **Collaboration.** Read the situation below. Then follow the directions.

Situation: You are known as "the problem-solving committee" because you always make good suggestions. Working together with another pair of students, write responses to the following email messages using language from the **Making Suggestions** chart. Then share your responses with the class.

Red panda

To: PSC
Subject: Our red panda pair

Dear Problem-Solving Committee:

We have a problem with the red pandas here at the National Zoo. We have an adult male and an adult female, and they're in the same enclosure together. So far, however, we have no baby red pandas. What do you suggest?

Best,
Dr. Nancy Hartl

To: PSC
Subject: Plant species

Dear Problem-Solving Committee:

When I say, "endangered species," what do you think of? A cute panda bear? Or an unusual kind of fish? Well, they're not the only species in danger. I'm a botanist, and I'm very concerned about the world's plants. Many, many species of plants are endangered—mostly because of human activities such as farming. How can I make the public more aware of this problem?

Thank you,
Mr. Silvio Rhodes

You are going to create and present a group plan for studying an endangered species.

 A | Form a group with two or three other students and read the information below.

Good news! Your group has received a large research grant to study an endangered species' reproductive behavior. You have plenty of money, so you can travel anywhere and study the species of your choice.

B | Fill out the questionnaire below to decide what species your group will study and where.

Research Project Questionnaire

1. We'd like to study . . .
   ❏ a plant species.   ❏ an animal species.

2. We'd prefer to study . . .
   ❏ a popular species.   ❏ a species that's not well known.

3. We'd like to travel . . .
   ❏ to a country that's far away.   ❏ within this country.

4. We'd prefer to travel . . .
   ❏ by plane or helicopter.   ❏ by car or boat.

5. We'd like to do . . .
   ❏ a short study (weeks).   ❏ a long study (months).

C | **Organizing Ideas.** Working as a group, make a plan for your study using the form below. Look back at your questionnaire for ideas, and practice making suggestions as you discuss your plan.

Study Plan

Species: _____

Purpose of Study: _____   Length of Study: _____

Study Location: _____   Travel Plans: _____

Presentation Skills: Using Specific Details

Specific details in your presentation help your audience understand your exact meaning. Using adverbs, adjectives, and adjective clauses are good ways to do this.
> *The Bengal tiger is the **largest** tiger sub-species, and it's **extremely endangered**. We chose a location **where very few people live.***

 D | **Presentation.** Share some of the details of your study plan with the class. Every person in your group should speak. Then invite the class to ask questions and suggest other ideas for your study. Decide how you will present your plan. You can use the board, paper, or PowerPoint.®

Human Migration

ACADEMIC PATHWAYS

Lesson A: Listening to a PowerPoint® Lecture
Discussing Case Studies
Lesson B: Listening to a Small Group Discussion
Giving a Group Presentation

Think and Discuss

1. This photo shows Hong Kong at night. What do you know about Hong Kong?

2. Hong Kong is a gateway city, home to people from many other countries. Why do you think so many people from other countries live there?

3. Do you know of any other cities with large foreign-born populations?

Lights fill the sky during Hong Kong's "Symphony of Lights." With approximately 3 million foreign-born residents, Hong Kong is one of the world's major "gateway" cities, or entry points for immigrants.

Exploring the Theme:
Human Migration

A | Look at the map and map key. Then answer the questions.

 1. What do the circles show? What do the arrows show?
 2. What is a gateway city?
 3. What information does this map show about your country?

B | Look at the photos and read the captions. Then discuss the questions.

 1. For how many years was Ellis Island the entry point for immigrants to the United States?
 2. According to the information on these pages, why did people immigrate to Germany? to Saudi Arabia? to Australia?

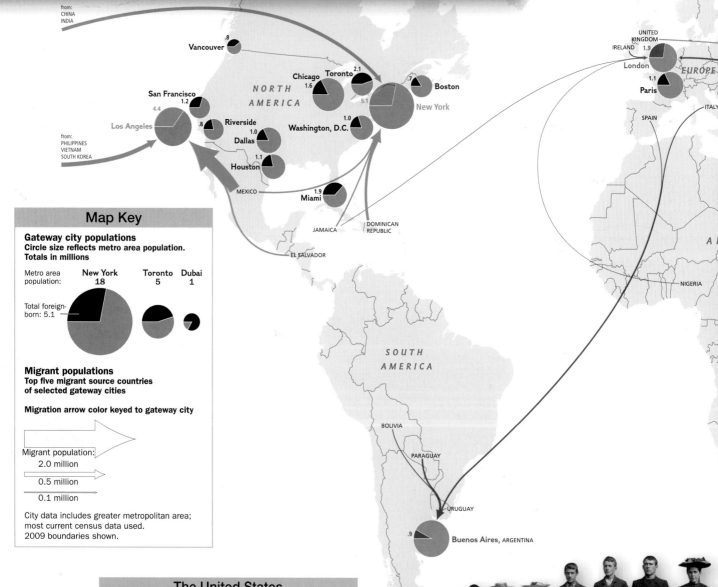

from:
CHINA
INDIA

Vancouver .8

Chicago 1.6   Toronto 2.1   Boston .7

San Francisco 1.2

NORTH AMERICA

New York 5.1

Los Angeles 4.4

from:
PHILIPPINES
VIETNAM
SOUTH KOREA

Riverside 1.0
Dallas .8
Washington, D.C. 1.0
Houston 1.1

MEXICO

Miami 1.9

JAMAICA   DOMINICAN REPUBLIC

EL SALVADOR

UNITED KINGDOM
IRELAND 1.9
London   EUROPE
Paris 1.1
SPAIN   ITALY

AF

NIGERIA

SOUTH AMERICA

BOLIVIA

PARAGUAY

URUGUAY

Buenos Aires, ARGENTINA .9

Map Key

Gateway city populations
Circle size reflects metro area population.
Totals in millions

Metro area population: New York 18   Toronto 5   Dubai 1

Total foreign-born: 5.1

Migrant populations
Top five migrant source countries of selected gateway cities

Migration arrow color keyed to gateway city

Migrant population:
 2.0 million
 0.5 million
 0.1 million

City data includes greater metropolitan area;
most current census data used.
2009 boundaries shown.

The United States

Ellis Island, New York, was the entry point for immigrants to the United States between the years 1892 to 1924.

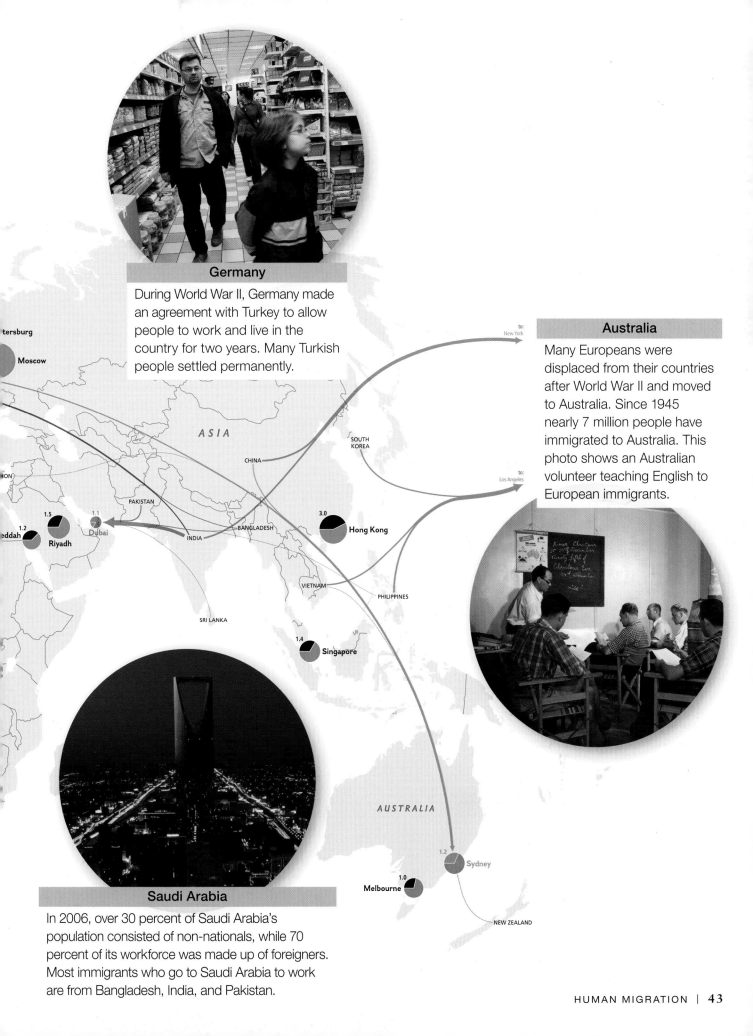

Germany

During World War II, Germany made an agreement with Turkey to allow people to work and live in the country for two years. Many Turkish people settled permanently.

Australia

Many Europeans were displaced from their countries after World War II and moved to Australia. Since 1945 nearly 7 million people have immigrated to Australia. This photo shows an Australian volunteer teaching English to European immigrants.

Saudi Arabia

In 2006, over 30 percent of Saudi Arabia's population consisted of non-nationals, while 70 percent of its workforce was made up of foreigners. Most immigrants who go to Saudi Arabia to work are from Bangladesh, India, and Pakistan.

Map labels: tersburg, Moscow, ASIA, SOUTH KOREA, CHINA, to: New York, to: Los Angeles, PAKISTAN, 1.5, 1.1, 1.2, eddah, Riyadh, Dubai, BANGLADESH, INDIA, 3.0, Hong Kong, VIETNAM, PHILIPPINES, SRI LANKA, 1.4, Singapore, AUSTRALIA, 1.2, Sydney, 1.0, Melbourne, NEW ZEALAND

A | **Meaning from Context.** Read and listen to the sentences. Then write each word in blue next to its definition below. These are words you will hear and use in Lesson A.

1. Erlinda's **native** language is Tagalog. She learned English in high school.
2. I have a **temporary** driver's license. I can use it for two months while I take driving lessons.
3. In the 1840s, more than 8 million people **emigrated** from Ireland to other countries because there wasn't enough food in Ireland.
4. Our university has programs for students who want to study **abroad** in France or Mexico.
5. There is a large **community** of Japanese people who live in São Paulo, Brazil.
6. Many **immigrants** bring traditions from their home countries to their new countries.
7. I'm working in Hong Kong for two years, but my **permanent** home is Beijing. I'll go back there to live with my family next year.
8. In my city, there is a **trend** toward hiring more foreign workers in hotels and restaurants. You can see more people from different countries working in those places.
9. Too many people in my country have **negative** ideas about foreigners. For example, some people think that foreigners don't work hard and that they can't learn our language.
10. His **original** job was operating a machine in a factory, but then he graduated from a technical college, and now he's an engineer.

a. _____ (n.) a general pattern

b. _____ (adv.) out of the country

c. _____ (v.) left your own country to live in another country

d. _____ (adj.) lasting for only a limited time

e. _____ (n.) people who come to live in a new country

f. _____ (adj.) lasting forever

g. _____ (adj.) first, earliest

h. _____ (adj.) bad, unpleasant, or harmful

i. _____ (n.) a group of people living in a certain place or who are alike in some way

j. _____ (adj.) related to the place where a person was born

B | **Using a Dictionary.** Find other forms and definitions of the vocabulary words in your dictionary to complete the chart below.

Vocabulary Word	Related Words	Definitions
immigrant (n.)	v: _immigrate_	_to come to live in a new country_
	n: _immigration_	_the process of immigrating_
emigrate (v.)	n: _____	_a person who emigrates_
	n: _____	_the process of emigrating_
temporary (adj.)	adv: _____	_____
permanent (adj.)	adv: _____	_____
original (adj.)	adv: _____	_____
negative (adj.)	adv: _____	_____
trend (n.)	adj: _____	_____

A | Look at the photo. Then discuss the questions below with a partner.

1. How would you describe the place where these young women are walking?
2. What do you notice about their clothes?

B | Read the article and fill in each blank with the correct form of a word from exercise **A** on page 44. Use each word only once.

Two young women go for a Sunday afternoon walk in the small town of Budesti, Romania—but their clothes say a lot about an important world (1) _____. Along with their traditional Romanian Sunday dresses, the women are wearing fashionable foreign jackets and shoes. People in the women's families went to live (2) _____ to work and then came back to their hometown, bringing money and foreign products—like these clothes.

More than 2.5 million Romanians have (3) _____ and are now living in countries such as Spain and Italy. For most of these people, the move is only (4) _____. They plan to work in a store or factory for several years and then return to Romania. They send money to their families and keep in contact with them by phone. Often, they live together in a Romanian (5) _____ with other people who speak their (6) _____ language.

Other Romanians have made a (7) _____ move to Canada or Australia, and they will never go back to live in their (8) _____ country. These (9) _____ often face difficulties in their new country with language, culture, and (10) _____ feelings from the local people. But their children usually learn to speak two languages and become comfortable in two cultures.

C | Write down notes to answer the questions below.

1. Are there many immigrants in your country? If so, where did they come from? Are most of them permanent or temporary? _____

_____

2. Do people ever emigrate from your country? Why? _____

_____

3. If you had a chance to live abroad for 10 years, where would you go? Explain.

_____

D | Discussion. Form a group with two or three other students and discuss your answers from exercise **C**.

Before Listening

A | **Predicting Content.** Look at the six slides on pages 46–47 from a professor's lecture about immigration and emigration. What topics do you think the professor will talk about for each slide? Discuss your ideas with a partner. *(See page 202 in the Independent Student Handbook for more information on predicting.)*

B | Form a group with another pair of students and share your predictions.

Listening: A PowerPoint Lecture

track 1-24 **C** | **Listening for Main Ideas.** Listen and number the photos in the order that you hear about them. How many of the topics that you predicted in exercise **A** were in the lecture?

Problems during the 1920s–1930s

1. _____

_____

2. _____

_____

CANADA

North Dakota

UNITED STATES

MEXICO

North Dakota 100 years ago:_____

_____

_____

North Dakota today: _____

_____

_____

Modern immigration → People moving to:_____

_____

_____

_____

_____

_____

Some people trying to preserve the old: _____

Every year, _____

are invited to this theater in Marmarth.

Importance of the railroad:

1. _____

_____

2. _____

_____

Town of Corinth, ND

Population in the past: _____

Population now: _____

🎧 **D** | **Listening for Details.** Listen again and complete the notes for each slide.

track 1-24

After Listening

👥 **Critical Thinking.** Discuss the questions with your group.

1. Why did immigrants go to western North Dakota? Why did they leave?
2. Are there places in your country that are losing population? Are the reasons similar to or different from the reasons people left North Dakota?
3. Do you think it's possible to save some of the towns that are disappearing? Should people try to save them?
4. Can you think of any ideas to help the towns that you heard about?

Grammar

Adjectives with *Enough*, *Not Enough*, and *Too*

We use **adjective + *enough*** to talk about something that is sufficient, or the amount we need or want.

> *The population is **big enough** to support a grocery store, a gas station, and a café.*

We use ***not* + adjective + *enough*** to talk about things that are insufficient, or when there is not the amount we want or need of something.

> *The farm isn't **big enough** to make much money.*

We use ***too* + adjective** to talk about something that is excessive, or more than we need or want.

> *North Dakota is **too cold** for many people. They prefer to live someplace warmer.*

***Too* + adjective** is often followed by a verb in the infinitive.

> *People believed that North Dakota was **too dry to grow** farm crops.*

A | Write sentences with *too*, *enough*, or *not enough*.

1. I can't go with you tonight. ___*I'm too busy to see a movie.*___
   (I/busy/see a movie)

2. I don't want to live in Marmarth, North Dakota.
   _____ (it/small/for me)

3. I can't hear the TV. _____ (it/loud)

4. My children are learning to cook. _____
   (they/old/make dinner)

5. People don't usually travel to North Dakota. They think
   _____ (it/interesting/for a vacation)

6. Very few people live in the center of Australia.
   _____ (the land/dry)

7. I like this bag. _____ (it/big/ to
   hold my laptop and my books)

B | Look at the activities below. Can you do these things? Tell a partner. Use an adjective with *enough*, *not enough*, or *too*.

> I'm not fit enough to run 5 miles. What about you?

> I'm too old to run 5 miles!

1. Run 5 miles
2. Buy a new car
3. Study abroad
4. Play chess
5. Take a month-long vacation
6. Get married

C | With your partner, think of three more ideas like the ones in exercise **B.** Then ask another pair of students.

Can you lift 100 pounds?

I'm not strong enough!

Enough, Not Enough, and Too + Nouns

We use **enough** + **noun** to talk about a sufficient amount of something, or the amount we need or want.

> The local farms are able to produce **enough food** to meet the needs of the population.

We use **not enough** + **noun** to talk about an insufficient amount or lack of something.

> There are **not enough jobs** in the town, so people are leaving.
> I have enough money, but **not enough time.**

We use **too** + **much/many** + **noun** to talk about an excessive amount of something, or more than we want or need.

> My city has **too many cars** and **too much pollution.**

A | Complete the sentences. Use *too much/many, enough,* or *not enough*.

1. Some people emigrate because there is __not enough__ food in their native countries.

2. Many people don't want to live in North Dakota because there is _____ snow in the winter.

3. My sister moved to a small town in the country because there was _____ crime in the city.

4. The problem with Boston is that there are _____ cars and _____ parking spaces.

5. Do we have _____ gas to get all the way to New Haven?

B | **Discussion.** Look at the topics below. Discuss your ideas and opinions about each topic with your group. Use *too, enough,* or *not enough* + nouns in your discussion.

1. Advantages and disadvantages of living in a big city
2. Greatest challenges faced by people in your country
3. Challenges you face in your everyday life

Living in a small town is nice because it's safe, but there are not enough good jobs or things to do on the weekends.

Language Function

Asking for Reasons

We ask for reasons in order to:

- find out more about a topic we are interested in
- get information and details we need for a research project, etc.
- keep a conversation going or show interest in what a speaker is talking about

Here are some ways of asking for reasons.

Why is that?

What is/are the reason(s) for that?

Really, why/why not?

What do you think the reason is for that?

That's interesting. Why not?/Why is that?

A | Fill out the questionnaire about immigration and emigration. Write two more questions of your own.

Question	Yes	No	Reason
1. Do many people emigrate from your country?	X	☐	*Not enough jobs, too much violence in big cities*
2. Do you like the city you live in now?	☐	☐	
3. Is there a problem with small towns disappearing in your country?	☐	☐	
4. Are immigrants and ethnic minorities treated well in your country?	☐	☐	
5. _____	☐	☐	
6. _____	☐	☐	

B | Interview a partner using the questionnaire from exercise **A**. Use the language from this lesson to ask about reasons and keep the conversation going.

Do many people emigrate from your country?

Yes, they do.

What are the reasons for that?

Well, there are not enough jobs right now. Also, there is a lot of violence in the big cities, so people want to leave.

Discussing Case Studies

A | Read these case studies about people who want to emigrate to other countries. Underline or highlight the most important information for each person.

Case Study 1 Ayu

Ayu lives in a village in Indonesia. She has two young children. Her husband died last year, and now she and her children live on her parents' farm. Five years ago, Ayu's friend Melati got a job in Singapore. Melati works as a housemaid, and she has saved enough money to send her son to college. She called Ayu to tell her that she knows another family that is looking for a housemaid. She is sure the family would hire Ayu. Ayu could save a lot of money if she took the job, but housemaids in Singapore can't get visas for their children.

Case Study 2 Luka

Luka is 30 years old and lives in Zagreb, Croatia. He was trained as an architect, but he hasn't been able to find a job in his field since he graduated from the technical university. One of his former professors told him that there are not enough architects in New Zealand. Luka's girlfriend, Maya, who is a nurse, thinks they should get married and emigrate to New Zealand. Luka really wants to work as an architect, but he is worried about his father, who is in very poor health.

Case Study 3 Ibrahim

Ibrahim is a 16-year-old boy from Nigeria. Five years ago, he was playing soccer in the street with his friends, and a foreign coach saw how well he was playing. Now the coach wants to take Ibrahim to France. He says he can get Ibrahim a visa and help him continue his soccer training in Paris. The coach says that if Ibrahim plays well enough, he can get a position on a European soccer team and make a lot of money. Ibrahim has always dreamed of playing for a foreign team, but his parents don't know whether they can trust the coach. His parents are worried that the coach isn't telling the truth.

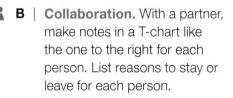

B | **Collaboration.** With a partner, make notes in a T-chart like the one to the right for each person. List reasons to stay or leave for each person.

Reasons to stay	Reasons to leave

C | **Discussion.** Form a group with another pair of students. Share your notes, and then agree on whether each person should stay or leave. Use expressions from page 50 when asking about reasons.

D | **Presentation.** Explain your group's decisions to the class.

Turkish Germany

Before Viewing

🎧 track 1-25 **A** | Read about Germany's guest worker program. Then look at the information in the line graph.

Moving to Germany

During World War II, many Germans emigrated from their country. Then after the war, when the country was rebuilding and the economy was growing, there was a shortage of workers. So Germany made agreements with several countries to allow workers, mostly men, to live in the country for two years and work at industrial jobs. After two years, the men were expected to return to their home countries, which included Italy, Spain, Greece, and Turkey.

The guest worker program began in 1955 and ended in 1973, when Germany's economic growth slowed. In contrast to the economy, the number of foreigners in Germany continued to grow as family members joined the workers. A new agreement among European Union countries also allowed Italians to enter Germany without any special permission. In addition, a second generation had been born, and those babies were still foreigners according to German law.

Turkish family arriving at the train station in Munich

Percentage of Foreigners in Germany

Year

Source: www.migrationinformation.org

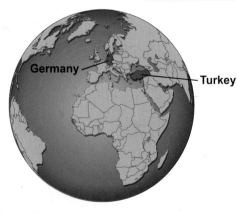

Germany
— Turkey

👥 **B** | **Understanding Visuals.** With a partner, talk about the information shown in the line graph. The *x* axis shows the year and the *y* axis shows the percentage of foreign immigrants. *(See page 216 in the Independent Student Handbook for more information on understanding graphs.)*

1. What was the immigration trend between 1960 and 1988?
2. Do you think this trend has continued in Germany? Why, or why not?
3. What do the people who immigrated to Germany during the guest worker program have in common with other people you learned about in Lesson A of the unit?

C | Complete each sentence with *enough, not enough,* or *too.*

1. The guest worker program began when there were
   _____ workers in Germany.

2. In 1955, German companies had _____
   money to pay foreign workers.

3. The government expected the guest workers to be temporary
   residents, so from the government's point of view, some of the
   workers stayed in Germany _____ long.

4. By 1973, there was _____ economic
   growth to support the program.

A Turkish family taking
a walk in Berlin

While Viewing

A | Watch the video and check (✔) the aspects of Turkish culture that you see.

❑ food ❑ music ❑ clothing ❑ religion ❑ language ❑ art ❑ other

B | Watch the video again and pay close attention to the part about the Rixdorfer Elementary
School. Then circle the correct word or phrase in each sentence.

1. The Turkish and German children are (together/separated).
2. The price there is (higher/lower) than average.
3. The teachers use (one language/two languages).
4. The success rate at the school is (higher/lower) than average.

After Viewing

Critical Thinking Focus: Analyzing Information

While you listen to or view information, it's important to think about what you're hearing
and seeing. For example, you might want to compare it with other information you've
heard on the same topic. Or you may need to make inferences about the information
you're *not* hearing in order to "fill in the blanks."

Critical Thinking. Discuss the issues below with two or three other students.

1. The video doesn't address specific problems faced by the Turkish community in
   Germany, but it does tell us that, *"Turkish fears grew when the Berlin Wall fell and
   the government focused on reunification rather than the needs of minorities."*
   Discuss the kinds of problems you think the Turkish people and other
   immigrant groups in Germany might face.

2. The woman who speaks in the video talks about the children at the Rixdorfer
   Elementary School. She says, *"They don't see the difference between the
   Turkish and the German, and so they have no problems with foreigners.
   They are not foreigners. They are kids."* Do you think bilingual and
   bi-cultural schools are an effective solution to Germany's problems?

🎧 track 1-26 **A** | Write the word from the box that can replace the words in parentheses. These are words you will hear and use in Lesson B. Use your dictionary to help you. Then listen and check your answers.

assimilate	settle	ancestors	minority	attitude
generation	positive	ethnic	discrimination	retain

1. My last name is Petrov. My _____ (grandparents and great-grandparents) were from Russia.

2. The Aborigines are a _____ (small group of people) in Australia.

3. Most of the younger _____ (people born in the same period of time) in my country can speak English well.

4. Carlos had a very _____ (good) experience studying in Beijing. He said his classmates were really friendly.

5. One day, I would like to _____ (make a permanent home) in Canada. It's a beautiful country with lots of opportunities.

6. My family came from Sweden a very long time ago, but we still _____ (keep) some of the old Swedish customs.

7. Malaysia is the home of many different _____ (racial and cultural) groups, including Malays, Chinese, Indians, and tribal people.

8. Some immigrants think that they should try very hard not to _____ (adopt the customs of new culture) or learn the language of the country they are living in.

9. In the past, there was a lot of _____ (unfair treatment) towards people from the southern part of my country. Today, the problem isn't as bad.

10. My grandmother didn't like foreigners, but then she had a doctor from India and she really liked him. That changed her _____ (way of thinking) about them completely!

👥 **B** | **Self Reflection.** Answer the questions in your notebook with your own ideas. Then discuss your answers with a partner. Use the vocabulary from exercise **A** in your answers.

1. Have you ever changed your **attitude** about anything? How did your **attitude** change? Why?

2. Where are your **ancestors** from? What do you know about them?

3. List three ways the older **generation** is different from the younger **generation** in your country.

4. Has your family **retained** any traditions and customs? Explain.

5. What ethnic **minorities** are there in your country? How are they treated? Do people **discriminate** against them?

A | Read the information about one group of immigrants. Your partner will read about the other group.

B | **Note-Taking.** Take turns telling your partner about the information you read. Take notes as you listen.

track 1-27

Student A — Hmong Americans

The Hmong are an ethnic minority from Vietnam, Laos, and Thailand. In the 1970s, after the war between the U.S. and Vietnam, many Hmong were forced to leave their homes, and a large number of them emigrated to the U.S. to settle permanently. The Hmong were mostly uneducated farmers in their native countries. When they emigrated to the U.S., many of them settled together in small towns and started vegetable farms. They retained many of their native customs and did not learn much English. The Hmong people mainly kept to themselves, but many of the local people did not like having them in their communities. Today, most young Hmong-Americans are bilingual and well educated, but their parents make sure the family retains the traditional culture and customs.

track 1-28

Student B — Japanese Brazilians

The first Japanese immigrants came to Brazil in 1908, and today Brazil has the largest Japanese community outside of Japan. Japanese immigrants came to work on coffee farms across Brazil. They planned to stay only a few years, make money, and then go home. However, very few returned to Japan. During the 1940s, there were many laws that restricted the activities and freedom of Japanese Brazilians. Life improved for the Japanese Brazilians in the 1970s. They moved into new fields of business and became very successful. Today, only the oldest people in the community still speak Japanese, and the majority of the youngest generation are of mixed race.

C | **Using a Graphic Organizer.** Discuss the questions below with your partner. Then create a Venn diagram comparing the Hmong Americans and the Japanese Brazilians. (*See page 214 of the Independent Student Handbook for more information on Venn diagrams.*)

1. How are the Hmong Americans and the Japanese Brazilians similar?
2. How are they different?

D | **Critical Thinking.** Discuss the questions below with your partner. Refer to the information in your Venn diagram from exercise **C** to help you.

1. Which group do you think had a more positive experience in their new country?
2. How much did each group assimilate into their new culture?
3. Do you think both groups of people were successful in their new countries? Why, or why not?

A foreign worker stacks fish traps near the Burj a Arab hotel in Dubai.

Emigrants leave Djakarta to resettle on less developed islands.

Before Listening

Prior Knowledge. Discuss the questions with a partner.

1. Do you know someone who has gone to live abroad? Why did that person go?
2. Did that person stay there or return home? Why?
3. Do you think that person was successful? Why, or why not?

Listening: A Small Group Discussion

track 1-29 **A** | **Using a Graphic Organizer.** Listen to a teacher give a discussion assignment. In your notebook, make a chart like the one below. Complete the left-hand column in the chart. (*See pages 214-215 of the Independent Student Handbook for information on using graphic organizers.*)

	Josh's	Nasir's	Emily's	Sunisa's
1. Who emigrated?	Grand parent	father	uncle	an uncle
2. Where did the person ~~come from~~?	Poland	Pakistan, Saudi Arabia	U.K. England	China
3. Where did the person ~~go to~~?	Chicago		Australia	Thailand
4. ~~Why~~ did the person leave?	Troubles in Europe	good money	cheap, no romance	population
5. Did the person ~~assimilate~~?	didn't, children did	No, move Pakistan	help, anything girls	Yes, mixed marriage, speak Thai

Parents upset slightly

track 1-30-33 **B** | **Listening for Details.** Listen to the group discussion and complete the chart.

After Listening

Discussion. Work with a partner. Discuss the questions.

1. What was the goal of each person emigrating? Who was successful in meeting his or her goals?
2. Who wanted to assimilate with the new culture? Who assimilated successfully?
3. Do you think all immigrants should try to assimilate? Why, or why not?

Pronunciation

Fast Speech

When we speak quickly, in English or in any language, certain sounds change. Here are two common patterns in English.

1. In questions, *do* and *did* are reduced (pronounced very quickly) to become '*d*.

Why did Patty leave?	*Why'd Patty leave?*
Where did John go?	*Where'd John go?*
What time do you wake up?	*What time d'you wake up?*

2. Words are linked together and not pronounced separately. We often link:

- *a consonant sound with a vowel sound*   *your address*   *six eggs*
- *a vowel sound with another vowel sound*   *my uncle*   *to India*
- *the same consonant sound*   *a big girl*   *that town*

A | Listen to five sentences from the listening passage. Write down each sentence.

1. _____
2. _____
3. _____
4. _____
5. _____

B | Circle the places where *do* and *did* are reduced. Underline the places where words can be linked together.

C | Practice saying the sentences from exercise **A** with a partner. Link and reduce the sounds.

Grammar

Using the Past Continuous Tense

We use the past continuous tense to talk about something that was in progress at a certain time in the past.

> *In 1990, my family **was living** in Tokyo.*

We can also use the past continuous with *while* to talk about two things that were happening at the same time in the past.

> *My brother **was working** full time **while** he **was earning** his college degree.*
> ***While** I **was trying** to study, my roommate **was talking** on the phone.*

The past continuous can be used to provide background information or "set the scene" for a story.

> *Everyone knew that a war **was coming**, and my grandparents were lucky to get out.*

A | Practice asking and answering the questions below with a partner. Use complete sentences in your answers.

> At 9:30 last night, I was . . .

1. What were you doing last night at 9:30?
2. What were you thinking about while you were coming to class today?
3. Where did your family live when you were growing up?
4. What was happening in your country the year you were born?
5. At the age of 10, what were you planning to do later in life?
6. Where were your grandparents living the year your mother/father was born?

B | The following sentences describe two things that were happening at the same time in the past. Complete each sentence with the past continuous and your own ideas.

1. While you __were having fun at the beach__ yesterday, I was studying for the English test.
2. While your ancestors were living in a castle, my ancestors _____.
3. While the first astronaut was walking on the moon, _____.
4. Last night, I _____ while my friend _____.
5. Your grandparents were working on a farm while my grandparents _____.
6. While we _____ last weekend, our teacher _____.

Language Function

Telling a Personal History

A personal history is a story with information about significant events in our lives or in the lives of people we know. We often talk about our own personal history in social situations or in more formal situations such as job or college interviews.

A | **Brainstorming.** Make a list of people you know who have emigrated to another country or immigrated to your country. Your list can include family members, friends, or yourself.

B | **Using a Graphic Organizer.** Choose one of the people from your list and write notes about the person that answer the questions in the graphic organizer below. Think about the type of information the students talked about on page 56.

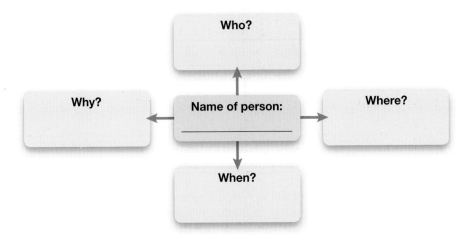

Who?

Why?

Name of person:
_____

Where?

When?

Storytelling Tips

Including smaller details will help make your story "come alive" and be more interesting for your listener. Here are some types of details you might include.

People's likes and dislikes
My dad and uncle were crazy about baseball.

People's funny or interesting habits
My sister cried every time my father left.

Specific details about the situation
When we drove my sister to the airport, it was snowing.

C | Look back at your graphic organizer in exercise **B**. Add some details to your story to make it come alive.

D | **Presentation.** Tell your story to your group. Use the notes from your graphic organizer to help you. Allow time to ask and answer questions about each other's stories.

Student to Student: Asking Sensitive Questions

When asking a question about information that may be very personal or sensitive, you can soften your question with these expressions:

I hope this isn't too personal, but . . .?
Do you mind if I ask . . .?
Would you mind telling me . . .?
Can I ask . . .?

You are going to give a group presentation to the class about a group of people who moved to a new place abroad or to another region of their own country (for example, Turkish people in Germany). You should include pictures, graphs, or other visual information to support your presentation. You can use paper, the board, or PowerPoint to help you present your information. Then your group will present the information to the class. Your presentation will teach your classmates about these topics:

1. When and why did this group leave their homes?
2. Why did they choose to go to this place?
3. How much did they assimilate? Why?
4. What is their situation today?

A | With your group, choose the group of people you will talk about. Your teacher can give you ideas.

B | **Researching.** Decide which person in your group will research each topic. Outside of class, research your topic online or in the library. (*See page 212 of the Independent Student Handbook for more information on doing research.*)

C | **Planning a Presentation.** As a group, organize the information on your topic. Then practice your presentation.

D | **Presentation.** Present your information to the class. When you give your presentation, all group members should speak. Answer any questions from your audience.

Presentation Skills: Using Visuals

When you use a visual in a presentation, you need to help your listeners focus on the most important part of the visual. You can do this with a pointer or your hand. Here are some expressions you can use when talking about visuals:

This chart/picture shows (the number of immigrants in 1900).
You can see here that (some people still wore traditional clothes).
Please notice that (the percentage of Chinese speakers is smaller now).

Fascinating Planet

ACADEMIC PATHWAYS

Lesson A: Listening to a Documentary
          Explaining Causes and Effects
Lesson B: Listening to an Informal Conversation
          Doing and Discussing Internet Research

Think and Discuss

1. Look at the photo. Would you like to visit this place? Why? Why not?

2. Why do people like to visit natural places?

New Zealand's Tongariro National Park has three active volcanoes and an ancient native forest.

Exploring the Theme:
Fascinating Planet

Look at the photos and read the captions. Then discuss the questions.

1. What do you find interesting or surprising about the information on these pages?
2. What do you think the environment and climate are like in the Tsingy?
3. What are some of the national parks in your country? What makes them special?

The dry upper parts of the Tsingy are the favorite places for some animals. This dragonfly is cooling itself.

The *Pachypodium* plant does not need much water, so it does well in the highest regions of the Tsingy.

The Tsingy de Bemaraha National Park in Madagascar

The Tsingy de Bemaraha National Park in Madagascar is a very unusual place. Its sharp pointed peaks are made from eroded limestone. The high peaks and low canyons here are home to many unusual species of animals and plants, such as the white *Decken's sifaka* lemur (shown on the left). Some of the species are so rare that scientists have not yet identified them.

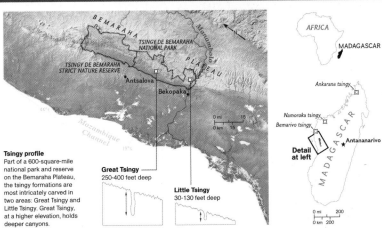

Tsingy profile
Part of a 600-square-mile national park and reserve on the Bemaraha Plateau, the tsingy formations are most intricately carved in two areas: Great Tsingy and Little Tsingy. Great Tsingy, at a higher elevation, holds deeper canyons.

Great Tsingy
250-400 feet deep

Little Tsingy
30-130 feet deep

Source: African Natural Heritage

A | **Using a Dictionary.** Work with a partner. Check (✔) the words you already know. Use a dictionary to help you with any words you don't know. These are words you will hear and use in Lesson A.

❏ crack	❏ deep	❏ dissolve	❏ erode	❏ form
❏ lack (of)	❏ protect	❏ rare	❏ sharp	❏ stone

🎧 track 1-36 **B** | Complete each sentence with the correct form of a word from exercise **A**. Then listen and check your answers.

1. Ancient people didn't have metal. They used _____ tools for farming and hunting.

2. This wall has a _____ in it. I can see light coming in from outside.

3. Sophie can't swim very well, so she won't go into _____ water.

4. A _____ knife can cut into an apple very easily.

5. After it rains, small streams of water come together and _____ a river.

6. I almost never eat sweets, so chocolate is a _____ treat for me.

7. If you put sugar in a cup of coffee, it will _____.

8. This mountain used to be much higher, but wind and rain have _____ it.

9. He's new at this job, but customers don't seem to notice his _____ of experience.

10. Most of the farmers wear hats to _____ themselves from the sun.

🎧 track 1-37 **C** | **Meaning from Context.** Read about Jiuzhaigou National Park and circle the correct word choice. Then listen and check your answers.

The lakes of Jiuzhaigou get their colors from dissolved stone and minerals.

It used to be more difficult to reach Jiuzhaigou, with its clean air and clear blue-green lakes, but nowadays, there is no (lack/form) of visitors to this national park in China's Sichuan province. Approximately 2 million tourists visit the park each year.

Water is the main attraction of Jiuzhaigou. Rivers flow down from the mountains and form beautiful waterfalls. The park's lakes are not (sharp/deep), so it's easy to see through the clean water to the bottom, brightly colored with (dissolved/cracked) minerals.

Jiuzhaigou is also a nature reserve, where panda bears and (stone/rare) bird species are (protected/eroded). The trees and other plant life in the reserve are also safe as long as this land remains a national park.

D | Discussion. Work with a partner. Discuss the questions.

1. Do you think Jiuzhaigou will stay clean and beautiful with 2 million tourists visiting every year? Why, or why not?
2. What do you think park officials could do to keep the park clean and beautiful?

E | Meaning from Context. Read about glaciers and circle the correct word choice. Then listen and check your answers.

track 1-38

The lakes in Jiuzhaigou National Park were (formed/dissolved) by glaciers—huge bodies of ice. Today there are glaciers high up in some mountains, but at other times in the earth's history colder temperatures allowed glaciers to exist in much larger areas.

As glaciers grow and move, they push dirt and (stone/rare) along with them. This material, along with the ice itself, is (lack/sharp) enough to (erode/protect) the land where the glaciers move. In this way, hills can become flat land, and flat land can become holes. Later, when temperatures become warmer and the glaciers melt, lakes are the result.

Glacial ice can become water in another way, too. At the bottom edge of a glacier, (cracks/forms) can develop, and large pieces of ice can fall into the water below. These pieces of ice then melt and become part of the body of water.

In British Columbia, Canada, a helicopter approaches the bottom edge of a glacier and the lake that it has formed.

F | Discussion. Work with a partner. Discuss the questions.

1. How is climate change affecting the world's glaciers?
2. How do changes to glaciers affect the world in general?

G | Critical Thinking. Form a group with two or three other students and discuss the questions.

1. National parks are rare in some countries and common in others. Which is true in your country?
2. Jiuzhaigou has no lack of tourists. What do you think is the greater benefit of this tourism: the money spent by tourists, or the love and respect for nature tourists feel when they visit the park?
3. The beautiful mountains and lakes in Jiuzhaigou took millions of years to form. How long do you think it would take for human beings to have a major effect on them?
4. Worldwide, there is a limited amount of money and resources for the protection of rare animals such as panda bears. How should people decide which species are worth protecting?

Before Listening

A | Look at the diagram showing how the Tsingy de Bemaraha was formed. Then write the sentence letters in the correct place on the diagram.

a. More water flows into the caves[1] and enlarges them.

b. Cracks form in the top of the limestone.

c. The tops of some caves collapse, forming larger caves.

d. Rain dissolves the top of the limestone and forms sharp points.

e. Water flows into the cracks and begins to form small caves.

f. The tops of other caves collapse, the water runs out, and deep canyons[2] are formed.

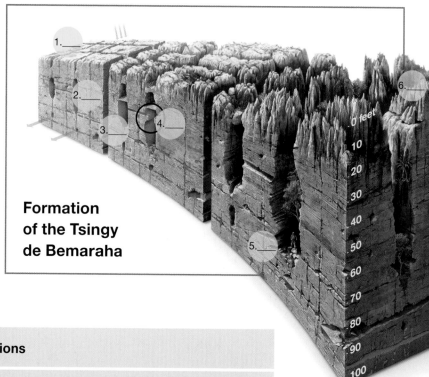

Formation of the Tsingy de Bemaraha

Tuning Out Distractions

In this lesson, you will hear a conversation and part of a television documentary about the Tsingy de Bemaraha. In the real world, there can be distractions while you're trying to listen. A door opens and closes when a student enters a lecture late. A telephone rings during a job interview. Someone talks loudly while you're watching a movie. In each case, your ability to tune out the distraction and concentrate will help you to understand more of what you're listening to.

 track 1-39 **B** | Listen to a conversation in a coffee shop and try to tune out the distractions. Then choose the correct word or phrase to complete each statement below.

1. The woman learned about Tsingy de Bemaraha from a _____.
   a. lecture   b. TV show   c. magazine article

2. The woman's friend asks about the _____ in Tsingy de Bemaraha.
   a. canyons   b. limestone   c. lemurs

3. The woman mentions _____ night.
   a. Tuesday   b. Wednesday   c. Thursday

4. The woman's friend answers the phone when her _____ calls her.
   a. sister   b. daughter   c. mother

[1] A **cave** is a large hole in the side of a cliff or under ground.

[2] A **canyon** is a long, narrow valley with very steep sides.

Listening: A Documentary

 A | Listen to part of a documentary about the Tsingy de Bemaraha.
track 1-40   What distractions do you need to tune out?

_____

_____

 B | **Note-Taking.** Listen again and complete the notes.
track 1-40

- Plants, animals protected in Tsingy because . . .   1. _hall path_____
                                                      2. _impossible to go_____
- Name means, "place where one cannot _walk barefoot_____."
- Walking into Tsingy difficult because . . .   1. _stone peaks_____ (above)
                                                2. _caves, water_____ (below)

Critical Thinking Focus: Using Graphic Organizers

Using graphic organizers, such as flow charts, can help you organize important information in a visual way.

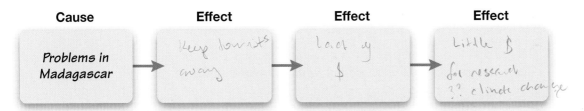

Cause	Effect	Effect	Effect
Problems in Madagascar	Keep tourists away	Lack of $	Little $ for research ?? climate change

An explorer in one of the deep canyons of the Tsingy de Bemaraha

C | **Using a Graphic Organizer.** Listen again and use your notes from exercise **B**
track 1-40   to complete the cause and effect flow chart above. (See pages 214-215 of the
Independent Student Handbook for more information on using graphic organizers.)

After Listening

A | The word *because* introduces a cause. Read the sentences below and underline
the causes. Then circle the effects.

1. The animals in the Tsingy are protected because it's a national park.
2. The peaks in the Tsingy are very sharp because rain has eroded the stone.
3. Because the Tsingy is almost impossible to get to, not many tourists visit it.
4. The caves became larger because the stone that had divided them collapsed.
5. Because there is little money for research, scientists aren't sure how climate
   change is affecting the Tsingy.

B | **Discussion.** Compare your sentences with a partner's. Then discuss the question.

1. What do you notice about the placement of the causes and effects in the sentences?

Grammar

A | **Prior Knowledge.** Read each sentence and answer the questions that follow.

1. At two o'clock, Olaf was reading the newspaper.
   How much time does it usually take for a person to read a newspaper?
   What time do you think Olaf started reading? What time did he finish?
2. Teresa fell while we were learning a new dance step.
   Did Teresa fall before, after, or during the dance lesson?

The Simple Past tense with the Past Continuous Tense

We use the past continuous tense to talk about something that was in progress at a certain time in the past.

*In the spring of 2007, I **was doing** research in Bolivia.*

To talk about something that happened while another event was in progress in the past, we can use the simple past tense.

*When I **found** my group, the tour guide **was talking** about glaciers.*

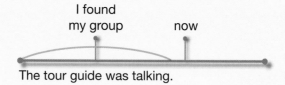

I found
my group   now

The tour guide was talking.

The word *while* often introduces a clause with the past continuous tense.

*We **saw** several kinds of birds **while** we **were walking** in the national park.*

The word *when* often introduces a clause with the simple past tense.

***When** the lights **went out**, Ronald **was giving** his presentation on penguins.*

A group of eco-tourists in Norway listening to birds

B | Read each situation. With a partner, say two different sentences about each situation using the simple past with the past continuous.

Example: Between six thirty and seven o'clock last night/you and your family/eat dinner. The telephone/ring/at six forty-one, six forty-eight, and six fifty-five.

> While we were eating dinner, the telephone rang three times.

> The telephone rang every few minutes while we were eating dinner.

1. In September of last year/you/do research in the Tsingy de Bemaraha.
   You/discover a new species of frog.
2. Yesterday at five forty-five in the evening/you/get home from work.
   Yesterday from five o'clock to six o'clock at night/your neighbor/paint the front of her house.
3. Debora/see a bear.
   Debora/hike at the national park.
4. The train/arrive/at seven forty-three.
   From seven forty to seven forty-five/Mitch and Jean/buy tickets at the ticket counter.
5. Last night/we/watch TV.
   The dog/start to bark.

Language Function

Talking about Historical Events

We often use the past continuous and the simple past together when talking about historical events that happened while another event (personal or historical) was in progress.

I **was playing** soccer with my brother when the first man **landed** on the moon.

Los Glaciares National Park in Argentina became a UNESCO World Heritage site in 1981.

A | Read about the National World Heritage Program. Then look at each date below and discuss with a partner what was happening in your life or in your country at that time.

> **United Nations Educational, Scientific, and Cultural Organization (UNESCO) World Heritage Program**
>
> The World Heritage program was created by UNESCO as a way to conserve places that have cultural or environmental importance for everyone in the world.

1. 1990 – Tsingy de Bemaraha and Tongariro National Park receive World Heritage status.
2. 1992 – Jiuzhaigou National Park receives World Heritage status.
3. 1993 – Tongariro National Park receives World Heritage status under new criterion.
4. 1997 – Lençóis Maranhenses National Park receives World Heritage status.

B | Read the information below about the history of the World Heritage program.

The History of World Heritage

The idea for the World Heritage program was first discussed during World War II, but it took many years to actually create the program:

UNESCO—United Nations Educational, Scientific, and Cultural Organization

History	1939–1945	World War II
	1942–1945	The Conference of Allied Ministers of Education in London hold meetings to discuss ways to re-establish their educational systems post-war.
	Nov. 1–16, 1945	After the meetings in London, the United Nations has a conference there to create an educational and cultural organization (later called UNESCO).
	Nov.–Dec., 1946	The first session of the General Conference of UNESCO is held. It marks the official beginning of the organization.
	1965–1972	UNESCO countries discuss a way to conserve places of global, cultural, and environmental importance.
	Nov. 16, 1972	UNESCO adopts the Convention Concerning the Protection of the World Cultural and Natural Heritage.
	1972–2010	Nine hundred and eleven places become World Heritage sites. The sites have cultural or natural importance, or both.

C | Take turns asking and answering the questions below with a partner. Use the information from the chart above and your own ideas in your answers. There may be more than one correct way to answer each question.

1. What was going on in 1941 when the movie *Citizen Kane* was released?

   > When *Citizen Kane* was released, World War II was going on.

2. When the first computer was built in 1945, what else was going on?
3. What was going on when Miguel Alemán became Mexico's president on November 1, 1946?
4. What was happening when Martin Luther King Jr. was killed in 1968?
5. When Neil Armstrong walked on the moon in 1969, what was happening on Earth?

Explaining Causes and Effects

Causes and Effects

To introduce *causes* you can use **due to, because of,** and **since.**

> **Due to** *an increase in tourism, more bus drivers are employed.*
> **Because of** *the rise in tourism, the company hired more bus drivers.*
> **Since** *there are more tourists, more souvenirs are being sold.*

Note: A comma is only needed if the explanatory phrase comes first.

> *More souvenirs are being sold* **since** *there are more tourists.*

To introduce *effects,* you can use **therefore, as a result,** and **so.**

> *Tourists walk on the rock formations.* **Therefore,** *some formations have been broken and won't be seen by future generations.*
> *The park charges an admission fee.* **As a result,** *it has enough money to build walkways.*
> *The park is beautiful,* **so** *many people want to see it.*

A | With a partner, look at the flow charts that show the advantages and disadvantages of places having World Heritage status. Then follow the steps below.

1. Choose one chart to talk about. Your partner will talk about the other.
2. Take turns explaining your flow chart to your partner. Practice using words and phrases from the chart at the top of the page.

Chart 1: Advantages

World Heritage status means more people hear about a national park. → More visitors go to the national park each year.

More people develop a love of natural places.

More money is spent in and near the park.

Chart 2: Disadvantages

More visitors go to places with World Heritage status. → The amount of trash and air pollution in the park increases.

The national park isn't a beautiful, natural place anymore. ← Ecosystems can be damaged by human activities.

B | Switch roles and explain the other chart to your partner.

C | **Critical Thinking.** Form a group with two or three other students and discuss the questions.

1. Do you think the advantages of World Heritage status outweigh the disadvantages? Why, or why not?
2. Do you know of any cultural or natural attractions that have been helped by tourism? Damaged by tourism?

THE GIANT'S CAUSEWAY

Located on the coast of Northern Ireland, the rock formation called the Giant's Causeway is the source of local legends.

Before Viewing

The Giant's Causeway, which is a huge and unusual-looking rock formation made of basalt columns, became Ireland's first UNESCO World Heritage site in 1986 due to its natural beauty and importance as a geological site.

A | Using a Dictionary. You will hear these words in the video. Match each word with the correct definition. Use a dictionary as needed to help you.

1. _____ A legend . . .
2. _____ A causeway . . .
3. _____ A giant . . .
4. _____ A geologist . . .
5. _____ Basalt . . .
6. _____ A column . . .

a. is a kind of gray stone that comes from volcanoes.
b. is a tall, solid cylinder.
c. is a person who studies the earth's structure and surface.
d. is a traditional story.
e. is a path or roadway built across water.
f. is an imaginary person who is very big and strong.

B | Critical Thinking. For each set of causes and effects below, create at least two different sentences with a partner. Use the words and phrases from page 71.

> Because pressure built up in a volcano, hot lava…

> Pressure built up in a volcano, so hot lava…

1. Pressure built up in a volcano. → Hot lava erupted and formed a thick layer on the ground.
2. The lava cooled slowly. → The basalt cracked and formed columns.
3. The basalt columns eroded. → Some of the stones we see today look like steps.
4. The stones looked like a causeway. → People made up a story about a giant.
5. The giant decided to go to Scotland. → He built the stone causeway.
6. The Giant's Causeway is interesting. → Many people visit the site each year.

C | Using the Simple Past with the Past Continuous. Ask and answer the questions below using the information from exercise **B**.

1. What was happening inside the volcano before it erupted?
2. What happened while the lava was cooling?

While Viewing

A | Watch the video. Then fill in the blanks with the numbers you hear.

1. For some people, these ___40,000___ pieces of basalt are a natural formation.
2. Dick then tells a story about how Finn was angry with a Scottish giant who lived ___25___ miles across the sea.
3. They say that a volcano made the Giant's Causeway about ___60___ million years ago.
4. Visitors have been coming to the Giant's Causeway and the nearby Irish coast since the ___1800's___.

B | Note-Taking. Watch again and take notes in the T-chart. (*See page 214 of the Independent Student Handbook for more information on using a T-chart.*)

Why the Giant's Causeway Was Built	How the Giant's Causeway Formed
According to the legend . . .	According to geologists . . . lava was like wet mud, dried & shrinks, forming columns

C | Use your notes from exercise **B** to tell a partner either why the Giant's Causeway was built, or how it formed. Then switch roles.

After Viewing

A | Collaboration. Legends often give an explanation for something in the natural world. Work with your partner to create a new legend about the Giant's Causeway rock formation, the mountains, valleys, and lakes of Jiuzhaigou, or the limestone peaks and caves in the Tsingy de Bemaraha.

B | Form a group with one or two other student pairs and tell each other your stories from exercise **A.** Be sure to use language from the unit to explain causes and effects.

The Giant's Causeway is a popular destination for children and tourists.

track 1-41

A | **Meaning from Context.** Look at the photo and maps. Read and listen to the information about New Zealand's Tongariro National Park. Notice the words in blue. These are words you will hear and use in Lesson B.

World Heritage

In 1887, a Maori chief gave Tongariro's three sacred[1] volcanoes and the land around them to the government and people of New Zealand, thus creating the country's first national park. It has been named a World Heritage site twice—first on the **basis** of its natural beauty. In addition, its cultural importance to the Maori was **sufficient** to earn the park World Heritage status.

Film Location

New Zealand's landscape is varied. It has dramatic **features** such as volcanoes, but also rolling green hills and beautiful lakes, so Peter Jackson had many **options** when he was choosing locations for his *Lord of the Rings* films.

Ring of Fire

The Ring of Fire is an area with numerous earthquakes and active volcanoes. New Zealand sits on the Alpine Fault, where the **edges** of the Australian Plate and Pacific Plate move sideways past each other. The movement of the plates along the fault line leads to earthquakes, and the release of hot material from under the earth's **surface** leads to volcanic activity.

The three volcanoes of Tongariro National Park. Furthest away is Mount Tongariro, and second is Ngauruhoe—"Mount Doom" in Peter Jackson's *Lord of the Rings* movie trilogy. In the foreground is Ruapehu.

RING OF FIRE

ASIA

PACIFIC OCEAN

AREA BELOW

▲ Volcano
▲▲ Subduction zone

RING OF FIRE

Auckland
Tasman Sea
AUSTRALIAN PLATE
North Island
★ Wellington
Alpine Fault
Christchurch
South Island
Plate movement
PACIFIC OCEAN
PACIFIC PLATE

0 mi 200
0 km 200

Invasive Species

In the 19th century, European immigrants began to arrive, along with foreign animals and plants. These species are a **threat** to New Zealand's native species. Cats, Australian possums, and even rats kill and eat native birds. Plants such as European heather and North American pine compete with native plants. To restore the **balance** of nature and encourage the survival of native species, much work has been done to kill the invasive species brought in from other parts of the world.

Tourism

The most popular ski areas on North Island—with their roads, ski lifts, hotels, and shops—are on Mount Ruapehu. This kind of development would not be allowed in a national park today, but the ski areas date from 1913, and they do bring money to the area. Staff members at the Department of Conservation are **constantly** trying to find **compromises** in park management that will keep skiers happy and protect the environment at the same time.

[1]Something is **sacred** if it has religious or spiritual importance.

B | Write each word in **blue** from exercise **A** next to its definition.

1. _____ (n.) an agreement where each side gets some, but not all of what it wants
2. _____ (n.) something that is likely to be harmful
3. _____ (n.) lines or borders where surfaces end
4. _____ (adv.) happening all the time, continuously
5. _____ (n.) the flat, top level of something
6. _____ (n.) possible choices or alternatives
7. _____ (adj.) enough
8. _____ (n.) important parts or special qualities of something
9. _____ (n.) equal amounts, a state of equilibrium
10. _____ (n.) the main reason for something

Volcanic material surrounds one of the Emerald Lakes on Mount Tongariro.

C | With a partner, choose the best vocabulary word from the box to complete each sentence. Then practice the dialog.

balance	compromise	options	basis	threat

Sonia: Did you know that in New Zealand, they have to kill some kinds of animals and plants?

Nick: That seems strange. What's the (1) _____ for killing them?

Sonia: They're invasive species. If people don't kill them, the invasive species take over.

Nick: So they're trying to keep some kind of (2) _____ between the different species. Otherwise, they'd end up with only invasive species, right?

Sonia: I guess so, but it isn't nice to think about.

Nick: I suppose they don't have many (3) _____. If they didn't kill some plants and animals, there would be a huge (4) _____ to others.

Sonia: True, but do you think some people disagree with the killing?

Nick: Maybe. They've probably had to make some kind of a (5) _____. They kill just enough of the plants and animals to protect native species.

D | **Brainstorming.** Brainstorm answers to each of the questions with your group.

1. How many of the earth's **surface features** can you think of? (e.g., volcanoes)
2. What are some things that **constantly** occur on Earth? (e.g., Animals are born and die.)
3. What are some typical fun activities that people do on weekends? (e.g., going to the movies) How much money is **sufficient** for each of these activities?

Before Listening

🎧 track 1-42 **A** | Listen and read about a national park in northeastern Brazil. What makes the park unusual?

Brazil's Lençóis Maranhenses National Park

Lençóis Maranhenses National Park

The name of this national park means the "bedsheets of Maranhão," the state in Brazil where the park is located. From the air, the park's white sand dunes[1] do look like sheets drying in the wind, and it's the wind that gives the dunes their half-moon shapes. However, this park features a lot more than sand. Green and blue pools of water are left behind by the rain, fishermen go out to sea in their boats, and local people take care of herds of goats.

So is the Lençóis a desert, or a seascape? Is it a park, or a place where people live? In fact, it's not a true desert because it receives around 42 inches (120 centimeters) of rain each year. Yet sand dunes as far as the eye can see, along with the lack of trees and other plants, suggest a desert. The park also has 90 residents—people in two villages who change their routines with the seasons. They raise chickens, goats, cattle, and crops such as cassava, beans, and cashews during the dry season. When it rains, residents go out to sea and live in fishing camps on the beach.

[1]A **dune** is a hill of sand near the ocean or in a desert.

Two large rivers, the Parnaíba and the Preguiças, carry sand from the interior of the continent to the ocean, where it is carried west to Lençóis Maranhenses.

🎧 track 1-42 **B** | Listen again and pay attention to the intonation in the underlined sentences.

Pronunciation

Intonation for Choices and Lists

🎧 track 1-43

When there are two choices, we use rising then falling intonation.

Do you prefer the aisle or the window?

With lists of three or more items, we use rising intonation except for the last item, which receives falling intonation.

My favorite colors are yellow, blue, and red.

C | Listen to each sentence and mark the intonation with arrows.

1. We have coffee, tea, and lemonade.
2. Do you think the salary they're offering is sufficient, or will you ask for more?
3. We could stay home, or we could stay out late, or we could compromise.
4. Would you rather go to Spain or to Portugal?
5. She's going to Korea, Japan, and China.

D | Practice saying the questions above with a partner.

Residents of the Lençóis lead a herd of goats up the side of a sand dune.

Listening: An Informal Conversation

 A | **Listening for Main Ideas.** Listen and answer the questions below.

1. What are the speakers trying to decide? _____
2. What are their two choices? _____
3. What do they decide to do? _____

 B | **Listening for Details.** Listen again and circle the letter of the correct answer.

1. What's one disadvantage of the man's vacation idea?
   a. not much to do there   b. long plane trip from Tokyo
2. Why does the woman not want to go to the beach?
   a. cool weather   b. too much sun
3. What would the woman prefer to do?
   a. go hiking   b. play golf
4. What's one advantage of going in August?
   a. low prices   b. hot weather
5. What is the man most interested in?
   a. seeing different cultures   b. seeing different scenery

After Listening

 Self-Reflection. Discuss the following questions with a partner. Be sure to use the appropriate intonation and explain your answers.

1. Do you prefer to spend vacation time in your home country or abroad?
2. Do you like vacations that are very active or very relaxing?
3. Do you prefer to travel by plane, by train, or by bus?
4. Would you rather go to a national park or to an interesting city?
5. Would your dream vacation be in Asia, Europe, Africa, or someplace else?
6. Would you prefer to have more money or more vacation time?

Grammar

A | **Prior Knowledge.** Read the conversation. Then answer the questions.

> **Makiko:** *I just got back from Alaska. It was really cold there.*
> **Tim:** *How cold was it?*
> **Makiko:** *It was <u>so cold that</u> my camera wouldn't work. I think it was frozen!*

1. After she says, "*so cold that*," Makiko _____.
   a. changes the topic   b. gives more details
2. The information that follows the phrase, *so cold that* is _____.
   a. a cause   b. an effect

So + Adjective + That

We use *so* + adj + *that* to talk about results or give more details.

> *The car was going* **so fast that** *it couldn't stop at the red light.*
In other words, because the car was going very fast, it couldn't stop.

> *The room was* **so quiet that** *I could hear myself breathing.*
In other words, because the room was very quiet, I could hear myself breathing.

B | With a partner, think of at least two possible endings for each sentence.

1. The movie was so popular that _____.
2. Emilio is so strong that _____.
3. That year, food was so scarce that _____.
4. The instructions are so clear that _____.
5. The park is so beautiful that _____.

C | Make a list of eight adjectives in your notebook. Then write a new sentence with *so* + adj + *that* for at least six of your adjectives.

1. _____
2. _____
3. _____
4. _____
5. _____
6. _____

Presentation Skills: Making Eye Contact

Even if you are using notes, it's important to look up and speak directly to your audience. When you make eye contact with your audience, it helps you connect with them. This will make your presentation more interesting for your audience because you are speaking to them.

D | **Presentation.** Stand up and say two of your sentences from exercise **C** to the whole class. Be sure to make eye contact with your audience rather than down at your book.

E | **Brainstorming.** As a class or in a small group, brainstorm places in the world that match the descriptions below. One has been done as an example.

dry _____the Sahara Desert_____   beautiful _____

cold _____   mountainous _____

rainy _____   hot _____

F | Use *so* + adj + *that* + noun to make sentences about the places you listed in exercise **E**.

> It's so dry in the Sahara that few plants grow there.

> It's so dry that very few people live there.

Language Function: Responding to Suggestions

With a partner, take turns making suggestions about the topics below. Go along with some of your partner's suggestions, and don't go along with others. Refer to Making Suggestions on page 38 in Unit 2 if you need help.

Student A
- Doing homework together
- Walking somewhere
- Talking to the instructor after class
- Buying a new car

Student B
- Getting something to eat or drink
- Wearing warmer or cooler clothes
- Joining a study group
- Taking a class together

Student to Student: Responding to Suggestions

When someone you're talking to makes a suggestion, you are expected to respond. If you want to go along with the suggestion, you can say for example:

OK./Sure./All right.
That's a great idea!/That sounds good.

If you don't want to go along with the suggestion, your response needs to be polite.

I'd rather not . . . I'll . . .
Well, I don't really like to . . .
I'm not sure about that.

You are going to practice doing Internet research on the national parks you learned about in this unit. You will work with a partner.

When you look for information on the Internet, ask yourself:

1. Do I need recent information?

   The answer depends on your topic. If you want to learn about current events in the world or the latest technology, look for a recent date on the Web sites you visit.

2. Where can I find relevant information?

   Again, think about your topic. General information might be found in an online encyclopedia. Current news stories are in online newspapers. Statistics about a country's population and income may be included on a government Web site. And with every topic, choosing relevant key words for your search is very important.

3. Is the information on this Web site accurate and reliable?

   The Internet provides good information—and bad. Good Web sites often have:
   a. *an identifiable source for the information (Where does it come from?)*
   b. *the date of the most recent update (Is the information current?)*
   c. *the URL suffix .edu or .gov (These sites aren't making money online.)*

 A | Work with your partner to find the missing information about the places below online. As you do your research, use the questions and tips above to guide you.

Jiuzhaigou National Park, China	The Tsingy de Bemaraha, Madagascar	Tongariro National Park, New Zealand	Lençóis Maranhenses National Park, Brazil
Became a national park in _____.	Became a national park in _____.	Became a national park in _____.	Became a national park in _____.
Size of park: _____	Size of park: _____	Size of park: _____	Size of park: _____
Number of tourists each year: _____	Number of tourists each year: _____	Number of tourists each year: _____	Number of tourists each year: _____
World Heritage status: yes/no If yes, year(s): _____	World Heritage status: yes/no If yes, year(s): _____	World Heritage status: yes/no If yes, year(s): _____	World Heritage status: yes/no If yes, year(s): _____

B | **Discussion.** Form a group with another pair of students and discuss the questions. Were you able to find all of the information? How do you know that the information is accurate? What kind of Web sites were the most helpful to you? What key words did you use in your searches? (*See page 212 of the Independent Student Handbook for more information on doing online research.*)

Making a Living, Making a Difference

ACADEMIC PATHWAYS
Lesson A: Listening to a Guest Speaker
          Making Comparisons
Lesson B: Listening to a Class Question and Answer Session
          Giving a Presentation Based on Internet Research

Think and Discuss

1. What is the man in this picture selling? Do you think he made them himself?
2. Do you know many people who are self-employed? How do they make a living?

A man sells balloons in a busy Hanoi intersection.

Exploring the Theme:
Making a Living, Making a Difference

Look at the photos and read the captions. Then discuss the questions.

1. What is the difference between entrepreneurs and members of a co-op?
2. What are some handmade products that are sold in your country?
3. Have you ever been to a market like the one in this photo? What kinds of things were sold there?

Crowds gather at the Djemma El Fna square in Marrakesh, Morocco, for food and entertainment.

Entrepreneurs start their own small businesses or make products to sell. This photo shows textiles, which are the main creative art form in Bhutan.

In **cooperatives** or **co-ops**, farmers or workers join together to create one large business. The co-op members also own the business.

A | Using a Dictionary. Check (✓) the words you already know. Then use a dictionary to look up any words that are new to you. *(See page 209 of the Independent Student Handbook for tips on using a dictionary.)* These are words you will hear and use in Lesson A.

❑ owners   ❑ cooperate   ❑ wealth   ❑ diverse   ❑ enterprises

B | Read the article and fill in each blank with a word from the box. Use each word only once.

A cheese maker salts wheels of Swiss cheese at a dairy cooperative in Monticello, Wisconsin, USA.

Agricultural Cooperatives

Cooperatives, or co-ops, are different from corporations or other business (1) _____ in several ways. First, they're made up of members who are also the (2) _____ of the cooperative.

In the case of an agricultural co-op, a number of farmers may decide to (3) _____ and sell their products together, rather than separately. As co-op members, the farmers make decisions democratically. They also share their (4) _____ among themselves. Instead of going to stockholders and executives, profits in cooperatives are returned to their members, who may also share machinery and borrow money from the co-op.

Perhaps the most important benefit of co-ops is the pooling of farm products because large quantities may be more attractive to buyers.

Farmers in agricultural cooperatives are a (5) _____ group. They can be found in numerous countries, and they produce everything from cotton and soybeans to flowers and fruit.

C | Listen and check your answers from exercise **B**. *(track 2-2)*

D | Discussion. With a partner, discuss the questions below.

1. According to the article, what are the benefits of agricultural cooperatives to farmers?
2. What might some of the responsibilities be for farmers in cooperatives?

E | **Using a Dictionary.** Check (✓) the words you already know. Then use a dictionary to look up any words that are new to you. These are words you will hear and use in Lesson A.

❏ entrepreneurs   ❏ effective   ❏ poverty   ❏ earn   ❏ assess

F | Read the article and fill in each blank with a word from the box. Use each word only once.

Peruvian Weavers: A Profitable Cottage Industry[1]

In the Andes mountains of Peru, people in the village of Chinchero, not far from Cusco, were living in (1) _____. Their agricultural products—potatoes, barley, sheep—were not bringing in much money.

That's when the women of Chinchero became (2) _____. They started the Chinchero Weaving[2] Cooperative, and they began selling their traditional handmade textiles[3] to tourists. The women may not (3) _____ a lot of money for their work, but at least the money they make stays within the cooperative and within the community.

Starting a co-op was an (4) _____ way for villagers in Chinchero to bring in more money. However, co-ops are not the answer for every cottage industry.

Before deciding to start or join a cooperative, home-based industries need to (5) _____ their situation carefully. If a small business is already doing well, it may have the customer base it needs. It may not want to spend time going to co-op meetings and money on co-op dues. On the other hand, joining together with others can be the answer for businesses that are struggling.[4]

In Chinchero, Peru, children pose for a photo with their llamas. In their spare time, many children make traditional textiles for the Chinchero Weaving Cooperative.

[1] A **cottage industry** is a small business that is run from someone's home.
[2] **Weaving** is the process of making textiles.
[3] **Textiles** are fabrics.
[4] A business that is **struggling** is not doing well.

G | Listen and check your answers from exercise **F**.

H | **Discussion.** With a partner, discuss the questions below.

1. Why did the Chinchero villagers decide to become entrepreneurs?
2. Why do you think a cooperative works well for these weavers?

I | Take turns asking and answering the questions with a partner.

1. Who are some of the most famous **entrepreneurs,** and which businesses did they start?
2. In your country, do you think more people live in **wealth** or in **poverty**? How much money do people need to **earn** in order to be considered wealthy?
3. What are some of the responsibilities of business **owners**?
4. Do the students in your English class usually have **diverse** opinions, or do they usually agree on things?
5. Besides business, in what other parts of life do we need to **cooperate** with other people?

Before Listening

A | Look at the photo and read the caption. Then read and listen to the article about an unusual cooperative in India.

track 2-4

Snake Hunters Find Cure for Joblessness

Most people run away when they see a poisonous snake—but not the Irulas of India. For generations, the Irulas made their living catching wild snakes. The snakes' skins were sold and made into luxury goods such as handbags and boots.

These members of the Irula tribe in India catch snakes and "milk" them for their venom.

Then in 1972, the Indian Parliament adopted the Wildlife Protection Act, and the basis of the Irula's economy was suddenly illegal. Some Irulas got jobs as farm laborers, but many found themselves out of work.

The solution came in 1978 with the creation of the Irula Snake Catchers Industrial Cooperative Society, whose members use their snake hunting skills to catch snakes. However, the snakes are no longer sold for their skins. The cooperative has found a better use for the dangerous snakes.

B | **Discussion.** Form a group with two or three other students and discuss the questions below.

1. Why did the Irulas need to change the way they made a living?
2. How were the snakes used in the past, and how are they used now?
3. What might be some of the benefits of this change?

Critical Thinking Focus: Identifying the Speaker's Purpose

In this lesson, you will hear a presentation about the Irula snake venom cooperative. Whenever a speaker gives a prepared talk, that speaker has a purpose—something he or she wants to accomplish. Being aware of the speaker's purpose can help you understand the information that is presented and make a judgment about it.

C | **Critical Thinking.** Working with a partner, think of a possible speaker and situation for each speaking purpose.

1. To give information
   a lecture by a university professor

2. To persuade you to do something

3. To entertain you

4. To change your opinion

Listening: A Guest Speaker

 A | **Listening for Main Ideas.** Listen to the talk and answer the questions.

1. Who is the speaker?

_____

2. Who is in the audience?

_____

3. What is the speaker's purpose?

_____

Indian cobras were once hunted for their skins. Now, their venom is carefully obtained, and the snakes are returned to the wild.

B | Compare your answers in exercise **A** with a partner's. Explain the reasons for your answer to question #3.

 C | **Listening for Details.** Listen again and choose the correct answer.

1. According to the speaker, what does Worldwide Co-op offer to cooperative enterprises?
   a. loans   b. support   c. health insurance

2. Each year, how many people in India die from snakebites?
   a. 20,000   b. 30,000   c. 40,000

3. The speaker encourages the audience members to assess their own situations in order to understand the reasons why _____.
   a. wildlife are being killed
   b. people are earning more than before
   c. snakes are being milked for their venom

4. According to the speaker, Worldwide Co-op has information resources, including _____.
   a. books   b. journal articles   c. a Web site

After Listening

Critical Thinking. With your group members, think of an endangered animal that is being killed by humans. Discuss why the animal is being killed. Then think of another way that people might earn money from the animal.

> People hunt the rhinoceros because they can get a lot of money for its horn.

> Maybe they could take tourists to see the animals—from a distance.

Language Function

A | Practice saying the numbers in the box below.

Using Numbers and Statistics	
200	Two hundred
4000	Four thousand
36,000	Thirty-six thousand
700,000	Seven hundred thousand
1,000,000	One million
1,500,000	One million five hundred thousand (or 1.5 million: one point five million)
7,000,000,000	Seven billion

B | Write these numbers in words.

1. 50,000 _____

2. 3,200,000 _____

3. 400 _____

4. 740,000 _____

5. 8,000,000,000 _____

6. 1,297,300 _____

C | Cover the words in exercise **B**. Take turns pointing to any number and asking your partner to say it.

D | Look at the photo and read the caption. Then listen to some statistics about *kudzu* and write the numbers you hear.

An invasive species in the southeastern U.S., *kudzu* plants can grow as much as 12 inches (30 centimeters) in one day and up to 60 feet (18 meters) in one growing season.

1. Imported to the U.S. from Japan in 1876, *kudzu* grows from large underground tubers[1] that can weigh almost _____300_____ pounds (136 kilograms).

2. During the 1930s, the U.S. government planted ___70 million___ *kudzu* seedlings.

3. *Kudzu* was such a popular plant that at one time, the Kudzu Club of America had ___20,000___ members.

4. *Kudzu* can cover as many as ___150,000___ acres of land each year.

5. Currently, *kudzu* covers around ___8 million___ acres of land in the U.S.

E | Write down three "facts" with large numbers. They can be real facts or made up. Then form a group with two or three other students and take turns reading your "facts." Try to guess which facts are real.

> The population of the earth is 13 billion.

> Hmm . . . there isn't enough space for that many people!

[1] **Tubers** are thick plant roots such as the potato.

F | Read about an entrepreneur who is making a profit from *kudzu*.

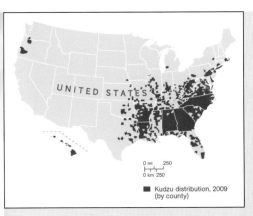

Nancy Basket is a Native American artist who runs Kudzu Kabin Designs from her home in South Carolina, USA. She is one of a few people who see the benefits of the vine that most North Americans hate. "It's very invasive. It grows 12 inches (30 centimeters) every single day, and people haven't been able to use it. But I use it for everything, and people can buy it (from me) in a form that's guaranteed to never grow again," Basket said.

Items for sale at Basket's design studio include her namesake baskets (she is named for a basket-making great grandmother) made from *kudzu* vines, and cards and posters made from

kudzu paper. Basket also makes everything from *kudzu* quiches and breads to jellies and candies. Even her studio is made out of *kudzu* bales[1]—the only such structure of its kind.

G | **Discussion.** Form a group with two or three other students and discuss the questions.

1. What do you think about Nancy Basket's small business idea?
2. Do you think that *kudzu* entrepreneurs can effectively reduce the amount of *kudzu* in the U.S.?

Small Business Statistics

Kudzu Kabin Designs has been in business for over 20 years, but not all small businesses in the U.S. are successful. The statistics in the **Quick Facts** table on page 90 come from the U.S. Federal Reserve Board.

H | Look at the information in the **Quick Facts** table on page 90 and take turns asking and answering the questions with a partner.

1. How many businesses were there in the U.S. in 2009?
2. About how many U.S. workers are employed by small businesses?
3. How many new jobs were created in the U.S. between 1993 and 2009?
4. How many businesses were started in the U.S. in 2006?
5. How many businesses in the U.S. closed in 2006?
6. How many businesses in the U.S. went bankrupt in 2006?
7. Can you see a trend in the number of bankruptcies over the years? Explain your answer.
8. Can you see a trend in new business start-ups over the years? Explain your answer.

[1] **Bales** are large cubes of material such as hay, paper, or *kudzu* tied together tightly.

Quick Facts

- In 2009, there were 1,275,000 businesses in the United States.
- Small firms with less than 500 employees represent 99.9 percent of the total.
- There were 18,311 large businesses in 2007.
- Small businesses employ about half of the 120,600,000 U.S. workers.
- Small firms accounted for 65 percent (or 9.8 million) of the 15 million net new jobs created between 1993 and 2009.

Starts and Closures of Employer Firms, 2005–2009

Category	2005	2006	2007	2008	2009
Starts	644,122	670,058	668,395	626,400e	552,600e
Closures	565,745	599,333	592,410	663,900e	660,900e
Bankruptcies	39,201	19,695	28,322	43,546	60,837

Notes: e = estimated number   bankruptcy = legal inability to pay bills

 I | Discussion. With a partner, discuss the questions below.

1. What surprises you about the statistics in the table?
2. How do you think these statistics compare with those in other countries you know about?

Grammar

Making Comparisons with *As . . . As*

We use the expression *as . . . as* (or *not as . . . as*) to talk about things that are (or are not) equal to each other. These *equative* sentences can be formed in several different ways.

Adjectives	*These textiles are **as beautiful as** the others.* *My brother isn't **as tall as** I am.*
Adverbs	*The large cobra was carried **as carefully as** the small one.* *Lenny didn't run **as quickly as** usual.*
Quantifiers + Count Nouns	*She owns **as many baskets as** her sister owns.* *Pat didn't eat **as many cookies as** Mary did.*
Quantifiers + Non-Count Nouns	*We sold **as much bread as** we could carry to the market.* *They don't earn **as much money as** the other workers.*

With a partner, take turns making true statements with *(not) as . . . as* and the words below.

1. Argentina/large/Brazil
2. I/tall/you
3. The weather here in spring/good/the weather in summer
4. We/complete this exercise/quickly/the rest of the class

Making Comparisons

A | Look at the market scenes and read the captions. With a partner, say as many sentences about the pictures as you can using *(not) as . . . as.*

A shopper walks past a variety of fruit at St. George's Market in Belfast, Northern Ireland.

Food stalls in Beijing, China, selling everything from seafood and vegetables to sweets.

> The market in Ireland isn't as organized as the market in China.

> There are as many people at the Irish market as there are at the Chinese market.

B | **Discussion.** In a group, discuss the questions for each of the entrepreneurial enterprises from Lesson A of this unit. Use *as . . . as* when possible and give reasons for your answers.

1. Who are the owners of each enterprise, and why did they start their businesses?
2. Which enterprise probably employs the largest number of workers?
3. How would you assess the earning potential of each business? (i.e., Which one probably makes the most money?)
4. Which enterprise do you think is most effective in terms of easing poverty for its workers?

The Chinchero Weaving Cooperative

The Irula Snake Catchers Industrial Cooperative Society

Kudzu Kabin Designs

C | **Presentation.** Take turns sharing your group's ideas with the rest of the class and discuss any differences of opinion.

THE BUSINESS OF CRANBERRIES

Before Viewing

A | **Using a Dictionary.** You will hear these words and phrases in the video. Work with a partner and match each word or phrase with the correct definition. Use your dictionary to help you.

1. marsh (n.) _____   a. something that is a result of a period of time or history
2. harvest (n.) _____   b. a sudden drop in temperature that often kills plants
3. legacy (n.) _____   c. water supplied to land to help plants grow
4. vine (n.) _____   d. a wet, muddy area of land
5. corral (v.) _____   e. a plant that grows over things and often produces fruit
6. irrigation (n.) _____   f. to trap, or gather things in a group
7. hard frost (n.) _____   g. an unusually large harvest
8. bumper crop (n.) _____   h. the crop that is gathered

B | **Prior Knowledge.** You are going to watch a video clip about Mary Brazeau Brown, the owner of a cranberry company. Like the people discussed in Lesson A, she makes a living by using the resources around her. How much do *you* know about cranberries? Take the quiz below and find out.

CRANBERRY QUIZ: Circle the correct answer for each question.

1. Cranberries are a native fruit to which continent?
   a. North America   b. South America   c. Europe   d. Africa
2. The Algonquin Indians used cranberries for all of the following purposes except _____.
   a. food   b. a symbol of peace   c. money   d. medicine
3. What is the average number of cranberries needed to make one can of cranberry sauce?
   a. 200   b. 500   c. 1000   d. 2000
4. Americans traditionally eat cranberry sauce with which kind of meat?
   a. beef   b. turkey   c. chicken   d. lamb
5. John Lennon repeated the words "cranberry sauce" at the end of which Beatles song?
   a. *Tax Man*   b. *I Am the Walrus*   c. *Strawberry Fields Forever*   d. *Penny Lane*

Source: www.cranberryfarmers.org

ANSWERS: 1. a, 2. c, 3. a, 4. b, 5. c

While Viewing

A | Read the statements. Then watch the video and circle **T** for *true* or **F** for *false*.

1. Mary has always wanted to work outdoors.   **T**   **F**
2. Glacial Lake Cranberries is in Wisconsin.   **T**   **F**
3. Mary oversees every aspect of the business.   **T**   **F**
4. Cranberries are harvested in early fall.   **T**   **F**
5. A hard frost is good for cranberries.   **T**   **F**
6. Cranberries require lots of water.   **T**   **F**

B | Watch the video again and number the steps of the cranberry-harvesting process in the correct order.

_____ The cranberries are corralled.

_____ Berries are knocked from their vines by machines called beaters.

_____ Cranberries ripen to a glowing red.

_____ The cranberry beds are flooded.

_____ The berries float to the surface.

C | Close your book and take turns explaining the cranberry harvesting process to a partner.

After Viewing

A | Write sentences in your notebook using *as . . . as* and the words below. Use your own ideas and opinions.

1. Growing cranberries/dangerous/collecting snake venom
2. Working outdoors at a cranberry company/stressful/working in an office
3. Owning a family business/difficult/working for a company
4. *Kudzu* vines/useful/cranberries

B | **Discussion.** Explain your ideas and opinions from exercise **A** to a partner.

C | **Critical Thinking.** Discuss these questions in a group.

1. Do you think growing food is a good way to make a living? Why, or why not?
2. What are some advantages and disadvantages to owning your own business?
3. Do you think starting a business requires a lot of money? Explain.

A | **Meaning from Context.** Read and listen to the conversation. Notice the words in blue. These are words you will hear and use in Lesson B.

Margo:	What are you reading?
Walter:	It's a letter from a charity organization. I've never heard of them before, but listen to this: "Just 10 years after our *Schools for Kids* program began, there has been a 27 percent drop in the rate of poverty among people in the region." That's pretty impressive!
Margo:	Sure. I mean, less poverty is a good thing. Are you thinking of sending them money?
Walter:	I'm thinking about it. After all, I have a pretty good job, and this is a good concept—invest in education now, and there will be less poverty in the future.
Margo:	That does seem like a good idea.
Walter:	Do you give any money to charities?
Margo:	Yes, there's one called Heifer International where you send enough money for a farm animal—like a chicken or a goat. The animal provides eggs or milk to a poor family, and if the animal reproduces, the babies are given to another poor family.
Walter:	That makes a lot of sense. Good nutrition is such a fundamental human need.
Margo:	It is indeed.

B | **Discussion.** Form a group with two or three other students and discuss the questions.

1. Which charity organizations do you know about? What do these charities do?
2. Do you give any money to charities? Why, or why not?
3. Do you think that charity organizations are an effective way to fight poverty?

C | **Using a Dictionary.** Practice the conversation with a partner and use a dictionary as needed.

D | **Meaning from Context.** Read and listen to the book review. Notice the words in blue. These are words you will hear and use in Lesson B.

Title: *Just Give Money to the Poor: The Development Revolution from the Global South*

Authors: Joseph Hanlon, Armando Barrientos, David Hulme

Review: Traditionally, help for poor people has come from large organizations such as Oxfam and WHO, and it has been in the form of complex projects such as dams, irrigation systems, schools, and hospitals. In this book, authors Hanlon, Barrientos, and Hulme present evidence in favor of a simpler approach. According to their data, making small, regular payments directly to poor people provides a better outcome—in other words better living conditions—than the large, complex projects provide.

Hanlon et. al. describe "cash transfer" programs in a number of countries where poverty is a major problem. People in need receive a small amount of money, sometimes as little as five to ten dollars each month, and they use the money in any way they choose. Almost always, the authors say, poor families make very responsible decisions about using the extra income, buying more or better food, buying a school uniform so a child can attend school, or saving a little each month to start a small business.

USING VOCABULARY

E | Write each word in **blue** from exercise **D** next to its definition.

1. _____ (n.) paper money or metal coins
2. _____ (adj.) trustworthy, proper, and sensible
3. _____ (n.) a result
4. _____ (n.) money paid
5. _____ (n.) the movement of something, such as money from one person or place to another

A father and son in the Dharavi area of Mumbai, India

F | Fill in each blank in the conversations with a word from the box. Use

drop	cash	charity	concept	fundamental
outcome	payment	rate	responsible	transfer

each word only once.

1. **A:** Do you take credit cards?
   B: Actually, we prefer _____ or checks.

2. **A:** Are you the person who's _____ for buying food at your house?
   B: Yes, I am. If I don't do it, nobody will.

3. **A:** Did you buy your car with cash?
   B: No, I have to make a _____ every month.

4. **A:** I need to change my Italian money for Australian dollars. What's the exchange _____?
   B: It's not very good, I'm afraid. There was a _____ in the value of the euro yesterday.

5. **A:** Our economy is a mess. What do you think is the _____ problem?
   B: I think we've borrowed too much money from other countries.

6. **A:** You sent them money? I never give away money unless I get something in return.
   B: Hmmm . . . I think I have a different _____ of charity than you do.

7. **A:** Hi, I'd like to make a money _____ from my checking account to my savings account.
   B: No problem. Can I see your ID?

8. **A:** What's your favorite _____?
   B: I like Doctors Without Borders. They give medical care in places where it's really needed.

9. **A:** I'm really unhappy with the _____ of yesterday's game.
   B: Me too! I can't believe they lost again!

G | Practice the conversations in exercise **F** with a partner.

Pronunciation

In Aceh, Indonesia, new houses were built by a charity organization for survivors of the 2004 tsunami.

Contractions

Contractions are short combinations of two or more words. The contracted word is usually a function word (pronouns, auxiliary verbs, etc.). Contractions can be difficult to hear, but they're important because they communicate the speaker's meaning.

There's no hospital in the town. (now)
There was no hospital in the town. (in the past—but there is one now)

track 2-9

Some Common Contractions

With *be*	With *have/has*
I am → I'm you/we/they are → you're/we're/they're he/she/it is → he's/she's/it's Linda's at the library.	I have → I've (you've/we've/etc.) he/she/it has → he's/she's/it's They've always wanted to go scuba diving.
With *will*	**With *would***
I will → I'll (you'll/he'll/we'll/etc.) She'll tell us when it's time to leave.	I would → I'd (you'd/she'd/they'd/etc.) We'd rather not have the party here.

 Practice saying the example sentences from the chart. Then think of some new sentences with contractions and practice saying them with a partner.

Before Listening

Review the information on page 86 of Lesson A about identifying a speaker's purpose.

Listening: A Class Question and Answer Session

track 2-10 **A** | Listen to part of a class question and answer session. Then answer the questions below.

1. Who is the speaker? _____

_____

_____

2. What is the speaker's purpose? _____

_____

_____

🎧 **B** | Listen again and write the contractions you hear. Then decide which two words make up
track 2-10 each contraction.

    1. Hi, everyone. _____ like to start by thanking you for inviting me here.

    2. _____ always happy to get out of the office.

    3. Your _____ right.

    4. _____ worked for several charitable organizations over the years.

🎧 **C** | Listen to the rest of the question and answer session and complete only the questions that
track 2-11 the students ask. Write the exact words. You might have to listen more than once.

Question 1: Do you know whether _____?

Answer: _____

Question 2: Can you please explain why _____?

Answer: _____

Question 3: I'd like to know who _____.

Answer: _____

Question 4: I was wondering how _____.

Answer: _____

🎧 **D** | **Note-Taking.** Listen again and take brief notes on the guest speaker's answers to the
track 2-11 students' questions.

After Listening

👥 **Critical Thinking.** Discuss the questions with a partner.

    1. Is the speaker working for a charity organization now? Explain.

    2. Do you think the speaker is a reliable source of information? Why, or why not?

    3. What do you think poor people in your country would buy with cash payments?

The purchase of an animal can improve a farm family's diet and contribute to their income.

Grammar

Indirect Questions

An indirect question is a question inside another question or statement. We use indirect questions because they are often more polite than direct questions.

When does class begin?	(Direct Question)
Can you tell me when class begins?	(Indirect Question)

Indirect questions are often in the form of statements.

I'd like to know *who makes decisions about money.*
I was wondering *how communities get things like new schools and roads.*

Indirect questions begin with a polite phrase. Here are some polite phrases we use for indirect questions.

Do you know *whether people really use the money for important things?*
Can you tell me *how cash transfer programs work?*
Can you please explain *why you don't ask people to work for the money?*
I'd like to know *how people make a living selling snake venom.*
I was wondering *how people start their own farms.*

A | Make these questions for a professor more polite by rewriting them as indirect questions in your notebook.

1. Where does the cash for the payments come from?
2. When will the final exam be given?
3. Are there any poor people in Japan?
4. Why did you give me a *C* on this paper?
5. How much money do elderly people in Namibia get?
6. Who is the director of that organization?

B | Imagine a speaker is coming to your class (you can choose the topic). With a group, brainstorm a list of questions you would like to ask him or her, and turn them into indirect questions. Talk about possible answers.

C | Role-play your discussion from exercise **B**. Use expressions from the box below to show interest in what the speaker is saying.

Student to Student: Showing Interest in What a Speaker is Saying

When you are listening to someone speak, it is important to show them that you are interested and paying attention to what they are saying. Using expressions like these can also help to keep a conversation going.

More formal:	*How interesting!*		*I didn't know that!*
Less formal:	*Wow!*	*Cool!*	*That's great!*

Language Function: Using Indirect Questions

A | **Collaboration.** Form a group with three or four other students and follow the steps below.

1. Imagine that your club, Students Against Poverty, has raised $125,000 to help fight poverty.
2. Read about four charity organizations that might receive the money.
3. To help you decide which charity to give the money to, think of one or two polite, indirect questions to ask a representative from each organization.

A Sweeter World

- Gives bees to families, and teaches them how to start a home-based honey business.
- Bees can produce honey in the country or in cities.
- Honey is valuable, and people in every country love it.
- When the bees reproduce, the family gives their extra bees to a new family.

The Library Project

- Collects used science books, textbooks, and reference books in major languages (English, Spanish, French, etc.).
- Sends the books to small towns in developing countries to start public libraries.
- Every year, the libraries receive more books.
- The libraries are free for anyone to use.

Business Start-Up

- Helps women around the world start businesses by lending them a small amount of money (about $100).
- Women start very small businesses, such as sewing or baking and selling bread at the market.
- When the women pay back their loans, the money is used again for more loans.
- The organization gives advice and helps women with their businesses.

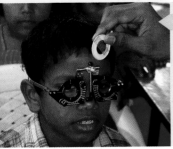

Clear Vision

- Collects used eyeglasses, and gives them to people with vision problems in poor countries.
- Children who can't see well don't succeed in school, and workers with bad vision can't get good jobs.
- Doctors travel with the group to make sure each person gets the right glasses.
- The doctors also help people with eye diseases.

B | Get together with another group. Share the questions that you plan to ask each organization and explain the reasons for each question.

5

You and your group are going to give a presentation about a non-governmental organization (NGO) that works to help people in your own country or another country. Two very large and famous NGOs are the Red Cross/Red Crescent and Oxfam, but there are many, many other NGOs that are doing interesting and effective work.

A | **Planning a Presentation.** Follow these steps to prepare your presentation.

1. Choose an organization that you think is effective and is making a difference in people's lives.

2. Go online to find the answers to the questions below. If the organization has an office in your country, you can also call to ask for information. Try to find photos showing the group at work. *(See page 212 of the Independent Student Handbook for more information on doing online research.)*

   - Where do they work?
   - What is their goal?
   - How do they work towards this goal?
   - How can people know if they're effective?
   - What can your audience do to support them?

B | Plan and practice your section of the group's presentation. Your group's presentation should be 8–10 minutes long, and each member should present a part of it. You can present from your notes or use PowerPoint®.

Presentation Skills: Practicing and Timing Your Presentation

Before you give a formal presentation, you should practice it several times and make sure the length is suitable. The average native speaker gives a presentation at a rate of 100–120 words per minute. It's OK for non-native speakers to speak a little more slowly than this.

Many people speak faster when they feel nervous, so their actual presentation takes less time than they expected. If you tend to speak too quickly, remind yourself to speak *slowly* and *carefully* during your presentation. Leave short pauses between your sentences.

C | **Presentation.** Take turns giving your presentations to the class. After each presentation, the audience should ask questions to get more information. Try to use indirect questions.

> Could you please tell me how many countries they work in?

A World of Words

ACADEMIC PATHWAYS
Lesson A: Listening to a Lecture
Discussing Fairy Tales
Lesson B: Listening to a Class Discussion Session
Giving a Summary

Think and Discuss

1. Where do you think this man is, and why?
2. What kind of book do you think he's reading?
3. What are some different types of literature that you know about?

A man sits on a desert ledge reading a book in his sleeping bag.

Exploring the Theme:
A World of Words

Look at the timeline and the photos and read the captions. Then discuss the questions.

1. Of the three pictured writers, whose work would you be most likely to read? Why?
2. Which of the major writers on the timeline were alive at the same time?
3. Who are some of the most famous writers from your country? Where would they fit on the timeline?

Three of the World's Major Writers

The poet Li Po once worked for the Chinese emperor. He influenced many generations of later poets, including Matsuo Bashō. Some of the subjects he wrote about were nature, friendship, and the passage of time.

Lewis Carroll is the pen name of England's Charles Dodgson. He studied logic and mathematics, yet his most famous book, *Alice's Adventures in Wonderland,* is pure fantasy.

Chile's Isabel Allende has published stories for children, plays, and several novels. Her stories are often about the lives of women and sometimes combine elements of myth and reality.

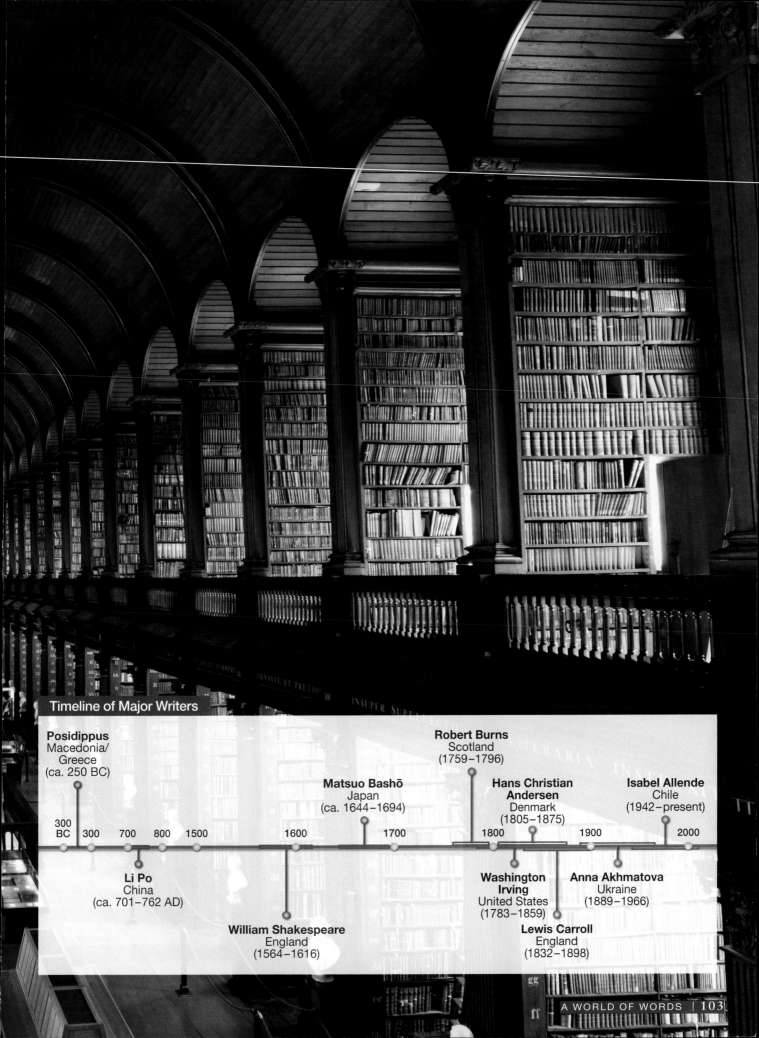

Timeline of Major Writers

Posidippus
Macedonia/
Greece
(ca. 250 BC)

Robert Burns
Scotland
(1759–1796)

Matsuo Bashō
Japan
(ca. 1644–1694)

**Hans Christian
Andersen**
Denmark
(1805–1875)

Isabel Allende
Chile
(1942–present)

300 BC	300	700	800	1500	1600	1700	1800	1900	2000

Li Po
China
(ca. 701–762 AD)

**Washington
Irving**
United States
(1783–1859)

Anna Akhmatova
Ukraine
(1889–1966)

William Shakespeare
England
(1564–1616)

Lewis Carroll
England
(1832–1898)

A | Meaning from Context. Read and listen to the information about three poets from three different time periods. Notice the words in blue. These are words you will hear and use in Lesson A.

Matsuo Bashō, Japan, ca. 1644–1694

Bashō is famous for his *haiku*, short **poems** with three lines. Each line in a *haiku* has a set number of syllables—five in the first line, seven in the second, and five in the last line. A *haiku* does not need to rhyme, but it should **capture** a moment of one's life. Nature is often the subject of a *haiku*, but the meaning can be as much about human emotion as the **external** world. Bashō's most famous book, *Narrow Road to a Far Province*, was **published** after a long journey on foot.

Robert Burns, Scotland, 1759–1796

Robert Burns's first book, *Poems, Chiefly in the Scottish Dialect*, was published in 1786—just one year after the first of his 14 children was born. The book contained Burns's **observations** of the lives of ordinary people. He watched them doing farm work, going to church, and falling in love, and his humor and **insights** on everyday life made him a very popular writer. Robert Burns only lived to the age of 37, but he continues to have an **influence** on writers today.

Anna Akhmatova, Ukraine, 1889–1966

Anna Akhmatova—poet, translator, and literary critic—was born in the Ukraine but spent much of her life in Russia. Much of her writing was **political**, and many of her poems, including the well-known *Requiem*, **reflected** the difficulties that Russians faced during the time of Joseph Stalin and World War II. Family life was also difficult for Akhmatova, who married three times, and whose one child was **raised** by grandparents. Akhmatova is remembered for her original writing style, as well as her ideas.

B | Write each word in blue next to its definition.

1. _____ (adj.) outside
2. _____ (v.) be taken care of until grown up
3. _____ (n.) things one sees or notices
4. _____ (n.) pieces of writing with carefully chosen words in short lines
5. _____ (v.) printed to be sold
6. _____ (n.) accurate and deep understanding of something
7. _____ (adj.) having to do with government
8. _____ (v.) to represent or express something successfully, to catch
9. _____ (n.) something that has an effect on a person or situation
10. _____ (v.) showed that an attitude or situation exists

USING VOCABULARY

👥 **A** | Take turns asking and answering the questions with a partner.

1. In what year was this textbook **published**? Have you **published** anything (in print or online), or do you think any of your writing will be **published** in the future?
2. Who was Anna Akhmatova's child **raised** by? Do you think that was difficult for her? Why, or why not?
3. The meaning of *haiku* can be as much about human emotion as the **external** world. What are some examples of the **external** world?
4. Have you ever written a **poem**? If so, what did you write about? If not, what kind of poetry do you like to read?
5. Are there any writers who have had an **influence** on you? Explain.

B | Fill in each blank with the correct form of a word from the box. You will use some words more than once.

capture	observation	reflect	insight	influence

1. Toby's friends were doing very well in school. They must have had a good _____ on him, because Toby's own grades soon improved.
2. Bob is a very talented photographer. He is really able to _____ people's emotions in his photos.
3. In class today, Hannah made a good _____. She noticed that the light in the classroom is better in the afternoon, so we're going to move our reading time to 2 o'clock.
4. Parents usually gain valuable _____ into child development as they watch their children grow up. People who don't have children don't always have these _____, so they might not understand why children do certain things.
5. The next morning, Julian saw his face in the bathroom mirror. He was definitely getting older. The story he wrote in class that day _____ that fact. It was about a man who was trying to accept the aging process.

Before Listening

Understanding Sidetracks

A lecture or other talk isn't always a direct journey from point A to point B. Even a well-planned lecture can include sidetracks—thoughts that are on a different topic than the rest of the talk. In some cases, sidetracks are a way to add ideas that might be interesting to the audience; for example, a personal experience or a funny story. Other sidetracks are unplanned thoughts that occur while the speaker is talking.

For the listener, sidetracks can be entertaining or a chance to relax for a moment. On the other hand, sidetracks can be confusing, so it's helpful to be able to identify them.

Expressions that signal sidetracks include:

That reminds me . . .	*By the way . . .*	*This is off the subject, but . . .*
As an aside . . .		*On a different topic . . .*

Expressions that signal a return to the main topic include:
Getting back to what I was saying . . .
Returning to the topic . . .
As I was saying . . .

 track 2-15   Listen to an excerpt from a lecture and check (✔) the expressions from the box that you hear.

Expressions That Signal Sidetracks

❑ That reminds me . . .
❑ As an aside . . .
❑ By the way . . .
❑ This is off the subject, but . . .
❑ On a different topic . . .

Expressions That Signal a Return to the Main Topic

❑ Getting back to what I was saying . . .
❑ Returning to the topic . . .
❑ As I was saying . . .
❑ Getting back to our topic . . .

Listening: A Lecture

 track 2-15   **A** | **Listening for Main Ideas.** Listen again and circle the topics in the left-hand column of the chart that are discussed in the lecture.

Part of the path that Bashō walked on can still be seen on the Natagiri Pass in Japan.

Topic	Notes
Syllables in *haiku* Origin of *haiku*	from haikai
Bashō's early life Bashō's marriage	studied haiku in Kyoto, 伊賀 poetry
What are *haikai*? What are *haibun*?	longer form of poetry · sonnet?, 17 · haiku & prose
Bashō's 1684 journey Bashō's 1689 journey ✓	Sea · Minzawa Kenji 日本 · Narrow Road · "The v. soul of Japan had .."
Bashō's insights Bashō's death	haiku philosophy, death

🎧 track 2-15 **B** | **Note-Taking.** Listen to the lecture again and take notes either in the right-hand side of the chart from exercise **A** or in your notebook. Remember to write down only key words and to use abbreviations and symbols whenever possible.

After Listening

A | Take the professor's quiz using your notes from exercise **B** above.

Quiz

1. The form *haiku* came from the _____ verse of *haikai* poems.
   a. first   b. second   c. third

2. _____ was **not** an important influence in Bashō's early life.
   a. Shakespeare   b. Chinese poetry   c. Taoism

3. Shakespeare's poems can be compared to _____.
   a. *haiku*   b. *haikai*   c. *haibun*

4. Bashō's journey took him _____ of Edo.
   a. east   b. west   c. north   d. south

5. Basho is **not** remembered for his insights on _____.
   a. nature   b. education   c. death   d. life

B | Compare your notes and quiz answers with a partner's.

C | **Discussion.** Read the *haiku* under the photograph and discuss the following questions.

1. Do you like *haiku*? Why, or why not?
2. What does this *haiku* make you think of?

D | **Critical Thinking.** Bashō's master work, *Narrow Road to a Far Province,* includes *haibun* about the everyday problems of travel. Brainstorm some specific things you think he might have written about.

*an ancient pond
a frog jumps in
the splash of water*
~Matsuo Bashō

Language Function

Making Sidetracks and Returning to a Topic

Earlier in this unit, you heard a professor make sidetracks during a lecture. In this section, you will practice making sidetracks and returning to your original topic. Please refer to the expressions on page 106.

A | **Note-Taking.** Choose one of the following texts and read it while your partner reads the other. While you read, take brief notes on the following points:

- Literary genre (fiction, non-fiction, poetry, biography, etc.)
- Setting (when and where it takes place)
- Author's style (style of language)
- Content (information)

A sculpture of the Little Mermaid, from a fairy tale by Hans Christian Andersen, in Copenhagen, Denmark

Text A track 2-16

Published in 1847, The True Story of My Life *by well-known fairy-tale writer Hans Christian Andersen, begins with his birth:*

My native land, Denmark, is a poetical land, full of popular traditions, old songs, and an eventful history, which has become bound up with that of Sweden and Norway. The Danish islands are possessed of beautiful beech woods, and corn and clover fields: they resemble gardens on a great scale. Upon one of these green islands, Funen, stands Odense, the place of my birth, [. . .]. Odense is the capital of the province and lies twenty-two Danish miles from Copenhagen.

In the year 1805 there lived here, in a small mean room, a young married couple, who were extremely attached to each other; he was a shoemaker, scarcely twenty-two years old, a man of a richly gifted and truly poetical mind. His wife, a few years older than himself, was ignorant of life and of the world, but possessed a heart full of love.

Text B track 2-17

Published in 1865, Alice's Adventures in Wonderland *by Lewis Carroll begins with a day in the life of Alice, the story's main character:*

So she was considering, in her own mind (as well as she could, for the hot day made her feel very sleepy and stupid), whether the pleasure of making a daisy-chain would be worth the trouble of getting up and picking the daisies, when suddenly a White Rabbit with pink eyes ran close by her.

There was nothing so *very* remarkable in that; nor did Alice think it so *very* much out of the way to hear the Rabbit say to itself, "Oh dear! Oh dear! I shall be too late!" (when she thought it over afterward, it occurred to her that she ought to have wondered at this, but at the time it all seemed quite natural); but, when the Rabbit actually *took a watch out of its waistcoat-pocket,* and looked at it, and then hurried on, Alice started to her feet, for it flashed across her mind that she had never before seen a rabbit with either a waistcoat-pocket, or a watch to take out of it, and, burning with curiosity, she ran across the field after it, and was just in time to see it pop down a large rabbit-hole under the hedge.

B | Making Sidetracks. Use your notes to tell your partner about the text you read. While you are speaking, make one or two sidetracks and return to your original topic.

> By the way, yesterday I went to . . .

> Getting back to what I was saying, . . .

C | Discussion. Was it easy or difficult to follow your partner's sidetracks? Were you still able to understand what your partner said about the reading passage?

Grammar

The Simple Past vs. the Present Perfect

We use the simple past tense to talk about completed actions or states in the past.
> She **published** her first novel in 2004.
> Tim **left** the house at around six o'clock.
> My grandmother **was** married twice, and she **died** when she **was** 93 years old.

We use the present perfect tense to talk about:
1) Things that began in the past and continue to the present
> They **have lived** next door to us for 12 years.

2) Things that have happened several times before now
> I **have traveled** to Venice four times.

3) Things that happened at some indefinite time in the past and are connected to the present
> He has **studied** a lot, so he's ready for the exam.

The present perfect tense is formed with *have* or *has* + the past participle of a verb.

Regular Past Participle
*We **have decided** to eat dinner at home tonight.*
*Ms. Rowling **has influenced** many writers.*

Irregular Past Participle
*Mr. Lofgren **has written** three books.*
*The students **have taken** two quizzes so far.*

A | Discuss each sentence with a partner and choose the correct verb tense.

1. Andersen (lived/has lived) in Denmark during the 19th century.
2. Several generations of children (loved/have loved) Carroll's stories.
3. Ms. Springer (published/has published) several articles in her field, and I think she's working on a new article now.
4. Luke (made/has made) a good observation in our discussion section yesterday.
5. Bashō (wrote/has written) and published a large number of *haiku* and *haibun*.
6. I (didn't read/haven't read) any good books lately.

 track 2-18 **B** | Listen to the conversation. Practice it with a partner. Then switch roles and practice it again.

Amanda:	Have you decided what your research paper is going to be about?
Tyler:	Not yet. I'm interested in Akhmatova's poetry, but I don't know much about it.
Amanda:	Maybe the professor can recommend some good sources of information. Yesterday she said we could go to her office for help any time today.
Tyler:	But I'm also interested in fiction. Have you read anything by Isabel Allende?
Amanda:	No, I haven't. She's a modern-day novelist, isn't she?
Tyler:	She is, and she's really popular. Her books have been translated into a lot of different languages, including English.
Amanda:	That's lucky for you since you don't speak Spanish!
Tyler:	Very funny. The problem is—I haven't read any of her books either, and I don't think I have enough time before the paper is due.
Amanda:	Didn't the professor say something about books of literary criticism? Maybe you can just read *about* Allende.
Tyler:	I'd still have to do a lot of reading.
Amanda:	Well, sure—it's a research paper.
Tyler:	I think I'll go with the poet, and I think I'll go to the professor's office now.
Amanda:	Good ideas. Now I need to decide on *my* topic . . .

C | Read the statements about the conversation and notice the use of the simple past and the present perfect. Circle **T** for *true* or **F** for *false*.

1. The professor has assigned a research paper, but we're not sure from the conversation exactly when she gave the assignment.   **T**   **F**
2. Tyler has read several books by Isabel Allende.   **T**   **F**
3. Yesterday, the professor told the students when they could go to her office.   **T**   **F**
4. Amanda has read one book by Allende.   **T**   **F**
5. By the end of the conversation, Tyler has made two decisions.   **T**   **F**

Discussing Fairy Tales

A | Read and listen to a synopsis of *The Little Mermaid,* a fairy tale written by Hans Christian Andersen.

Andersen's Little Mermaid is the daughter of the Sea King, and she must wait to get married until her older sisters have been married—and she has a lot of older sisters! When it's finally her turn, she goes to the surface of the sea, rescues a prince from drowning, and falls in love. She's not human, however. In fact she has a tail, so marriage to the prince seems unlikely. It turns out that in order for the mermaid to become human, the prince must love her with all his heart and marry her, and she must give up her beautiful mermaid voice in order to lose the tail.

The fairy tale doesn't end the way you might expect. The prince does get married, but to a human princess, and the little mermaid becomes a spirit, one of the "daughters of the air" as a reward for her good deeds as a mermaid.

On and around a statue of Hans Christian Andersen, children listen to a storyteller in New York City's Central Park.

B | **Discussion.** Look at a few of the titles of some of Andersen's other stories and answer the questions below with a partner.

The Princess and the Pea   *The Ugly Duckling*
The Snow Queen   *The Emperor's New Suit*

1. Have you heard or read any of these fairy tales? If so, which ones? If not, do the titles remind you of other fairy tales you've heard or read?
2. Why do you think people tell their children fairly tales?
3. What do you think is the meaning of Andersen's mermaid story?

C | **Collaboration.** Form a group with two or three other students. Follow the directions below with your group members.

1. Think of a fairy tale you all know and recall as many of its details as possible. If you don't have a fairy tale in common, one group member can tell the group a fairy tale.
2. Discuss the fairy tale as a work of literature; for example: Why was it written or told? Who is the intended audience? If it teaches a lesson, what is that lesson? Have you (or would you) tell the story to your children?
3. Tell the rest of the class about the fairy tale your group discussed.

Sleepy Hollow

The historic Philipsburg Manor in Sleepy Hollow, NY

New York

Sleepy Hollow

CANADA

New York

UNITED STATES

MEXICO

Before Viewing

Using the Simple Past and Present Perfect. Read the information below and fill in each blank with the simple past or present perfect form of the verb in parentheses.

The Author: Washington Irving _____ (publish) *The Legend of Sleepy Hollow* in 1820. By that time, he had moved to England, but he still _____ (love) the beautiful New England landscape near Sleepy Hollow, New York. Readers _____ (enjoy) the story for nearly two centuries, and it's still a favorite at Halloween.

The Setting: When he wrote the story, Irving _____ (describe) Sleepy Hollow as a beautiful place where Dutch settlers enjoyed the autumn harvest. There, the people have a legend: A soldier whose head was shot off by a cannonball during the Revolutionary War rides around on a horse each night in search of his head.

American author Washington Irving lived from 1783 to 1859.

The Main Characters:

Ichabod Crane—*the comically tall, thin schoolmaster from the state of Connecticut*
Katrina van Tassel—*the daughter of a farmer in Sleepy Hollow*
Abraham "Brom Bones" van Brunt—*the local man who wants to marry Katrina*
The Headless Horseman—*the mysterious horseback rider that frightens Ichabod Crane*

While Viewing

A | Watch the video and choose the correct phrase to complete each sentence.

1. Dutch settlers (immigrants) came to the Sleepy Hollow area in the
   _____.
   a. 1600s   b. 1700s
2. Sleepy Hollow is well known for _____.
   a. its location on the Hudson River
   b. being the setting for Irving's story
3. Irving used the names of real Sleepy Hollow people and places in his
   story, including _____.
   a. Ichabod Crane   b. Katrina van Tassel
4. Washington Irving _____ as a boy.
   a. lived in Sleepy Hollow   b. visited Sleepy Hollow

B | Watch the video again and pay attention to the Sleepy Hollow tourist attractions.
Then circle **T** for *true* and **F** for *false* for each sentence below.

1. Tourists can visit a historic manor to see what life was like in the 17th and 18th centuries.	**T**	**F**
2. Tourists can visit the old cemetery.[1]	**T**	**F**
3. Tourists can attend the town's Halloween festival each year.	**T**	**F**
4. Tourists can see a man playing the role of the Headless Horseman and carrying a real jack-o-lantern.	**T**	**F**

After Viewing

A | **Discussion.** Discuss the questions below.

1. In the video, the narrator says, "It's a fun place to visit, but it's the tale of a gangly[2] schoolmaster and a headless horseman that really put Sleepy Hollow on the map." This means that the story made Sleepy Hollow famous, and makes Sleepy Hollow a tourist destination today. Would you visit Sleepy Hollow? Why, or why not?

B | **Critical Thinking.** In Lesson B of this unit, you will listen to a class discussion session. During the discussion session, students ask questions about a lecture in an informal setting. Working with a partner, write three questions to ask a literature professor about this video or about *The Legend of Sleepy Hollow*.

1. _____?
2. _____?
3. _____?

[1]A **cemetery** is a place where dead people's bodies are buried. *Graveyard* is a synonym for *cemetery*.
[2]A person is **gangly** if he or she is tall, thin, and not graceful-looking with his or her long arms and legs.

A | **Meaning from Context.** Read and listen to the interview with a bookstore owner. Notice the words in **blue**. These are words you will hear and use in Lesson B.

track 2-20

Q: You're the owner of a successful bookstore. What's the secret of your success?

A: Well, there's no magic **formula** that works for everyone. I bought this bookstore from the **previous** owner over 20 years ago. **Eventually**, a store like mine builds up a customer base. I know a lot of the customers by name, and some of them come in every day.

Q: What challenges do bookstores face nowadays?

A: As you know, in the digital age, almost everything my bookstore sells is available online. Instead of buying **printed** media like books and magazines, people can download them onto their electronic devices. The same goes for music. When was the last time you bought a CD?

Q: Do you have any regrets?

A: Absolutely not. You have to be fearless and follow your dreams. **Otherwise**, you might get to the end of your life and feel as if you haven't really lived.

 B | Discuss the questions with a partner. Use context clues to help you understand the words in **blue**. Then use your dictionary if you need to.

1. Do you think the woman had a good customer base 20 years ago? Why does she use the word *eventually*?
2. Is the woman the first owner of the bookstore? How do you know? What does the word *previous* mean?
3. What's a different way for the woman to say *otherwise* in her last answer? (You might need to use more than one word to say the same thing.)
4. The woman says there is no **formula** for success, but what are some things that every business needs to do in order to be successful?
5. Do you prefer reading **printed** books or reading books on an electronic device?

In Buenos Aires, Argentina, the Libreria El Ateneo Grand Splendid bookstore is housed in an old theater.

C | **Meaning from Context.** Read and listen to the interview with a librarian. Notice the words in blue. These are words you will hear and use in Lesson B.

ack 2-21

Q: You **mentioned** that you're a librarian at a public library. Tell us more about that.

A: That's not quite **accurate**. I do work at a public library part time, but I also work at a university library, and I teach a class once a week. Everyone has access to the materials at the public library, **whereas** only students and staff can use the university library.

Q: I see. And do you think it's fair for taxpayers to have to pay for the public library?

A: I used to wonder about that, but I've **gained** some insight since I've been working there. The public library really does make the city a better place, and taxpayers don't mind paying for that.

Q: Are people reading **contemporary** authors these days, or do they prefer the classics?

A: Both, really. They read the contemporary authors when their books are first published, but the older authors will never go out of style. They've already stood the test of time.

D | Discuss the questions with a partner. Use context clues to help you understand the words in **blue**. Then use your dictionary if you need to.

1. What do you think a city **gains** from having a public library? Does it lose anything?
2. When you **mention** something, do you say a lot or a little about it?
3. Does an **accurate** statement reflect the facts 75 percent or 100 percent?
4. What **contemporary** author can you think of who is popular now?
5. Does the word "**whereas**" signal an addition, an explanation, or a contrast?

In Madrid, Spain, commuters can borrow books from BiblioMetro, a public library in a metro station.

E | **Discussion.** Form a group with two or three other students and discuss the questions.

1. Do you think more people in the world have access to bookstores or to libraries?
2. In your opinion, will printed books and newspapers eventually be replaced by digital forms of information? Why, or why not?
3. Where do you look when you need to find accurate information? When you want something entertaining to read?

Pronunciation

The coast of the Sea of Japan, where Bashō walked for nine days during his journey in 1689

Review of Question Intonation

In *yes/no* questions, the speaker's voice rises on the last content word or phrase.

Is this information accurate?

Have you talked with the professor?

In questions with *wh-* words, the speaker's voice rises then falls on the last content word.

Where was the article published?

Why are you comparing them?

In questions that offer choices, the speaker's voice rises on the first choice(s), then rises and falls on the last choice.

Do you prefer to read poetry or prose?

Will you write your paper on Bashō, Burns, or Akhmatova?

A | Listen to the example questions from the chart. *track 2-22*

B | Read the questions below. Mark the intonation in each question. Then practice saying the questions with a partner.

1. Do you want to go to the bookstore or the library?
2. Are you writing your research paper?
3. Have you read chapter 3?
4. Where did you see him?
5. Would you like to walk or take the bus?
6. How was your presentation?

Before Listening

With a partner, discuss what you remember about the lecture from Lesson A.

Listening: A Class Discussion Session

A | **Listening for Main Ideas.** Listen to a discussion session with the professor from Lesson A of this unit and take brief notes on the question(s) each student asks the professor. *track 2-23*

Student #1: _____?

Student #2: _____?

Student #3: _____?

B | Listening for Details. Listen again and take brief notes on the professor's answers.

Topic	Notes
Haibun	haiku + prose, ~ prose dram~
Bashō's *haibun*	not invented by, wrote a lot, pioneer, master of form
Shakespeare	contemporary, no influence haiku/sonet, strict form, set verses, lines
Bashō's *haiku*	influenced by Chinese, poetry, Dao, Zen Buddhism, reflections of truth

C | Compare your notes with a partner's and ask your instructor any questions you have about the listening passage.

After Listening

A | Collaboration. Using your lecture notes from page 106 and the information from the discussion that you just heard, work with a partner and write four questions that might appear on the exam.

1. _____?
2. _____?
3. _____?
4. _____?

B | Critical Thinking. Form a group with one or two other student pairs and follow the directions below.

1. Share your questions from exercise **A**.
2. Choose two questions you think would definitely appear on the exam.
3. Explain your choices to the rest of the class.

C | Discussion. Discuss the questions.

1. In what ways might this discussion session help the students understand the material and do well on the exam?
2. Do you think an informal discussion session such as this one is necessary, or was the lecture sufficient to cover the material?
3. Did the professor make any sidetracks during the discussion session?

Grammar

👥 **A** | Practice the conversation with your partner. Then switch roles and practice it again.

Writers Jaan Kross and Ellen Niit on the balcony of their home in Estonia

Interviewer:	What are some of the good things about life as an author?
Author:	I don't know about other writers, but for me, the best part is that I can spend my time thinking and being creative every day.
Interviewer:	Don't you miss having co-workers?
Author:	Sometimes. Co-workers give you some social contact, but they're usually not true friends. When I do get together with my friends, I really value our time together.
Interviewer:	Have you ever had anything published that you're not proud of now?
Author:	Well, several years ago I wrote some short stories, and they were not my best work. I'm much more proud of my novels.
Interviewer:	Speaking of your novels, didn't I hear something about a new one?
Author:	You probably did, and the rumors are true. My next novel is being printed right now, and it should be in bookstores next month.
Interviewer:	I look forward to reading it, and I thank you for talking to me today.
Author:	It was my pleasure.

👥 **B** | Discuss the questions.

1. Does the interviewer think that the author probably misses having co-workers?
2. Is the interviewer certain about hearing something about a new novel?
3. Look at the interviewer's questions. Why do you think he or she uses negatives?

Negative Questions

Negative questions are most often used in informal speaking, and they have two main functions.

1. Showing that the speaker expects a certain answer.
Don't *you get lonely working at home?*   (The speaker thinks the answer is probably yes.)
Isn't *that your coat?*   (The speaker thinks the answer is probably yes.)

2. Checking the accuracy of information.
Doesn't *the flight leave at 9:25?*   (The speaker thinks that it probably does.)
Aren't *you in my philosophy class?*   (The speaker thinks that you probably are.)

👥 **C** | **Discussion.** Change the questions below to negative questions. Then with a partner, discuss the possible function of each negative question in a conversation.

1. Did you send an invitation to the Martins?
2. Are you worried about the exam?
3. Do you wish you lived someplace with a warmer climate?

Language Function

👥 **A** | **Discussion.** Read the information about vacation packages to the UNESCO Cities of Literature.[1] In a group, discuss some of the pros and cons of traveling to each place for a book festival.

Edinburgh, Scotland $1400 per person
- Population 450,000
- Located in the northern part of the UK
- Four days, three nights, hotel included
- Home of historic literary figures such as Sir Arthur Conan Doyle, author of the Sherlock Holmes stories
- Poetry competition
- More than 45 bookstores in the city center

Melbourne, Australia $2300 per person
- Population 3.5 million
- Located on Australia's southern coast
- Seven days, six nights, no hotel
- Known as Australia's cultural capital
- Home of one of Australia's most valued literary awards, the Melbourne Prize for Literature
- Discounts at bookstores and free admission to area museums

Princes Street, Edinburgh, Scotland

Iowa City, USA $1050 per person
- Population 70,000
- Located in the rural midwest region
- Home of world-famous Iowa Writers' Workshop
- 25 Pulitzer prizes won by Iowa authors
- Four days, three nights, includes home-stay with local family
- Appearances by contemporary authors from 11 countries

Dublin, Ireland $1650 per person
- Population 500,000
- Located on Ireland's east coast
- Five days, four nights, hotel included
- Home of four winners of the Nobel Prize for Literature, including George Bernard Shaw and W.B. Yeats
- Featuring seven films based on books
- Hundreds of pubs and cafés in the city center

👥 **B** | As a group, choose one vacation package from exercise **A** for your own travel. Use negative questions to try to persuade your group members.

> Don't you want to go to a big city like Melbourne? Iowa City is quite small.

[1]The four **Cities of Literature** are part of UNESCO's Creative Cities Network, which allows cities to share their experiences with cultural development.

In this activity, you will listen to a news report and take notes on specific information from the report. You will then give a brief summary to your group.

A | **Note-Taking.** Form a group with two other students and follow the instructions.

track **2-24**

1. Assign each group member a question from the chart below: A, B, or C.
2. Listen to a news report about ancient Greek poems that were found with an Egyptian mummy.
3. As you listen, select information that is relevant to your question. Take brief notes in one column of the chart below—only on information that answers your question.

Ancient Greek Poems Found with Egyptian Mummy

A: What did Posidippus write? Was it similar to any modern writing?	**B:** Why were Greek writings found with an Egyptian mummy?	**C:** What made this discovery unusual and significant?

The mummy of Egyptian Pharaoh Ramses II was placed inside this sarcophagus after his death.

B | Read the information below about summaries.

> ## Critical Thinking Focus: Selecting Relevant Information
>
> A summary is a shorter version of the original information you hear, watch, or read. It should include the most important or main ideas. It should not include small details or your own opinions about the information or topic. A summary should be brief and focus on the main ideas.

C | **Critical Thinking.** Look at your notes from exercise **A**. Cross out any information that should not be included in your summary.

D | **Organizing Ideas.** Prepare a summary with your group. Use your notes from exercise **C**.

E | **Presentation.** Present your summary to another group. Then give each other feedback. Did the summary only include relevant information and the most important ideas?

The Greek poet Posidippus worked in the Aegean region from about 280 to 240 BC.

> ## Presentation Skills: Giving a Summary
>
> When you give a summary, it's important to think about your purpose—what are you summarizing, and why? When you give a summary, you should provide the most important information about your topic clearly. You should keep your summary brief and avoid giving details or sidetracking.

After Oil

UNIT

7

ACADEMIC PATHWAYS

Lesson A: Listening to a Current Affairs Club Meeting
Giving an Informal Presentation
Lesson B: Listening to a Conversation between Students
Developing Materials for a Promotional Campaign

Think and Discuss

1. Look at the photo. How old do you think these gas pumps are?
2. How much do you think a gallon of gas cost when these pumps were in use?
3. How would your life be different if gasoline cost twice as much as it does now?

A pair of vintage gas pumps in a desert landscape

121

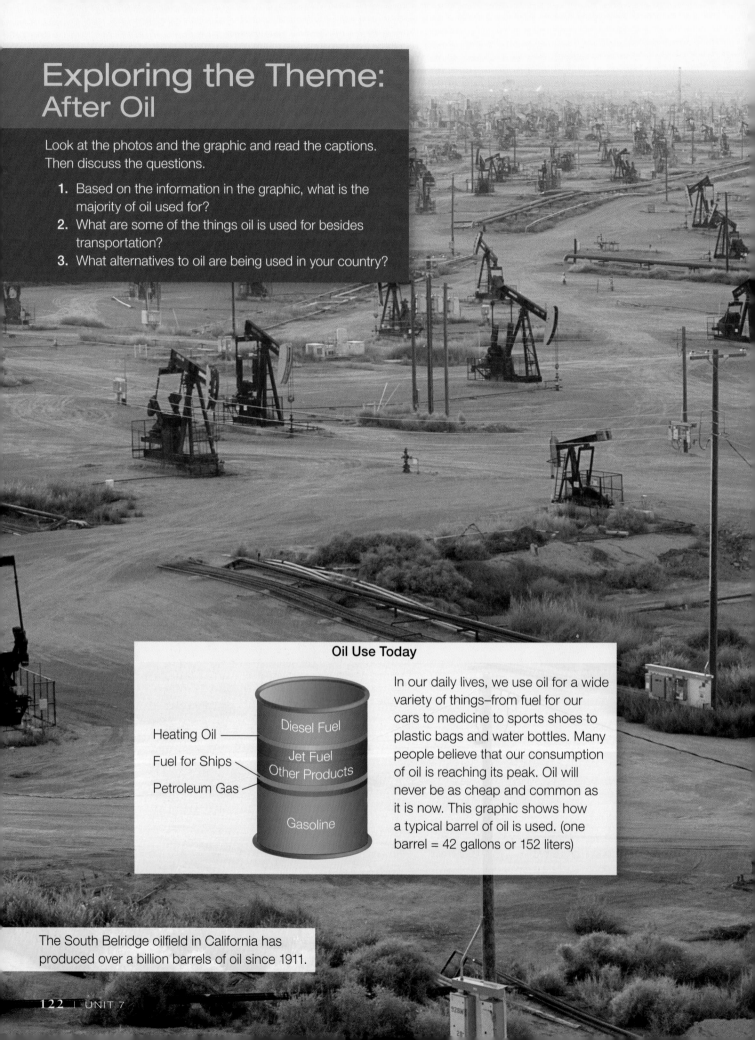

Exploring the Theme:
After Oil

Look at the photos and the graphic and read the captions.
Then discuss the questions.

1. Based on the information in the graphic, what is the majority of oil used for?
2. What are some of the things oil is used for besides transportation?
3. What alternatives to oil are being used in your country?

Oil Use Today

Heating Oil — Diesel Fuel

Fuel for Ships — Jet Fuel
Other Products

Petroleum Gas —

Gasoline

In our daily lives, we use oil for a wide variety of things–from fuel for our cars to medicine to sports shoes to plastic bags and water bottles. Many people believe that our consumption of oil is reaching its peak. Oil will never be as cheap and common as it is now. This graphic shows how a typical barrel of oil is used. (one barrel = 42 gallons or 152 liters)

The South Belridge oilfield in California has produced over a billion barrels of oil since 1911.

The Cost of Oil

Marina Wilson's award-winning steer weighs 1250 pounds (567 kilograms) and is about to be sold at an auction. The red barrels represent the amount of oil it took to raise the steer, including oil for agricultural chemicals and machinery, as well as the transportation of the animal's food.

Alternatives to Oil

Some scientists say we must shift to alternative forms of energy to prepare for the time when our supply of oil will be depleted. Finding substitutes for oil will be a priority for scientists and countries in the coming years.

A | Work with a partner. Match each word with its definition. Use your dictionary to help you. These are words you will hear or use in Lesson A.

1. shift (v.) _____
2. deplete (v.) _____
3. priority (n.) _____
4. enormous (adj.) _____
5. era (n.) _____
6. substitute (n.) _____
7. essential (adj.) _____
8. peak (n.) _____
9. extract (v.) _____
10. variety (n.) _____

a. to use up your supply of something
b. a period of time in history
c. a number of different kinds of the same thing
d. the highest amount or value of something
e. absolutely necessary
f. extremely large in size and amount
g. to remove a thing or substance from a place
h. to move slightly or gradually
i. the most important thing you have to achieve
j. the use of one thing instead of a different thing

B | **Understanding Visuals.** Look at the pictures below. Read the sentences. Then use the information to help you number the sentences in the correct order.

The History of Petroleum

OCEAN
300–400 million years ago

OCEAN
50–100 million years ago

Sand & Silt Rock

Plant & Animal Remains

Sand & Silt Rock

Oil & Gas Deposits

___4___ Oil wells **extract** the petroleum from under the sand and silt rock.

___1___ In a geological **era** 300–400 million years ago, sea plants and animals died, and their remains[1] fell to the bottom of the ocean.

___2___ The remains were covered with sand and silt.

___5___ The petroleum is used to make an **enormous variety** of products.

___3___ Heat and pressure under the sand were **essential** in making the remains into petroleum.

___7___ Many people now believe that scientists are right and **shifting** to **substitutes** for petroleum is an important **priority**.

___6___ Some scientists think that our supply of oil has reached a **peak** and will be **depleted** in the future.

[1]The **remains** of a person or animal are the parts that are left after it dies.

 C | Listen and check your answers.
track 2-25

A | Complete the conversation with the words from the box. Use each word only once.

shift	extract	substitute	era	variety
essential	peak	deplete	enormous	priority

Sara: Hey, Jamie. There's a guest speaker at the Current Affairs Club tonight, and I think you should go with me.

Jamie: Really? What's the topic?

Sara: Dr. Ron Steinberg is going to talk about (1) _____ oil.

Jamie: I don't even know what that means!

Sara: Well, that's the time period when the world is producing as much oil as possible. It means we're starting to (2) _____ our supplies of oil, so we're going to have less, and it'll be scarcer and more expensive.

Jamie: Expensive oil doesn't sound good.

Sara: You're right, but it looks like the (3) _____ of cheap oil is almost over.

Jamie: Is oil cheap now? I hadn't noticed at the gas station.

Sara: It might seem expensive now, but prices are going to go up.

Jamie: But aren't scientists working on new fuels—some kind of (4) _____ for oil? We can just (5) _____ from oil to the new fuel, and we'll have solar-powered airplanes or something, won't we?

Sara: Maybe, but oil isn't just important for transportation. In fact, it's (6) _____ for a wide (7) _____ of things.

Jamie: Like what?

Sara: Well, diesel fuel runs farm machines, so no more cheap oil means no more cheap food. And what about plastic, or ballpoint pens, or MP3 players . . . ?

Jamie: I see what you mean, but I'm sure there's still a/an (8) _____ amount of oil in the ground. They'll find ways to (9) _____ it. I can't believe you're so worried about this.

Sara: It's not just me. A lot of scientists are worried too. There's going to be less oil in the future, so finding solutions is a really high (10) _____ for everyone now.

Jamie: OK, OK—I'll go and hear the speaker with you tonight.

Sara: That's great. It starts at seven o'clock.

B | **Discussion.** Practice the conversation with a partner. Then discuss the questions below.

1. Why does Sara want to go to the lecture?
2. Why doesn't Jamie want to go?
3. Would you go to this lecture? Why, or why not?

Before Listening

Critical Thinking Focus: Considering Viewpoint and Bias

Bias refers to the pre-conceived ideas we carry with us based on our personal experiences and opinions. An unbiased speaker, therefore, would have no prejudices. The speaker would be completely fair and would consider all sides of every issue. In the real world, almost everyone has some degree of bias.

Thinking critically about a speaker's viewpoint and bias will help you to better understand the information that he or she presents. For example, an environmentalist and a petroleum company president would probably give very different lectures on "The Future of Oil." (*See page 205 in the Independent Student Handbook for more information on recognizing a speaker's bias.*)

Making Inferences. Look back at the conversation on page 125, and think about the speakers' viewpoints. Mark each statement below with the speaker who would probably agree with it: **J** for *Jamie* and **S** for *Sara*.

_____ People spend too much time worrying about the future.

_____ If we don't find substitutes for petroleum now, we will soon face serious problems.

_____ Science has always found solutions for our problems.

_____ The problems that we face now are different from problems in the past.

Listening: A Current Affairs Club Meeting

 A | **Listening for Main Ideas.** Listen to the meeting of the Current Affairs Club, and answer the questions below.

track 2-26

1. What does each speaker's organization do?

   Dr. Ron Steinberg, Future Fuels International: _____

   Dr. Leila Sparks, Lomax Petroleum: _____

2. What did Dr. M. King Hubbert's theory of peak oil say about U.S. oil production?

   _____

3. According to each speaker, what do Hubbert's models say now about world oil production?

   Dr. Sparks: _____

   Dr. Steinberg: _____

4. According to Dr. Steinberg, what are the problems with new oil discoveries?

   _____

   _____

Dr. M. King Hubbert (left) in 1933

B | Listening for Details. Listen again and circle the correct word to complete each sentence.

1. Peak oil production in the U.S. was in (1956/1970).
2. As the level of oil in a well goes down, the oil gets (harder/easier) to extract.
3. Dr. Steinberg thinks oil production will (increase/decrease) in the next two decades.
4. It's likely that many (small/large) oil fields haven't been discovered yet.
5. Dr. Sparks thinks Dr. Steinberg sounds (optimistic/pessimistic).

Plastic from petroleum provides soles for the Melli Shoe Company in Tehran, Iran.

After Listening

A | Critical Thinking. Mark each statement below with the speaker who would probably agree with it: **R** for *Ron Steinberg* and **L** for *Leila Sparks*.

_____ Oil supplies are slowly being depleted, so a gradual shift to other fuels is a good idea.

_____ The era of cheap oil is ending soon, and we'll have serious problems if we don't act now.

B | Read the statements. Circle **T** for *true* or **F** for *false* for each statement, or **M** for *maybe* if the statement could be based on a speaker's bias.

1. Dr. M. King Hubbert tried to predict the future of oil.   **T**   **F**   **M**
2. Hubbert thought that all the oil in the U.S. would be depleted by 1970.   **T**   **F**   **M**
3. It will be many years before world oil production reaches its peak.   **T**   **F**   **M**
4. The huge, easily accessible oil fields have already been discovered.   **T**   **F**   **M**
5. Some of the earth's oil supply is difficult to extract.   **T**   **F**   **M**
6. We must prepare now for the big changes in our near future.   **T**   **F**   **M**

C | Discussion. Form a group with two or three other students and compare your answers in exercise **B.** If you have any differences of opinion, discuss which speaker might or might not agree with the statements and why.

Grammar

Oil companies are extracting oil in deeper and deeper water as large oil fields become harder to find. This worker is trying to save an oil-covered pelican after the 2010 explosion of an offshore oil rig in the Gulf of Mexico.

Reported Speech

Quoted speech is most often used in writing. The words are exactly what the person said. In reported speech, we talk about a person's words with a reporting verb such as *say* or *tell*.

Quoted Speech

"Finding more oil **is** a high priority."
"New discoveries **will** be pretty small."
"I **saw** our teacher at the gas station."

Reported Speech

Sparks **said** *that finding more oil* **was** *a high priority.*
Steinberg **told** *us that new discoveries* **would** *be pretty small.*
She **said** *she* **had seen** *our teacher at the gas station.*

In reported speech, the word *that* after the reporting verb is optional.
"*You* **look** *tired.*"   *She said (***that***) I* **looked** *tired.*

Verbs and modal verbs usually change to a different (past) tense in reported speech.
"*I* **take** *the bus every day.*"   (simple present → simple past) *He said he* **took** *the bus every day.*
"*Jamie* **went** *home.*"   (simple past → past perfect)   *He told us that Jamie* **had gone** *home.*
"*I* **can** *help you carry the boxes.*"   (can → could)   *She* **said** *that she* **could** *help me carry the boxes.*

Changing the verb tense is optional in sentences about general facts or things that are still true.
"**I** *miss* **my** *friends very much.*"   *Ted said* **he** *misses his friends very much.*

Pronouns may need to change in reported speech.
"**I'm** *tired and* **my** *head hurts.*"   **She** *said* **she** *was tired and* **her** *head hurt.*

Verbs

simple present → simple past
present progressive → past progressive
present perfect → past perfect
simple past → past perfect

Modals

can → could
will → would
must/have to → had to
should → should (no change)

A | After the talk on peak oil, the speakers made these comments. Decide which speaker said each sentence. Then work with a partner to re-write the sentences as reported speech.

1. I drive an electric car to save gasoline. *He said he drove an electric car to save gasoline.*

   _____

2. I started this organization six years ago. _____

   _____

3. I am going to have a meeting with the president of the university. _____

   _____

4. I have given my presentation in eight countries. _____

   _____

5. I will travel to Ireland next summer. _____

   _____

Grammar

Changing Time Expressions in Reported Speech

When using reported speech, it may also be necessary to change time expressions in order to keep the speaker's original meaning, especially if some time has passed since the original statement.

"*I saw my friend* ***yesterday.***" → *She said she had seen her friend* ***the day before.***
"*I was in Los Angeles* ***last week.***" → *He said he had been in Los Angeles* ***the previous week.***
"*I'm leaving* ***tomorrow.***" → *She said she was leaving* ***the following day.***
"*I will be in Buenos Aires* ***next week.***" → *He said he would be in Buenos Aires* ***the following week.***

 B | Form a group with two other students and take turns role-playing the conversations below.

Student #1: asks a question
Student #2: answers using a complete sentence and the word or words in parentheses
Student #3: imagines that it's a few days later and reports on what Student #2 said

1. When did you call the airline? (yesterday)
2. When is your brother visiting? (next week)
3. When are you buying a hydrogen car? (next year)
4. When did you give your presentation? (last week)
5. When are you going to see the movie? (tomorrow)

Language Function: Reporting What Someone Has Said

A hybrid car

 A | Practice the conversation with a partner. Then switch roles and practice it again.

track 2-27

Grace:	Who was that on the phone?
Steve:	It was Michael. He said they'd decided to buy a hybrid car.
Grace:	*They* decided? I thought Laura loved fast, powerful cars.
Steve:	She does, but she told Michael she was concerned about the environment.
Grace:	Well, that sounds like a good change.
Steve:	I agree. He also said that with four children, they'd been worried about finding a big enough hybrid vehicle.
Grace:	Did they find one?
Steve:	Yes, he said it's some kind of a mini-van with three rows of seats.
Grace:	That sounds perfect. Maybe we should think about getting a hybrid.
Steve:	I think I'd rather wait for hydrogen cars. Those don't use any gasoline at all.
Grace:	True, but where are we going to get hydrogen fuel?
Steve:	Actually, there are already some gas stations in Germany that sell it.

B | Discussion. With a partner, discuss the questions below.

1. Which sentences in the conversation from exercise **A** contain reported speech? <u>Underline</u> them.
2. Do you think that hybrid vehicles, electric vehicles, or hydrogen vehicles will be more common 10 years from now?

C | Think of the last phone conversation you had with a friend. Tell your partner about it using reported speech. Your partner will make comments.

> He said he wanted to see *Race Through Time*. I told him it sounded like a really boring movie.

> Really? My brother said it was great.

D | Critical Thinking. Carbon dioxide, or CO_2, comes from a variety of sources, but mostly from burning fossil fuels such as oil and coal. Look at the pie chart below, and discuss the questions in a group. (*See page 216 of the Independent Student Handbook for more information on reading pie charts.*)

1. Which fossil fuel do you think is mainly used in each of the sectors shown in the chart?
2. Do the percentages in the chart surprise you in any way? Explain.
3. If Laura (from the conversation on page 129) is concerned about the environment, what are some things she can do to reduce carbon emissions[1] besides buying a hybrid vehicle? Consider every sector in the chart, and take brief notes on your group's ideas.

Fossil Fuel Use by Sector

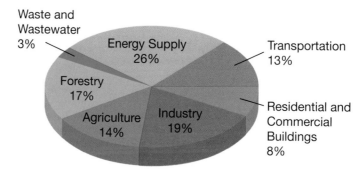

Waste and Wastewater 3%
Energy Supply 26%
Transportation 13%
Forestry 17%
Residential and Commercial Buildings 8%
Agriculture 14%
Industry 19%

E | Presentation. Share some of your group's ideas with the rest of the class. Use reported speech to tell the class about some of the most interesting ideas the members of your group had.

> Samir said that Laura could use public transportation instead of driving every day.

---

[1]An **emission** of something is its release into the atmosphere.

Giving an Informal Presentation

A | **Brainstorming.** Imagine it is one year from now and the price of oil is ten times higher than it is now. With a partner, use the left-hand column of the T-chart to list the changes that this increase in the price of oil has caused.

Changes	Adjustments
Bus fares have gone up.	We ride our bicycles everywhere.

B | In the right-hand column of the T-chart, list the adjustments you have made in your life because of the changes you listed in exercise **A**.

C | **Presentation.** Use the T-chart to share your ideas with the rest of the class. While you are speaking, the rest of the class will take brief notes so that they can ask you questions after your presentation (see exercise **D**).

> Bus fares have gone up.

> Right, so we ride our bicycles everywhere.

An oil rig at sunset

D | After each informal presentation, use the notes you took to ask the speakers questions. Use reported speech when possible to let the speakers know which part of their presentation you are curious about.

> You said you ride your bicycles everywhere now. I'm wondering if you both rode your bicycles before the price of oil increased.

Presentation Skills: Using an Appropriate Volume

Think about the last time you listened to a presentation. Could you hear the speaker easily, or was it an effort to hear the speaker? Or was the speaker's voice so loud that you wanted to cover your ears?

When you give a presentation, think about the size of the room, the distance between you and your audience, and any background noise in the room.

Before a formal presentation, consider making arrangements with someone in the audience to give you a signal to let you know if your voice is too soft, too loud, or just right. It's also fine to stop during a presentation and ask your audience if they can hear you.

Canadian Oil Sands

Western Canada is known for its enormous wilderness areas. The boreal forest is a huge ecosystem covering more than 1.2 billion acres (nearly 500 million hectares).

Alberta Canada

In strip mining, all of the topsoil is removed to access the oil sands—a mixture of a form of oil called bitumen and sand.

Before Viewing

A | Meaning from Context. Look at the photos and read the captions. Then discuss the questions with a partner. Use context clues to understand the meanings of new words whenever possible.

1. Are <u>wilderness</u> areas developed areas or undeveloped areas?
2. Does <u>strip mining</u> take place on the earth's surface or deep underground?
3. Do Canada's <u>oil sands</u> contain conventional <u>crude oil</u>, like the oil from oil wells, or <u>bitumen</u>?
4. Is the <u>processing</u> of oil sands a small business operation or a large one?
5. Do you think a <u>boom</u> is a period of slow growth or rapid growth?

B | Critical Thinking. Discuss the question with a partner.

In Dr. Hubbert's model of peak oil, the post-peak period includes reduced oil production and a worldwide shift to sources of oil that are more difficult and expensive to extract. Do you think the video you will see will support Hubbert's peak oil theory or refute it?

While Viewing

A | Read the statements. Then watch the video and circle **T** for *true* or **F** for *false*.

		T	F
1.	Canada and Saudi Arabia may have about the same amount of oil.	**T**	F
2.	Canada has been extracting oil for nearly 200 years.	**T**	**F**
3.	Fuel prices in Canada have been lower in recent years.	**T**	**F**
4.	The oil boom has had positive and negative effects in Canada.	**T**	F
5.	Strip mining has an effect on the earth's temperature.	**T**	F
6.	Canada is planning to stop mining the oil sands.	**T**	**F**

B | Considering Viewpoint and Bias. Read the quotations on page 133 from the people in the video. Then watch again and decide which of the topics below the chart each person is talking about. Write the letter of the topic next to each person's name.

Celina Harper, resident _____B____:	"I could just cry when I see what they've done to our land. You just could see . . . that's all you could see, just as far as you could see. Nothing, just nothing—not even one stick, not even just one tree standing."
Peter Essick, National Geographic photographer _____B____:	"You can take pictures (sort of) of the wilderness part, which is (sort of) the trees and the muskeg[1] which hasn't been developed yet, and then you can take pictures of some of the mining—the big trucks—but I was trying to show some ways you could see (sort of) the connection between (sort of) the wildlife, or the nature, and the mining."
Mike Noseworthy, resident _____B____:	"You're looking at high rent costs, high food costs, and high fuel costs."
Brenda Hampson, truck driver _____A____:	"It's just money, and it's all over the place, and the jobs are all over the place. In Alberta there's ten jobs for one person."
Steve Kallick, Pew Environment Group _____B____:	"This is the peat. It's spongy[2], and there's no strength to it. This is the accumulated carbon from millennia[3]. It's been exposed now to the surface. The protective cover has been removed, and all the carbon that's been stored has come back out into the atmosphere."

Topic A: Economic consequences of Canada's oil boom
Topic B: Environmental consequences of Canada's oil boom

After Viewing

A | Discussion. With a partner, talk about the quotations from people you saw in the video. Was it easy or difficult to understand the people's statements? Explain.

This processing facility in Alberta, Canada, extracts bitumen from the sand, water, and clay from the strip mining operation. Canada's oil boom has created numerous jobs.

B | Role-Playing. Form a group with three to five other students and role-play an informal debate between Canadians who support mining the oil sands and Canadians who oppose it. Follow the steps below.

1. Divide your group into two smaller groups and assign a role to each.
   Sub-group A: Canadians who support mining because of the economic development it brings
   Sub-group B: Canadians who oppose mining because of the environmental consequences
2. With your sub-group, brainstorm several points you would like to make in the debate.
3. Get together again with the other sub-group and have an informal debate about the following statement: *Canada should continue to extract oil from Alberta's oil sands.*
4. Decide which side won the debate.

[1]**Muskeg** is a type of soil found in northern forest areas.
[2]**Spongy** means soft.
[3]**Millenia** means thousands of years.

track 2-28 **A** | **Meaning from Context.** Read and listen to the information about hydrogen vehicles. Notice the words in blue. These are words you will hear and use in Lesson B.

In Germany, the Clean Energy Partnership is working to promote hydrogen-powered vehicles and hydrogen fueling stations.

Hydrogen Fuel Question & Answer

Q: Will there be cars that are powered by hydrogen in the future?

A: Yes, in fact, there are hydrogen vehicles now. Engineers have **designed** them to either **burn** hydrogen in an engine[1] or to react with oxygen in fuel cells[2] to run an electric engine.

Q: What are some of the advantages of hydrogen vehicles?

A: Unlike **conventional** gasoline or diesel-powered vehicles, hydrogen vehicles produce no carbon emissions. In addition, compared to electric cars, hydrogen cars can go a much longer **distance** before they need refueling, and the refueling process takes minutes instead of hours. Hydrogen fuel cells can also power larger vehicles such as buses.

Q: Are there any problems associated with hydrogen vehicles?

A: Unfortunately, there are. Although hydrogen doesn't need to be **refined** from crude oil like gasoline does, it does need to be manufactured. At present, it's **manufactured** either from natural gas or by using a lot of electricity. In places where electricity comes from fossil fuels such as coal, hydrogen isn't a great advantage—especially since hydrogen currently requires more energy to produce than it provides to the vehicle.

Q: Does that mean hydrogen vehicles might not be the energy **solution** that the transportation **sector** is looking for?

A: Maybe not right now, but eventually, technological **advances** should make hydrogen vehicles more practical and more efficient. Recently, a group of vehicle manufacturers and oil companies launched[3] a **campaign** to convince more people to drive hydrogen cars. If more people buy the cars, there will be more reasons to develop new technologies and solve the problems.

[1]The **engine** is the motor or the part of the car that converts fuel to motion.

[2]**Fuel cells** are devices that store electricity for later use.

[3]If you **launch** a campaign, you begin a campaign.

B | Match the sentence beginnings to their endings. Use context clues from exercise **A** to understand the words in blue, or use your dictionary if necessary.

1. An **advance** is _____
2. If something is **burned**, _____
3. A **campaign** is _____
4. If something is **conventional**, _____
5. When you **design** something, _____
6. **Distance** refers to _____
7. To **manufacture** something _____
8. If something is **refined**, _____
9. A **sector** is _____
10. Once you have a **solution**, _____

a. it is normal or usual.
b. you plan what it will be.
c. you no longer have a problem.
d. is to make it, often in a factory.
e. it is consumed by fire.
f. it is made pure; all other substances are removed.
g. some kind of progress, often in technology.
h. one of the parts that something is divided into.
i. how far away something is.
j. an organized promotion of something.

A | Fill in each blank with a word from the box. Then practice the conversation with a partner.

| distance | burn | solution | conventional | refined | manufacturing |

Victor: This is discouraging. The car dealerships around here only sell
(1) _____ cars. Don't they know that electric cars are the
(2) _____ to our oil problems?

Mi Young: Maybe there aren't many people who want electric cars, so the car
companies aren't (3) _____ very many.

Victor: You're probably right.

Mi Young: Besides, don't a lot of electric power plants (4) _____ coal?
That's no better than gasoline.

Victor: True, but gasoline has to be (5) _____, so they have to
ship it all over the world, and sometimes there are huge oil spills. Definitely
not good.

Mi Young: I see your point. But you work in another city, and you have to drive a long
(6) _____ every day. Electric cars can't go very far, you know.

Victor: That's true. I guess I could wait and buy a hydrogen car.

B | **Critical Thinking.** Discuss the questions in a group.

1. Do you think that hydrogen vehicles are an important technological **advance**? What
   other **advances** in the transportation **sector** do you know about?

2. If you were in charge of a **campaign** to promote hydrogen vehicles, how would you
   communicate with the public? What would your message be?

3. If you were in charge of **designing** the vehicle of the future, what would the vehicle
   be like?

Hydrogen fuel-cell busses in Hamburg, Germany,
share the road with gas-guzzlers.

Before Listening

A | Prior Knowledge. Read the information about ethanol. What other facts do you know about ethanol?

Quick Facts: Ethanol

- Ethanol is a type of alcohol that can be used as fuel.
- Crops such as sugarcane and corn are used to manufacture ethanol, but recent advances may lead to "cellulosic ethanol" made from plants such as wild grasses and crop waste material.
- Brazil and the United States are the largest producers of ethanol.
- New cars in Brazil are "flex-fuel" vehicles, and drivers can choose between 100 percent ethanol fuel or a blend that is 80 percent gasoline.
- The U.S. has few flex-fuel vehicles, and most of the gasoline sold in the country is blended with 10 percent ethanol.

A man harvests sugar cane in the state of São Paulo in Brazil.

B | Discussion. Is ethanol used in vehicles in your country? Would you rather drive (or ride in) a car powered by gasoline or by ethanol?

Listening: A Conversation between Students

track 2-29 **A |** Look at the notes taken by a student during a lecture. Then listen to a conversation about the lecture and check the notes for accuracy.

But you know,

Actually, I don't think.

It is ... Bore, tha

Su-

refining ethanol	
1. milling	sugarcane trucked to mills; remove juice → burn plant waste (why?) *power used to mill, electricity*
2. molasses	sugar crystals separated from juice, used as sugar (remaining liquid called "molasses") *molasses in cooking (cheaper than sugar)*
3. fermenting	yeast added to molasses; ferments → creates ethanol

track 2-29 **B |** Listen to the conversation again and answer the questions.

1. What part of the lecture did the student miss? How would you complete the notes?

_____

2. Does the conversation sound like polite disagreement or a real argument? Explain.

_____

After Listening

 Discussion. Work with a partner. Discuss the questions. Which of these concerns about ethanol as fuel seems the most important to you? Explain.

- Farmers may plant crops for ethanol instead of for food.
- A gallon of ethanol provides less power than a gallon of gasoline, yet the price of ethanol isn't much lower than the price of gasoline.
- Sugarcane can only be grown in very warm climates.

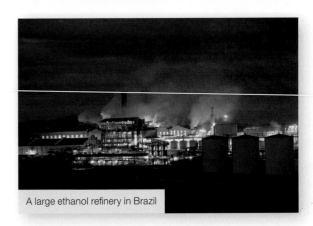

A large ethanol refinery in Brazil

Pronunciation

Reduced /h/ in Pronouns

In fast speech, the /h/ sound in pronouns such as *her* and *him* is usually not pronounced. The remaining vowel sounds in the pronouns are then linked to the preceding word.

track 2-30

Examples: *give + her* sounds like "giver"   *Please give her the message.*
is + his sounds like "izzes"   *Is his brother here?*

 A | Replace each "word" in parentheses with the verb and pronoun that are being reduced. Then practice saying the sentences with a partner.

1. His parents (tookim) _____ to the doctor's office.
2. (Hazzy) _____ finished the project yet?
3. (Wuzzer) _____ presentation good?
4. (Doowiz) _____ friends live in Jakarta?

track 2-31
B | Listen to the sentences from exercise **A**.

track 2-32
C | Listen and complete the sentences from the conversation with full (not reduced) words and the other missing information.

1. I believe she ___Said ad___ research was on ___Corn___ ethanol.
2. ___In my___ presentation slides, Professor Anderson showed them ___math ach___ different kinds of sugar.
3. ___Did he___ ask what they used to do with the ___molasses___ before they started making ethanol?
4. She ___told him___ it used to be used in ___cobhuji___ a lot more than it is now.

AFTER OIL | 137

Grammar

Future Time with Adverb Clauses

Some sentences about the future include time expressions.
> *I'll see you **at 5:00.***   *We're taking the exam **tomorrow morning.***

Other sentences about the future include two clauses—a main clause and a time clause (a type of adverb clause).

> *I'll see you **when your plane arrives.***   *We're taking the exam **before we eat lunch.***
> (main clause)   (time clause)   (main clause)   (time clause)

In sentences about the future with two clauses, the main clause is usually in a future tense, and the time clause is usually in the present tense.

The adverbs in adverbial time clauses have different functions. Here are some ways that adverbial time clauses are used:

- to talk about an event that happens <u>before</u> another future event
  *Helen will visit her parents **after/when/as soon** as she finds some free time.* (She'll find some free time, and then she'll visit her parents.)
- to talk about an event that happens <u>after</u> another future event
  *I'm going to finish reading this book **before** the library closes.* (The library will close sometime after I've finished reading the book.)
- to talk about an event that's in progress <u>at the same time</u> as another future event
  *Jerry is going to study **while** he's on the plane.*
  *I'll get some exercise **while** I'm walking the dog.*

The time clause can also be before the main clause.
> ***When the rain stops,** I'm going to ride my bike to the store.*

A | Work with a partner to finish the following sentences in at least two different ways.

> I'll buy a new car when I have enough money.

> I'll buy a new car when hydrogen cars become available.

1. I'll buy a new car when . . .
2. Oil is going to be more expensive after . . .
3. Before this year is finished, . . .
4. As soon as I get home, . . .
5. I'll practice this grammar point while . . .
6. When I'm older, . . .

B | **Critical Thinking.** Discuss the questions in a group.

1. What do you think will happen before Canada stops mining the oil sands? For example, will they mine all the bitumen in the country? Will they decide that wildlife is more important than oil?
2. As soon as oil becomes significantly more expensive, what do you think will happen?
3. What do you think will happen after substitutes for oil are found?

Language Function: Making Judgements about the Future

Discussion. Look at the photos and read the captions. Then discuss the questions below.

1. Which form of alternative energy shown in the photos on this page seems the most promising to you? Why?
2. How do you think scientists and engineers will solve the problems with these forms of energy?
3. Use adverb time clauses and your answers from question #2 to talk about the future of energy.

> When engineers figure out good ways to store solar power, it will be more practical for more people.

Student to Student: Softening Assertions

Sometimes you may want to "soften" your statements or assertions, especially if the topic is sensitive or if you're not completely certain about something. You can do this with certain introductory phrases or with modals.

It's possible that . . . **It seems to me** that . . .
I think/believe that . . . Ethanol **could/might/may** someday . . .

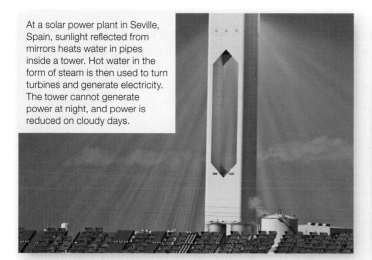

At a solar power plant in Seville, Spain, sunlight reflected from mirrors heats water in pipes inside a tower. Hot water in the form of steam is then used to turn turbines and generate electricity. The tower cannot generate power at night, and power is reduced on cloudy days.

In France, the daily motion of the ocean's tides into and out of the Barrage de la Rance River is used to generate electricity. In this photo, water whirls into a turbine at the power station. Scientists have noticed a reduction of some fish species in the river since the power plant was built.

Wind power in the Netherlands—past and present. Some people who live near large modern wind turbines complain that their appearance, their motion, and their sound is upsetting.

You are going to create materials to help promote an alternative energy source.

A | Read the information below and complete the steps that follow.

Drawbacks of Plant-Based Biofuels

Plant-based biofuels such as ethanol may be able to replace some petroleum products. However, biofuels don't actually reduce CO_2 in the atmosphere if the crops they're made from replace natural ecosystems such as forests, which remove CO_2 from the air. In Malaysia and Indonesia alone, millions of acres of forests have been cut down and replaced with palm oil plantations.

Biofuel Crop:	Replaces:	
Palm	Peat Forest & Rainforest	Ecosystem absorbs much CO_2
Soy	Rainforest	
Corn	Grassland	
Sugarcane	Woodland	
Prairie Grass	Abandoned Cropland	Ecosystem absorbs little CO_2

Overcoming the Drawbacks

The solution to the problem of crops replacing natural ecosystems may come in the form of "cellulosic" ethanol made from grasses, plant waste, or even waste wood. However, research is needed to find a way to extract the sugars from these materials easily and inexpensively. It's probable that money for such research needs to come at least partly from governments.

B | **Discussion.** Form a group with two or three other students and discuss the questions.

1. Which types of natural ecosystems are most beneficial to the environment?
2. What is the problem with using prairie grass as biofuel?
3. What problems are associated with other forms of alternative energy discussed in this unit (electric or hydrogen-powered cars, solar/wind/tidal energy, etc.)?

C | **Collaboration.** With your group, create a piece of promotional material for use in a campaign to support government funding for technological advances in the energy sector. Follow the directions below.

1. Decide which form of alternative energy you want to promote.
2. Brainstorm reasons the public should support government funding of research for that form of energy.
3. Decide on a form for your promotional material (poster, brochure, TV commercial, PowerPoint, etc.).
4. Develop your promotional material in such a way that the whole class will be able to see it.

D | **Presentation.** Share your promotional material with the class and explain why you chose the form of alternative energy that you did. Then ask your audience for feedback on your material. Do your classmates think it would convince the public to support government-funded research?

Traditional and Modern Medicine

ACADEMIC PATHWAYS

Lesson A: Listening to a Conversation in a Professor's Office
Evaluating Claims about Public Health
Lesson B: Listening to a Conversation between Friends
Preparing and Presenting a Group Summary

Think and Discuss

1. Look at the photo and read the caption. Do you think this will be an effective medicine?

2. Which do you trust more when you're sick—natural medicines from plants or medicines from a doctor?

3. What do you think the advantages or disadvantages are of knowing which diseases you are more likely to get because of your DNA?

This Cambodian man is harvesting lotus for food and medicine.

141

Exploring the Theme:
Traditional and Modern Medicine

Look at the photos and read the captions. Then discuss the questions.

1. What information on this page surprises you?
2. How has modern medicine improved patients' lives?
3. What is your experience with these or other home remedies?

Home Remedies: Traditional Cures

Green Tea
Studies have shown it to be a cancer fighter.

Red Chili Pepper
Eat it when your nose is stuffed up, and you'll breathe easily.

Garlic
It can kill a virus, so eat it to help prevent colds and flu.

Ginger
It's tasty, and it prevents travel sickness and other nausea.

Modern Medicine: High-Tech Solutions

Modern medical engineering has made it possible, in some cases, for a blind person to see, a deaf person to hear, and a person without a hand to pick up a key. The patient in this photo is picking up a key with the Proto 1 arm.

Night falls over lavender fields in northeast Tasmania. Lavender has been used for hundreds of years as a natural remedy for a variety of health problems, including colds and headaches.

track 3-2 **A** | **Meaning from Context.** Look at the photos and read the captions. Then read and listen to the article. Notice the words in blue. These are words you will hear and use in Lesson A.

New Respect for Old-Fashioned Medicines

Using plants as natural remedies for health problems is nothing new. In fact, almost two-thirds of the earth's population still rely on the healing power of plants. For them, nothing else is affordable or available. Plant-based medicine has also captured the attention of many scientists, who are studying plants' ability to restore health and fight diseases such as cancer.

An herbalist in Lucknow, India, prepares plant-based medicines.

In India, where many people talk about their symptoms with a traditional healer instead of a medical doctor, Darshan Shankar has created the Foundation for Revitalisation of Local Health Traditions. He says that preserving the knowledge of these healers is as crucial as conserving the plants they use. "The world has realized it should be concerned about saving biodiversity. But cultural knowledge is just as important."

A woman in Madagascar harvests the rosy periwinkle plant.

Nat Quansah, an ethnobotanist who lives in Madagascar, studies plants such as the rosy periwinkle. A synthetic version of the active chemical from that plant is now produced in laboratories and made into drugs that inhibit cancer growth. Quansah knows about hundreds of other promising plant species that could be the basis for future medicines.

Jim Duke, now retired from the U.S. Department of Agriculture, still teaches and writes about medicinal plants such as chicory, which contains chicoric acid—a chemical that may someday be used to fight a deadly virus. Duke says that empirical studies of medicinal plants are needed. "We can use science to test plants, to find what works best. The issue is [. . .] how to use science to get the best medicine, be it natural or synthetic."

B | Write each word in blue from exercise **A** next to its definition.

1. _____ (n.) medicines, or things that make an illness better
2. _____ (adj.) something that seems likely to be very good or successful
3. _____ (adj.) based on scientific observations and experiments
4. _____ (adj.) extremely important
5. _____ (n.) a serious illness in which tumors grow in or on the body
6. _____ (v.) to slow or prevent something
7. _____ (v.) to return something to its original condition
8. _____ (n.) a tiny germ that causes an illness
9. _____ (adj.) artificial, human-made
10. _____ (n.) signs of an illness

In Madagascar, a healer squeezes sap from a leaf for the relief of earache.

A | Fill in each blank with the correct form of a word from the box. Use each word only once.

symptom	restore	virus	empirical	remedy

> **A:** How are you doing?
>
> **B:** Not very well. I think I may have caught a (1) _____. My roommates are sick, too.
>
> **A:** I'm sorry you don't feel well. What are your (2) _____?
>
> **B:** I have a sore throat and a fever, and my muscles ache.
>
> **A:** I know about a natural (3) _____ you could try. It's based on Chinese herbs, and it's supposed to help (4) _____ balance to the body.
>
> **B:** Does it work?
>
> **A:** I don't really know. I read about it on the Internet.
>
> **B:** Well, an Internet article probably isn't based on (5) _____ research, but I'm willing to try anything if it makes me feel better.

B | Practice the conversation with a partner. Then switch roles and practice it again.

C | Take turns asking and answering the questions with your partner.

1. What do you think is the most **crucial** skill for succeeding in school?
2. What are some foods and activities that cause **cancer**?
3. What can people do in their daily lives to **inhibit** the spread of **viruses**?
4. What **promising** signs do you see in the children you know? (e.g., Do you think they'll grow up to be great artists or famous professors?)
5. Look around you. Are the clothes you're wearing or is anything in the room made from a **synthetic** material? (e.g., polyester, nylon, plastic)

D | Choose five words from exercise **A** on page 144. In your notebook, write a sentence using each word.

E | Share your sentences from exercise **D** with a partner.

Before Listening

Listener Response: Asking Questions While Listening

In some listening situations, you're not expected to do anything except understand the speaker. In other situations, however, it's important to respond to what you hear. Asking questions while listening makes you an active participant in the conversation or presentation. You might ask questions to get clarification, to give a reaction such as surprise or interest, or to add new ideas. (*See page 202 in the Independent Student Handbook for more strategies for improving your listening skills.*)

track 3-3   **A** | Read and listen to part of a conversation in a professor's office.

Professor: First of all, it costs a lot of money to develop any new drug and then to do empirical studies on it and get government approval. It's just a long, expensive process.

Student: Sure, but isn't it worth it if the new drug can save lives?

B | **Discussion.** With a partner, discuss the questions below.

1. Is the professor explaining benefits or problems connected with new drug development?
2. What do you think is the purpose of the student's question?

C | Take turns saying the sentences below to your partner. Then your partner should respond to each sentence with a question. Try to ask different types of questions (clarification, reaction, new idea).

> My daughter got a role in the school play. I'm so proud of her.

> Which play are they doing?

1. I heard that there's a bad virus going around.
2. I felt awful yesterday, so I tried a natural remedy.
3. My chemistry course is a lot of work, but it's really interesting.
4. I don't know what to do. My paper is not going to be finished on Friday.
5. A new restaurant opened up in my neighborhood.
6. My father got a promotion at work.

Listening: A Conversation in a Professor's Office

A | Listen to the whole conversation between the professor and student. Then write answers to the questions.

1. Why has the student gone to talk with the professor? _____

_____

2. What questions does the student ask while the professor is giving her explanation?

a. <u>Sure, but isn't it worth it if the new drug can save lives?</u>

b. _____

c. _____

d. _____

A medication used to treat heart disease comes from the leaves of the *digitalis* plant.

B | **Listening for Details.** Listen again and complete the student's notes.

Developing new drugs from plants:

Problems   1. studies ($$$) <u>cost a lot</u>

         2. government <u>approval</u> _____ (takes a long time)

         3. many variables w/trad. <u>remedies</u>

            a. might get the wrong <u>subspecies</u> of plant

            b. might pick at wrong <u>time of day</u>

            c. (age) plant might be too <u>old / young</u>

            d. <u>other plants</u> might be growing nearby

Scientists 1. must identify active <u>chemicals</u> from plant

         2. same <u>amount / standards</u> in tablet or injection

         3. test drug's effects with large <u>clinical</u> trials

After Listening

Take turns explaining to your partner why it's so difficult to develop new medications from plant-based remedies. Use your notes, as well as your own words and ideas.

A | Two friends are talking. Listen to the conversation. Then practice the conversation with a partner. Switch roles and practice it again.

track 3-5

Nico:	Hi, Bill. What's up?
Bill:	I'm reading an article about olive oil.
Nico:	Really? What does it say?
Bill:	It says that olive oil can prevent heart disease and some cancers.
Nico:	I've heard that before, and of course we make and use a lot of olive oil in Greece.
Bill:	Maybe if I use more of it, I'll live a longer, healthier life.
Nico:	Maybe, but you know—olive oil isn't the only reason Greek people are healthy.
Bill:	Yeah? What are some other reasons?
Nico:	We eat a lot of vegetables and fruit—every day. And exercise is built into our lifestyle. The weather is good, so we walk everywhere, and in my family at least, we love to dance.
Bill:	I see what you mean. Here in the U.S., I take the bus most places, especially in winter.
Nico:	There you go. But at least you get to hang out with a Greek person.
Bill:	True. Maybe that will make me healthier.

Olive oil is the only vegetable oil that can be created simply by pressing the raw material—in this case, olives.

B | **Discussion.** With a partner, discuss the questions below.

1. In which country does the conversation take place?
2. What three reasons does Nico give for the good health of people in Greece?
3. What else do you know about the Mediterranean diet?

Grammar

Real Conditionals

We use the real conditional with the present tense to talk about things that are true in general.

> ***If** people **exercise**, their hearts **are** healthier.*
>   (condition)   (result)

> *I **feel** healthy **if** I **eat** fruits and vegetables every day.*
> (result)   (condition)

We use the real conditional with future tenses to talk about the future consequences of certain conditions.

> ***If** you **visit** my family in Greece, they **will feed** you a lot of seafood.*
>   (condition)   (result)

> ***I'll stay** with Nico's family **if** I **go** to Greece.*
> (result)   (condition)

Note: We generally do not use *will* in the *If* clause even though we are talking about the future.

One or both clauses can be negative in the real conditional.

> *People **don't get** as sick if they **take** a virus-inhibiting drug.*
> *If you **come** here next winter, you **won't be** able to walk everywhere because of the snow.*

A | Critical Thinking. With a partner, think of at least two different ways to end each real conditional sentence about the present or the future.

1. If I catch a bad cold, . . .
2. If I eat a lot of junk food, . . .
3. You will stay healthier if . . .
4. If you don't get enough sleep, . . .
5. If I have some free time this weekend, . . .

B | With your partner, take turns asking and answering the questions below using real conditional sentences. Discuss your reasons.

1. What happens if people exercise three times a week?
2. If you need medical help in the future, will you choose traditional or modern treatments?
3. If people don't have access to clean water, what happens?
4. What happens if someone eats a lot of fruits and vegetables?
5. What will happen if you don't learn the vocabulary in this unit?

Language Function: Discussing Health

A | Read and listen to the article about a National Geographic Emerging Explorer. How is he making his country a healthier place?

Fighting Disease with a Guitar

Feliciano dos Santos

As a child in Mozambique's Niassa Province, Feliciano dos Santos caught the polio virus from the dirty water in his tiny village. "When I was young," he recalls, "I never believed I would grow up, get married, have children, drive a car, and live such a full life . . ."

These days, Santos and his band *Massukos* use music to spread messages of sanitation and hygiene[1] to some of the poorest, most remote villages in Mozambique. Their hit song, *Wash Your Hands,* is part of a public health campaign created by Santos's non-governmental organization (NGO), Estamos. The project has successfully convinced villagers to install thousands of sustainable EcoSan latrines[2], dramatically improving sanitation and reducing disease throughout the region.

Santos's NGO also works on programs to install pumps for clean water, conduct health studies, and combat a new cholera epidemic. Says Santos, "Clean water is a basic human right, yet so many don't have it. I'm using my music to be the voice of people who have no voice."

[1]**Sanitation and hygiene** both refer to cleanliness.
[2]A **latrine** is a kind of toilet that is separate from a house and does not use water.

Women pumping water in the Mozambican town of Mpelane

B | Discussion. With a partner, discuss the questions below.

1. What kinds of public health campaigns have you seen or heard about? For example, have you seen TV commercials or outdoor signs with health messages? If so, for which health issues?
2. Do you think a popular song would work well in a public health campaign? Explain.
3. The article mentions polio and cholera, two diseases spread by dirty water. What other negative health effects can dirty water have?

C | Collaboration. Form a group with three or four other students and follow the steps.

1. Brainstorm some of the public health issues in your native country or the country where you're studying now. Examples might include tobacco use, sanitation, diet, air quality, and so on.
2. Decide on one public health issue that you all agree is very important.
3. Think of the title of a song that the band *Massukos* could perform to spread a message about your issue. Then write some of the lyrics of the song.
4. Tell the rest of the class why you decided on the issue that you did.
5. Then tell the rest of the class about your song and read the title and lyrics aloud. Make sure all the members of your group do some of the speaking.

Critical Thinking Focus: Evaluating Claims

A claim is a statement that is presented as true. When you make a claim, or when you hear or read one, it should be logical and it should be supported with evidence.

Example #1: *Poor air quality is the worst threat to public health in this city.*

That claim might be true, but we don't have any reason to believe it, especially if we don't live in your city and we haven't experienced the air quality for ourselves.

Example #2: *A recent study suggests that air quality may be the worst threat to public health in this city.*

The second claim uses more tentative language (*suggests, may be*), which is reasonable if the speaker isn't 100 percent certain, and it is based on research.

There are several questions you can ask yourself in order to decide whether a claim is true or not.

1. Does the speaker provide statistics, expert opinions, or some other evidence that I can trust?
2. Is the claim reasonable and logical based on what I know?
3. Is the claim current, or is it outdated or based on outdated evidence?
4. What is the speaker's motive? Does he or she have anything to gain by making the claim?

Evaluating Claims about Public Health

A | **Critical Thinking.** With your group, evaluate the claims on the business cards by asking yourselves the questions from page 150.

Scott Phelps
Advertising Sales Coordinator

Hello, Low Blood Pressure!
Over a billion people use social networking sites. Our non-profit advertisements placed on social networking sites are encouraging more people than ever before to get their blood pressure checked.

Jamila Thomas
EDUCATION DIRECTOR

Flu Vaccines for All
Flu shots are most effective in healthy adults, so get your immunization before you feel sick and help prevent the spread of the deadly influenza virus to the people you love.

ANDREA WALKER
Director of New Membership

SOUTHWEST DENTISTS ASSOCIATED
Our dentists are the best in the region, and good dental care is the basis of good health. Give us a call and let Southwest Dentists take care of your teeth.

Max Rosas
Sales and Marketing

Good Company Health Solutions
Absent workers cost companies over $18 billion in 2006. Don't wait for your employees to call in sick. Call us about our employee wellness program. You're in Good Company.

B | **Critical Thinking.** Form a group with two or three other students. Imagine you are giving a presentation and making the claims below. You want your audience to believe your claims. Discuss the best kind of support for each claim. This could include statistics, expert opinions, images such as photos, personal experiences, and other convincing forms of information.

1. Fewer children have come down with malaria since the new water wells were installed.
2. Adults are often more afraid of injections than children are.
3. The streets are cleaner now, and there are much better places for children to play.
4. Anti-smoking campaigns haven't been as effective as doctors would like.
5. Parents noticed alarming symptoms after their children received the vaccine.
6. The children's clinic is comfortable and convenient.

> I'd give some current statistics.

> Right—what are the exact numbers before and after?

Wildebeests in Africa

Before Viewing

A | **Predicting Content.** Lesson A discussed medical solutions humans use to cure illnesses. The video you are going to watch, *Wild Health,* discusses what animals do to *self-medicate,* or cure themselves when they are sick or injured. What are some things you think animals might do to cure themselves when they are sick or injured? Write three ideas below.

1. _____
2. _____
3. _____

B | **Using a Dictionary.** You will hear these words and phrases in the video. Write each word or phrase in the box next to its definition. Use your dictionary to help you.

Some scientists believe that observing animal behavior can lead to important discoveries for human medicine.

| compounds (n.) | curative (adj.) | preventative (adj.) | avoidance (n.) |
| fermentation (n.) | lactation (n.) | ground breaking (adj.) | nausea (n.) |

1. _____ intended to make sure things like disease or crime don't happen
2. _____ a chemical change to a substance
3. _____ substances that consists of two or more elements
4. _____ able to make an illness or injury disappear
5. _____ the condition of feeling sick and like you're going to vomit
6. _____ the production of milk by female mammals
7. _____ the act of staying away from something
8. _____ new and important

While Viewing

📺 **A** | Watch the video. Then complete the sentences.

1. Cindy Engel studies zoopharmacognosy, or _animal self-medi_ _cation_ .

2. Early medicine was based on _observing_ the _behavior_ of sick animals.

3. Engel's book has received enormous interest in the scientific communities across _Europe_ and _N A_ .

4. Engel has concentrated on _3_ _main_ areas of animal self-medication.

Animals suffer many of the same aches and pains that humans do, and when they do, they have to find natural remedies.

B | What are the three main areas of animal self-medication mentioned in the video? Were any of your predictions from the Before Viewing section mentioned?

1. _Cnaking nicome_
2. _Preventative_
3. _avoidance_

📺 **C** | Engel uses different animals as examples to support her research. Watch the video again. Match each animal with the correct example.

1. Chimpanzees _D_
2. Snow leopards _A_
3. Wildebeests _B_
4. Cattle/cows _C_

a. eat grass to avoid nausea.
b. migrate to places that have essential minerals for lactation.
c. travel to find the right kind of dirt.
d. have helped scientists discover several new compounds.

Animals like this snow leopard have found ways to self-medicate when they are sick or injured.

After Viewing

A | **Using the Real Conditional.** Finish the sentences below using the real conditional.

1. If scientists observe animal behavior, _____.
2. If cows want to find the right kind of dirt, _____.
3. If a snow leopard wants to avoid nausea, _____.
4. If we learn more about plants, _____.

👥 **B** | **Critical Thinking.** Discuss the questions below in a group.

1. Based on what you learned in Lesson A about evaluating claims, do you think Engel's claim that observing animal behavior is important to human medicine is a believable claim? Why, or why not?
2. What advice do you think Engel would give medical doctors?

A | **Prior Knowledge.** What do you know about high-tech medicine? Read and listen to the statements. Circle **T** for *true* or **F** for *false*. Notice the words in blue. Use your dictionary to help you. These are words you will hear and use in Lesson B.

track 3-7

QUIZ: High-Tech Medicine

1. The human genome[1] **consists** of more than one million genes.	**T**	**F**
2. By looking at your genes, doctors can determine which **hereditary** diseases you will **tend** to get.	**T**	**F**
3. People who lose an arm or leg can get a **device** called a *prosthesis* that helps them to walk or lift things.	**T**	**F**
4. Prosthetic arms or legs can be operated by signals that the brain **transmits** to the device.	**T**	**F**
5. New technology allows patients to re-grow lost fingers and toes.	**T**	**F**

ANSWERS: 1. F (around 25,000 genes), 2. T, 3. T, 4. T, 5. F

A scientist uses ultraviolet light to read genetic information.

B | Complete each sentence with the correct form of one of the words in blue from exercise **A**.

1. Pencil sharpeners and cellular telephones are kinds of _____.

2. Your Internet service provider _____ your email messages to other people's computers.

3. I _____ to arrive late to class, so I try to be very quiet when I go in.

4. It's a _____ disease. My grandfather and my uncle had it, too.

5. The treatment _____ of two different drugs and an exercise program.

track 3-8

C | **Meaning from Context.** Read and listen to the conversation. Then practice the conversation with a partner. Notice the words in blue. Then switch roles and practice it again.

> **Lily:** I just saw the most **extraordinary** thing on television.
>
> **Charles:** What was it?
>
> **Lily:** It was this woman who had a **severe** injury and lost her arm.
>
> **Charles:** What's extraordinary about that? It sounds terrible.
>
> **Lily:** It was, but I haven't gotten to the extraordinary part yet.
>
> **Charles:** OK, go on.
>
> **Lily:** This woman didn't have enough **muscles** left to operate most prostheses. But luckily, they've come up with a **radical** new solution to the problem.
>
> **Charles:** Sounds interesting. Did they reattach her arm?
>
> **Lily:** No, they couldn't do that. But they gave her a prosthesis with a **mechanism** that receives signals from her brain. She just thinks about moving the synthetic arm, and it moves!

[1]The human **genome** is all of your DNA.

D | Write each word in **blue** from exercise **C** next to its definition. These are words you will hear and use in Lesson B.

1. _____ (n.) tissue in the body that's used for movement
2. _____ (adj.) bad, causing great damage
3. _____ (n.) a part of a machine that performs a certain function
4. _____ (adj.) good or special
5. _____ (adj.) different from what's normal, drastic, or extreme

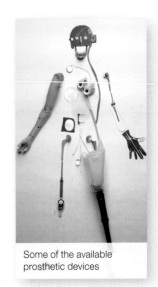

Some of the available prosthetic devices

E | Read the article and fill in each blank with one of the words from the box. (One word is extra.) Then listen and check your answers.

hereditary	extraordinary	transmit	tend	consists

Personalized Medicine: The Medicine of the Future

Imagine visiting your doctor for an annual exam—only this time the checkup
(1) _____ of a routine DNA test. Using information from
the test, your doctor not only predicts the (2) _____ health
problems you're likely to have in the future without having to ask about your personal
history, but also selects the best medications for you.

Although people (3) _____ to think of genetic mapping as
very expensive and time consuming, scientists can do genotyping—assessing one specific
part of the genetic information—rather than reading a person's entire genome. Since
genotyping can be done quickly and inexpensively, it's an (4) _____
tool for assessing a patient's risk factors.

F | Take turns asking and answering the questions with a partner.

1. Does anyone you know have a prosthesis (e.g., an artificial hip or knee)? If so, is the person happy with the **device**? Would you get a prosthesis if you needed one?
2. What was the most **severe** pain you ever experienced? Did you get any medical treatment for it?
3. How does a telephone **transmit** your voice from one place to another?
4. What are some things people can do if they want bigger or stronger **muscles**?
5. Our genes could be called the **mechanism** of **heredity** because they help us pass our DNA on to our children. What **mechanisms** in our bodies are involved in helping us get nutrition from food? getting oxygen into our blood?
6. The word *radical* is often used to describe ideas when they are new or extreme. Which famous people (scientists, artists, politicians, etc.) from the past can you think of who had **radical** ideas?

Pronunciation

Linking Vowels with /y/ and /w/ Sounds

When words that end in vowel sounds are followed by words that begin with a vowel sound, we link the words with a /y/ or /w/ sound. Examples:

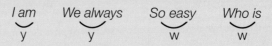

I am   We always   So easy   Who is
  y   y   w   w

track 3-10 **A** | Listen and circle the sound that links the underlined words in each sentence.

1. <u>She is</u> not going skiing this weekend.   /y/   /w/
2. <u>Who else</u> missed class today?   /y/   /w/
3. <u>He asked</u> a good question.   /y/   /w/
4. They did <u>two other</u> blood tests.   /y/   /w/
5. <u>Three of</u> his friends are sick.   /y/   /w/

B | Practice saying the sentences from exercise **A** with a partner.

Before Listening

Self-Reflection. You are going to hear two people talking about a family member who is going to have surgery. Has anyone you know had surgery? Did the surgery help them? Explain.

Listening: A Conversation between Friends

track 3-11 **A** | **Listening for Main Ideas.** Listen to a conversation between two friends and choose the correct answer to complete each sentence.

1. The woman's father has _____.
   a. cancer   b. arthritis   c. heredity
2. The woman says the surgery will be _____.
   a. radical   b. major   c. minor
3. After the surgery, the woman says there will be physical _____.
   a. therapy   b. disability   c. examinations

track 3-11 **B** | **Listening for Details.** Listen again and complete each sentence.

1. The surgery will be next _____.
2. The woman's father is having his _____ replaced with a prosthetic device.
3. The woman says _____ in her family gets the same condition as her father.
4. The physical therapy will take _____ weeks.

Amanda Kitts wearing her prosthetic arm.

C | **Making Inferences.** Read the statements below. Then listen again and circle **T** for *true* or **F** for *false*.

track 3-11

1. The man already knew that the woman's father was going to have surgery.

T   F

2. The man knows more about hip surgery than the woman does.

T   F

3. The woman has a positive attitude towards her father's surgery.

T   F

After Listening

A | **Discussion.** With a partner, discuss the questions below.

1. What kinds of questions does the man ask during the conversation?
2. Do all of the questions seem appropriate and polite to you?
3. What does the woman's attitude seem to be about her father's surgery?

B | **Pronunciation.** Read the sentences and underline six places where words are linked with /y/ or /w/ sounds. Then practice saying the sentences with a partner.

1. He only has to be in the hospital for a few days.
2. If he is in pain, I'll never know about it.
3. . . . the hip will be as good as new.
4. . . . he'll be able to take walks, or travel, or whatever.

C | **Brainstorming.** In a group, read the notes about Amanda Kitts and list as many differences as you can think of between her situation and that of the woman's father from the conversation you listened to. You can use a T-chart to help you.

- Developed at Johns Hopkins University and made of numerous high-tech materials, the Proto-2 is a neural prosthesis, controlled by the user's brain and nerves.
- Amanda Kitts received the prosthesis after losing most of her arm below the shoulder in a car accident.
- Small motors allow the Proto-2 to perform many kinds of movements, and since it's connected to Kitts' own nerves, she can feel how firmly she's holding something or whether she's touching a smooth or rough surface.

D | Join another group of students and compare your lists. Which group was able to think of more differences?

Grammar

A | **Prior Knowledge.** Read the sentences. Then answer the questions below.

> a. Today, many people have hip or knee replacements.
> b. A few of my parents' friends have had both kinds of surgery.
>
> 1. Which sentence talks about a greater number of people?
> 2. Which sentence is about people in general, and which is about specific people?

Quantifiers with Specific and General Nouns

- The words below are used to talk about quantities—*How much?* or *How many?*
- Except for *none* (0 percent) and *all* (100 percent), the words don't have a specific numerical meaning, so the quantities on the line below are only approximate.
- These quantifiers are normally used alone to talk about general nouns, and with *of* to talk about specific nouns.

0 Percent   100 Percent

←---→

none (of)   **a few** (of)   **some** (of)   **many** (of)   **most** (of)   **all** (of)

With General Nouns	**With Specific Nouns**
We saw a few nurses in the hospital cafeteria.	*None of the children in the study had cancer.*
Some patients don't mind getting injections.	*Maxine took some of the research papers home.*
Most people have a favorite natural remedy.	*Many of my friends have children.*
All birds hatch from eggs.	*He fed all of the mice before he left the lab.*

None as a quantifier is always used with specific nouns and *of*.
> **None of** the rabbits had been sick before.

Of is sometimes omitted when *all* is used with specific nouns in informal speech.
> **All the people in the study** were informed of the results by mail.

B | Write *of* if the sentence needs it, or else write Ø.

1. A few _____ my friends have needed to have surgery.
2. Many _____ men don't get annual checkups.
3. All _____ cats know how to hunt mice and other small animals.
4. Most _____ the time, I'm in my office.
5. None _____ the scientists noticed the dark clouds.
6. Some _____ people never seem to be happy.

C | With a partner, take turns asking and answering the questions using quantifiers from the chart and your own ideas.

1. How many medical doctors know about traditional herbal remedies?
2. How many of the men in your family have had surgery?
3. How many of your friends have their own car?

Language Function: Making Suggestions for Home Remedies

Cinnamon

Inhaling steam

Hot tea

A | **Brainstorming.** Follow the directions with a partner.

1. Make a list of several common, everyday health problems.
2. Decide on one health problem to role-play a conversation about.
3. Create a conversation between two friends. One has a health problem, and the other is suggesting some natural home remedies to try. What might they talk about?

Student to Student: Ending a Conversation

It's important to know how to end a conversation politely. Often ending a conversation involves three elements: a signal word to make a transition, an explanation, and a future plan. Here are some examples of polite ways to end a conversation.

Signal Words	An Explanation	A Future Plan
Well,	*I need to get going.*	*Give me a call tonight if you're not busy.*
So,	*My next class starts at 11:00.*	*I'll see you tomorrow at work.*
Anyway,	*It was nice talking to you.*	*Let's get together for coffee one of these days.*

B | Plan and practice your role-play with your partner.

1. Take brief notes on some of the things you'll talk about. Try to use:
   - the real conditional (e.g., *If you drink tea with honey, your throat will feel better.*)
   - quantifiers (e.g., *A few doctors even recommend this instead of aspirin.*)
2. Practice your conversation. Feel free to improvise (i.e., add details as you think of them), and be sure to respond by asking questions.
3. End the conversation politely.

> I have a headache.

> You should try drinking a cup of strong coffee.

C | **Presentation.** Form a group with another pair of students and perform your role-play for them. Give each other feedback on how well you used the language points covered in this unit.

Presentation Skills: Looking Up While Speaking

While speaking, some people keep their faces down and their eyes on their notes. One problem with this is that without eye contact, it's difficult to connect with an audience. In addition, the voice is projected downwards, so it can be difficult for an audience to hear the talk. A better technique is to look down at your notes only occasionally, and then look up and speak.

In this presentation, you will summarize information and work together as a group to present your summary to the rest of the class.

Form a group with three to five other students and follow the steps below.

1. Assign each group member one or more of the following roles below. (*See page 211 of the Independent Student Handbook for more information on group projects and presentations.*)

   Group Leader: Makes sure the assignment is done correctly and all group members participate.
   Secretary: Takes notes on the group's ideas (including a plan for sharing the work).
   Manager: During the planning and practice phases, the manager makes sure the presentation can be given within the time limit.
   Expert: Understands the topic well; invites and answers audience questions after the presentation.
   Coach: Reminds group members to perform their assigned roles.

2. Ask your teacher how long your presentation should be and how much time you'll have to prepare for it.

3. As a group, choose one of the options below for your summary. Take notes on the topic and decide which information to include in your presentation.

   Option #1: Do Internet research to learn more about one of the people mentioned in this unit.
   Option #2: Review the information in this unit about traditional and modern medicine.

4. As a group, create visual aids to use in your presentation. Use any media that are available to you (e.g., poster, PowerPoint® presentation, blackboard, personal items, etc.). You may want to review the information on talking about visuals in Unit 3 page 60.

5. Practice and time your presentation. Use the roles for group members above and make sure each person does some of the speaking during the presentation.

6. While you listen to other groups doing their presentations, evaluate them using the form below. (**Scoring key:** 5 = the highest score, 1= the lowest score)

EVALUATION FORM

The speakers looked up at the audience and were easy to hear.	**1 2 3 4 5**
The presentation was interesting and informative.	**1 2 3 4 5**
Group members worked together well.	**1 2 3 4 5**
The visual aid supported the presentation effectively.	**1 2 3 4 5**
Audience attention was directed to the visual aid effectively.	**1 2 3 4 5**

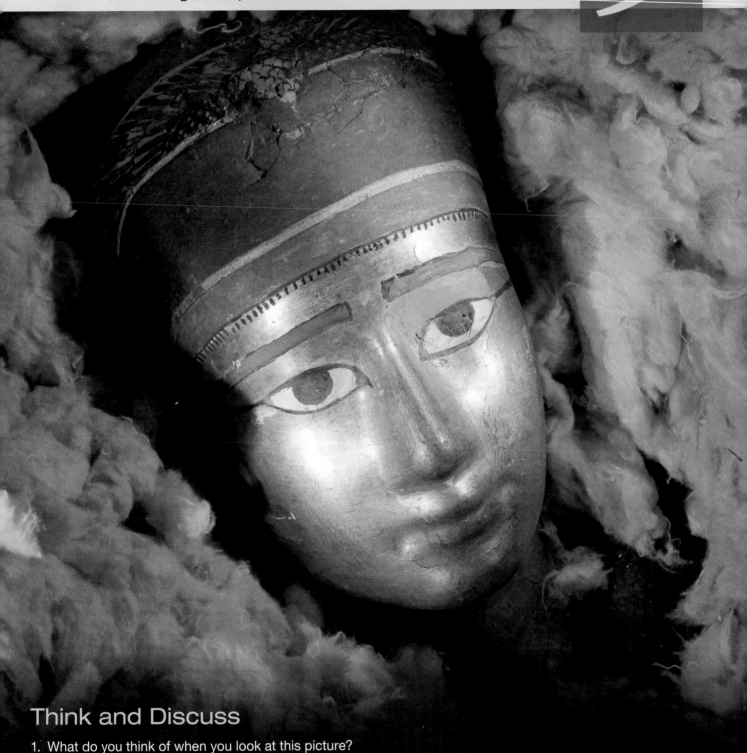

The Legacy of Ancient Civilizations

ACADEMIC PATHWAYS

Lesson A: Listening to a Lecture
            Discussing Timelines
Lesson B: Listening to a Discussion about a Group Project
            Giving a Group Presentation

Think and Discuss

1. What do you think of when you look at this picture?
2. What do you think this object was used for?

A woman's mask from Tell el Sowwah, Egypt

Exploring the Theme:
The Legacy of Ancient Civilizations

Look at the photos and read the captions. Then discuss the questions.

1. What do you know about the ancient civilizations shown on these pages?
2. What other ancient civilizations do you know about?
3. What can we learn from ancient civilizations?

The Ancient Egyptians

In order to provide everything a person would need in the afterlife, ancient Egyptians developed the art of mummy making. Animal mummies represented companionship for the dead person or had other symbolic meanings.

The Celtic People

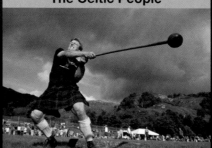

In Scotland, some ancient Celtic traditions are still alive and well, like the athletic event in this photo. Throwing heavy objects is a central part of the Highland games.

The Khmer Empire of Angkor

Every major king of the Khmer Empire had a temple constructed in Angkor, Cambodia. Angkor Wat is the largest and best known of these temples. In this photo, a man harvests lotus flowers in front of the Angkor Wat temple.

Choquequirau is located in the Vilcabamba
mountains of Peru.

A | **Using a Dictionary.** Check (✔) the words you already know. Then write each word next to its definition below. Use a dictionary to help you. These are words you will hear and use in Lesson A.

❑ adopt	❑ celebration	❑ invade	❑ surround	❑ appealing
❑ defense	❑ rebellious	❑ battle	❑ endure	❑ ruins

1. _____ a violent fight, especially between military groups

2. _____ to continue to exist for a long time

3. _____ describes a person who doesn't do what he or she is told

4. _____ to be located all around something or someone

5. _____ a festival or party

6. _____ to enter a country by force with an army

7. _____ action or structure to protect something or someone from danger

8. _____ likeable, pleasing and attractive

9. _____ to take on a new language, culture, etc., as one's own

10. _____ the parts of a structure that remain after great damage

B | Work with a partner. Write each vocabulary word in the correct column of the chart. Use the definitions from exercise **A** to help you.

Nouns	Verbs	Adjectives

C | **Discussion.** Work with a partner. Look at the map on this page. Which languages are spoken in this part of the world?

The modern Celtic world

USING VOCABULARY

A | Look at the photos and read the captions. Then complete the paragraphs with words from the boxes.

battles	ruins	surrounded
rebellious	invaded	defenses

Prehistoric Times: The Celtic languages spoken today date back at least 3000 years, and Celtic people have lived on the European continent much longer than that. Stone structures and the _____ of buildings and villages provide some information about the early Celtic people. Recent archaeological discoveries tell us that the well-known Stonehenge monument is _____ by buried human remains. Archaeologists now think the site may have been a cemetery for a powerful family.

Period of Invasions: First the Romans, then the Vikings, Normans, Anglo-Saxons, and English all _____ Celtic lands. Over the centuries, numerous _____ were fought, and the Celtic people became known for their _____ nature and strong military _____. The legends of King Arthur may be based on a real king who fought against the Anglo-Saxons, and William Wallace, the subject of the Hollywood movie, *Braveheart*, was killed by the English in 1305 after years of fighting for Scottish independence.

endure	celebrations	appealing	adopt

Modern Times: Today, Celtic languages and customs _____. Around 2.5 million people say they speak a Celtic language, and many modern people find ancient Celtic culture very _____. Some _____ religious traditions, while many others participate in Celtic _____ such as *Beltane*, which signals the beginning of summer.

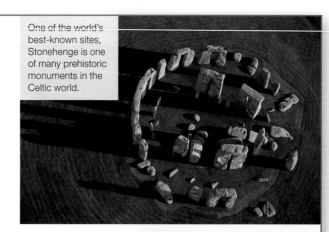

One of the world's best-known sites, Stonehenge is one of many prehistoric monuments in the Celtic world.

Wearing clothing that identifies their clan, or extended family, men compete in a tug-of-war at a Highland games—an athletic contest that originated in the Scottish Highlands.

A Japanese couple, the Yoshidas, getting married inside the ruins of an Irish monastery

B | Listen and check your answers.

THE LEGACY OF ANCIENT CIVILIZATIONS | **165**

Pronunciation

Voicing and Syllable Length

Every sound in English can be classified as voiced or voiceless. To hear the difference between the two, put your hands tightly over your ears and say *sssssss*. You shouldn't hear much at all. Now put your hands over your ears and say *zeeeeeee*. Both the /z/ and the /iy/ sounds are voiced, so you should hear them loudly. Common voiced and voiceless sounds include:

Voiceless Sounds

/p/   /t/   /s/   /f/   /k/   /th/   /ch/

Voiced Sounds

/b/   /d/   /m/   /n/   /z/   /v/   /g/   *all vowel sounds*

When words in English sound very similar except for the voicing of a consonant, it can be difficult to distinguish which word is being said. It helps to know that:

1. If a word ends with a voiceless sound, the vowel sound before it is short. (It actually takes less time to say it.)

2. If a word ends with a voiced sound, the vowel sound before it is long.

track 3-13

Examples:

Short	Long
leaf	leave
hat	had
advice	advise

track 3-14 **A** | Listen and repeat the words. Pay attention to the pronunciation of voiced and voiceless consonants, as well as long and short vowel sounds.

	Short	Long
1.	belief	believe
2.	pat	pad
3.	device	devise
4.	safe	save
5.	tap	tab

B | With a partner, decide whether each underlined word in the conversations below has a short or long vowel sound. Then practice the conversations.

1. **A:** Did you say you wanted some <u>ice</u>?
   B: No, I said my <u>eyes</u> are tired.
   A: Oh, I see.

2. **A:** Did you ask Ms. Choi for <u>advice</u>?
   B: Yes, I did.
   A: What did she <u>advise</u> you to do?

3. **A:** Is this CD-ROM ready for <u>use</u>?
   B: No, you need to format it before you <u>use</u> it.
   A: OK, I'll do that.

Before Listening

Prior Knowledge. Look at the photo and read the caption. Have you heard of these ruins? What do you know about them? Discuss your ideas with a partner.

Listening: A Lecture

A | **Listening for Main Ideas.** Listen to an excerpt from a lecture and choose the correct answer.

track 3-15

1. The previous lecture was about _____.
   a. invasions of Celtic lands
   b. Celtic languages and music
   c. the Celtic belief system

2. People inside Dun Aengus were safe except for _____.
   a. invaders arriving from the sea
   b. invaders getting inside the wall
   c. invaders taking the food supply

3. These Celtic languages have large numbers of speakers nowadays except for _____.
   a. Cornish   b. Welsh   c. Irish Gaelic

4. These Irish and Scottish writers are mentioned except for _____.
   a. Robert Louis Stevenson   b. James Joyce   c. Robert Browning

The ruins of Dun Aengus in Ireland

B | Listen to the lecture excerpt again and circle the word in each pair that you hear. The words are listed in the order that you will hear them.

track 3-15

1. believe belief
2. sat sad
3. peace peas
4. backs bags
5. safe save
6. leaf leave
7. half have
8. wrote rode

After Listening

Self-Reflection. Form a group with two or three other students. Read the information below. Then discuss the questions.

> To many people whose ancestors were Celtic, having a personal connection to the past is very important. For them, speaking a Celtic language, playing Celtic music, or attending Celtic celebrations is a source of pride and a way to be a part of long-lasting traditions.

1. Can you understand why people might want to connect with the past in this way?
2. Why might people want to connect with the past in this way?

Grammar

Now in ruins, the Ta Prohm monastery, once home to hundreds of monks, was part of Angkor, the capital of the Khmer Empire.

A| **Prior Knowledge.** Read the information and complete the sentences below.

In Lesson A of this unit, you learned about the invasions of Celtic lands, about the Celtic people's repeated defense of those lands, and about their independence. Eventually, however, the Celtic people were pushed to small pieces of land on the western edges of Europe and were ruled by the kings of England, France, and Spain.

What do you think would have happened . . .

1. . . . if the Celts had not been invaded repeatedly?
2. . . . if the Celtic people had not fought to defend themselves against the invasions?
3. . . . if the modern Celtic people had not maintained their cultural traditions?

The Past Unreal Conditional

We use the past unreal conditional to imagine a different past and to talk about things that might have been (if the situation had been different).

> **If** the invasions **hadn't happened,** the Celtic people **wouldn't have fought.**
> (The invasions did happen.)   (The Celtic people did fight.)

The past unreal conditional is formed with an *if* clause (the condition) and a result clause. The *if* clause uses the past perfect verb tense. The result clause uses *would + have +* the past participle.

If Clause	**Result Clause**

> **If** my grandfather **had been** rich, he **would have taken** his family to the city.
> (He wasn't rich.)   (He didn't take them to the city.)

The *if* clause can come first or last in the sentence.

> **I wouldn't have offered** to make coffee **if** **I had known** she was in a hurry to leave.

If the result is uncertain, we use *might have* or *could have.*

> **If** he **had studied** longer, he **might have become** a lawyer. (Or maybe a doctor, or . . .)

Could in the result clause can also be used to express ability.

> **I could have picked** you up at the airport **if I'd known** you were coming.

B | With a partner, think of at least two ways to complete each sentence.

1. If we had not taken this English course, . . .
2. I would have helped him with his homework if . . .
3. If the Roman armies had stayed in Rome, . . .
4. If I had not come to class today, . . .

C | Look at the photo and read the caption below. Then read and listen to the information.

Angkor Quick Facts

- In Southeast Asia, a short period of monsoon rains is followed by months of drought.
- The engineers of ancient Angkor designed a complex system of reservoirs and waterways to control flooding, support rice production, and provide transportation.
- Beginning around AD 900, every major king of the Khmer Empire had a temple constructed at Angkor. The largest and best known of the 50 temples is Angkor Wat, now a UNESCO World Heritage site and an important tourist attraction.
- By the early 1600s, the wealth of the empire had shifted from rice production to trading by sea.
- In the early 1700s, Vietnam took control of the Mekong River delta, and Angkor no longer had river access to the South China Sea.

Monsoon rain clouds gather over the Srah Srang reservoir at Angkor in modern-day Cambodia. This reservoir is tiny in comparison to two enormous man-made lakes nearby: East Baray and West Baray. The control of water was essential to Angkor, a city with a population of 750,000 at its peak in the 13th century AD.

D | Rewrite the facts below in your notebook as sentences with the past unreal conditional.

1. Before Angkor's engineers controlled the water, it was impossible to grow rice year-round.
   If Angkor's engineers hadn't been able to control the water, farmers wouldn't have been able to grow rice year-round.

2. Before Angkor's engineers controlled the water, there was serious flooding every year.

3. The Khmer built temples at Angkor. Now there are 50 large temples there.

4. King Suryavarman II ordered the construction of Angkor Wat. It was built during the 1100s.

5. Angkor Wat was rediscovered by the Western world in the late 1800s. It later became a UNESCO World Heritage site.

6. The Khmer Empire wasn't able to keep control of the Mekong River delta. They couldn't trade on the South China Sea anymore.

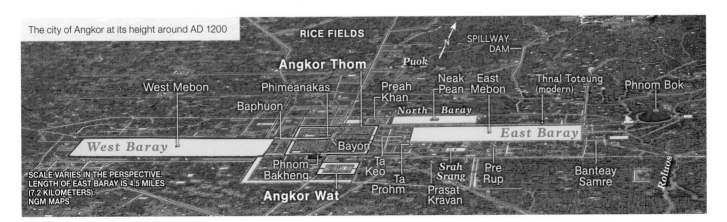

The city of Angkor at its height around AD 1200

RICE FIELDS
SPILLWAY DAM

Angkor Thom · Puok

N

West Mebon
Phimeanakas
Baphuon

Preah Khan

Neak Pean · East Mebon

Thnal Toteung (modern)

Phnom Bok

North Baray

Bayon

East Baray

West Baray

Phnom Bakheng

Ta Keo

Srah Srang

Pre Rup

Banteay Samre

Roluos

Ta Prohm

Prasat Kravan

Angkor Wat

SCALE VARIES IN THE PERSPECTIVE. LENGTH OF EAST BARAY IS 4.5 MILES (7.2 KILOMETERS). NGM MAPS

E | Practice the conversation with a partner. What regrets do the speakers have?

track 3-17

Paolo: What a great vacation. I'm so glad we decided to go to Angkor Wat.

Harold: I agree. It would have been so easy to stay a few more days in Thailand. But if we hadn't gone to Cambodia, we wouldn't have seen such a marvelous place.

Paolo: That's true, but it is a shame we didn't go to see the wildlife sanctuary.

Harold: Seeing the sanctuary would have been nice, but if we had gone there, we would have missed that beautiful sunset in Angkor.

Paolo: That was incredible! I got some great pictures.

Harold: You know, you really should have brought your good camera.

Paolo: If I had brought that one, I would have been worried about losing it. It's a really expensive camera.

West Baray, an enormous reservoir in Angkor, surrounds the temple of West Mebon.

Harold: That's a good point. And my camera wasn't working, so if you hadn't brought yours, we wouldn't have any pictures at all.

Paolo: This old camera has never let me down.

Harold: All in all, it was a really good vacation, wasn't it?

Paolo: One of the best.

Language Function: Discussing Conclusions

Critical Thinking Focus: Drawing Conclusions

When you draw a conclusion, you make a logical judgment about something based on the information you have. For example, *I might stop by your house. If there are no lights on, and when I knock on the door nobody answers, I'll probably conclude that nobody is home. I can't know this for certain since I can't go into the house and look around, but I do have enough information to reach a logical conclusion.*

A | In a group, discuss the information from this unit about Angkor and the Khmer Empire and list some conclusions you can draw based on this information. Consider the topics below.

- The length of time that Angkor was the capital of the Khmer Empire
- The art and architecture that can be seen at Angkor
- The number of temples built at Angkor
- The size and sophistication of the water control systems in and around Angkor

> We can conclude that there were a lot of workers in Angkor. Somebody had to construct those huge man-made lakes.

- The fact that Angkor's wealth and power declined after losing river access to the sea
- The fact that Angkor Wat is on UNESCO's World Heritage site list

B | **Discussion.** Discuss these questions as a class. Did your group have any unanswered questions about Angkor or the Khmer Empire? What would you want to find out if you were doing research on this ancient civilization?

Discussing Timelines

A | Look at the timeline showing some of the events in Carl's life. Then practice the conversation below with a partner.

ck 3-18

←– – – – – – – – – – – –|– – – – – – – – – – – →

Past
Lived in a very small village
Won an academic achievement award
Got a job at my aunt's company

Present
Working toward my MBA

Future
Will own my own business

Rick: Which of these events had the biggest impact on your life?

Carl: They all had a big impact, but the academic award was especially important.

Rick: Really? Why was it so important?

Carl: Well, I grew up in a small village. If I hadn't won that award, I wouldn't have gotten a scholarship to a private high school in the city.

Rick: Wow—good for you! That's quite an achievement.

Carl: Thanks, but there were some negative experiences as well.

Rick: Like what? Everything on your timeline seems good.

Carl: Actually, working for my aunt's company wasn't a good experience. I really didn't know what I was doing.

Rick: But if you hadn't had that bad experience, you might not have realized that you needed to study business.

Carl: That's a good point. Now that I'm studying for a master's degree in business, I'm learning all kinds of things that would have helped me back then.

Rick: You see? Your past has gotten you where you are today.

Carl: Right, and I hope that this degree helps me to run my own business someday.

B | **Discussion.** Discuss these questions with a partner. Which of the events on Carl's timeline was a negative experience for him? Does he seem to have any regrets about the experience?

C | **Self-Reflection.** Make a timeline of your own life in your notebook. The timeline should focus on your past. You can include any events—positive or negative—that you want to share with your classmates.

D | **Presentation.** Form a group with two or three other students and take turns explaining your timelines. Use the past unreal conditional to talk about your life and to make comments about your classmates' lives.

Mayan carvings from Alter Q depicting the sixteen rulers of Copan, Honduras

LOST TEMPLE

Before Viewing

A | Prior Knowledge. You will hear these words in the video. Check (✔) the words you already know. Then write each word next to its definition below. Use a dictionary to help you as needed.

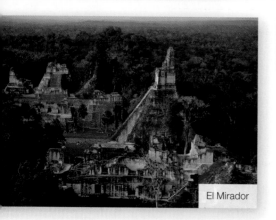

El Mirador

❑ chamber ❑ commission ❑ current ❑ elusive
❑ evidence ❑ setback ❑ solid ❑ suspect

1. _____ (adj.) difficult to find
2. _____ (n.) a large room
3. _____ (n.) something that causes a delay
4. _____ (n.) anything that makes you believe something
5. _____ (adj.) hard or firm
6. _____ (n.) a flow of electricity
7. _____ (v.) to formally arrange for someone to do a piece of work
8. _____ (v.) to believe something may have been done

B | Prior Knowledge. In Lesson A you learned about the Celtic and Angkor civilizations. The video you are going to see is about another ancient civilization, the Mayan. How much do you know about the Mayans? Take the quiz below to find out.

MAYAN QUIZ: Circle the correct answer.

1. Evidence of the Mayan civilization has been discovered in _____.
   a. the United States   b. Guatemala   c. Venezuela   d. Bolivia
2. The Mayan civilization existed _____ the classic period.
   a. 1000 years before   b. 500 years before   c. during   d. 200 years after
3. *El Mirador* is the name of _____.
   a. an ancient Mayan city   b. a Mayan king   c. a Mayan pyramid
4. The Mayans built pyramids _____.
   a. to live in   b. to honor important kings   c. to escape floods   d. to store food

---

OF THE MAYANS

Archaeologists working at a site that once was an ancient Mayan city.

While Viewing

A | Watch the video and check your answers from the quiz in exercise **B.**

B | Watch again and complete the sentences from the video with the words that you hear.

1. The "Classic Maya" grew across Central America _b/w AD 250- 900_.

2. He (Hanson) has been trying to solve the mystery of the Mayans. Who were they, and _how did they know so much_?

3. According to Hanson, the kings of Egypt were as important as the ancient _Maya kings_.

4. He (Hanson) feels that the work that archaeologists are doing in Mirador may help scientists get to know the kings _as people more personally_.

5. Hanson believes that this (one of the smaller pyramids) could be a temple; the tomb of an important king who ruled from _152 BC_ to _145 BC_.

6. He's preparing to dig at another _pyramid next year_.

7. Perhaps this archaeologist will achieve his goal of seeing the tomb of _an ancient Maya king_.

After Viewing

A | **Critical Thinking.** With a partner, think of some questions you would like to ask Hanson to learn more about his work and the Mayan civilization.

B | **Discussion.** Discuss the questions with a group.

1. What information did you find most interesting or surprising about the video? Explain.

2. Do you think that the mystery of the Mayan king was just a story? Why, or why not?

3. Why do you think the Mayans may have abandoned their cities?

4. This unit examines the ancient civilizations of the Celts, the Khmer, the Mayans, and the Egyptians. If you were an archaeologist, which of these cultures would you want to study. Why?

The pyramid of Danta

A | **Meaning from Context.** Look at the photos and read and listen to the information about animal mummies in Egypt. Notice the words in blue. These are words you will hear and use in Lesson B.

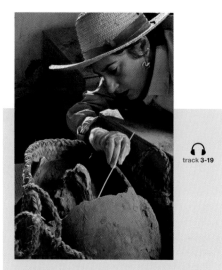

track 3-19

track 3-20

track 3-21

This mummy of an ibis reflects a time in the past when millions of these birds lived along the Nile River. Getting the mummy out of the jar[1] is **tough** because of the dried mud that surrounds it, but to Egyptologist Salima Ikram, it's worth the work. The popularity of the animal mummy exhibit that she's working on at the Egyptian Museum in Cairo has **exceeded** expectations. Visitors of all ages line up to look at the carefully preserved[2] mummies.

The Egyptian Museum in Cairo is home to some of the world's best-known mummies, including that of King Tutankhamen, his parents, and his grandparents. Ancient Egyptians knew that death was **inevitable**—all living things eventually **die**—but in an **attempt** to make the afterlife as comfortable as possible, mummies were **accompanied** by things they would need in the future; in other words, for all **eternity**. Much of the art and other valuable objects at the museum were found in Egyptian tombs.

This mummy of a cat wearing a painted face mask stands next to a cat-shaped wooden coffin[3] with a mummified kitten[4] inside. The items buried with ancient Egyptians represented important **aspects** of their daily lives—everything from furniture to cooking oil. They believed that in the afterlife, these items became real and useful to the dead person. That idea may not seem **rational** nowadays, but Ancient Egyptians didn't **distinguish** between human needs before and after death. They even mummified pieces of meat to represent the food the dead person would need.

[1]A **jar** is a glass or earthenware container to store things in.
[2]When a body is **preserved** as a mummy, it is treated to prevent decay over time.
[3]A **coffin** is a box in which a dead body is buried.
[4]A **kitten** is a baby cat.

B | Write each word in **blue** from exercise **A** next to its definition.

1. _____ (v.) to stop living
2. _____ (v.) to understand how two or more things are different
3. _____ (adj.) based on reason and logic
4. _____ (v.) was with someone or something
5. _____ (n.) parts of the character or nature of something
6. _____ (n.) a period of time that lasts forever
7. _____ (adj.) difficult (informal usage)
8. _____ (adj.) not possible to avoid
9. _____ (n.) the act of trying to do something
10. _____ (v.) was more than something else, went beyond

C | Take turns asking and answering the questions below with a partner.

1. Where was the last place you traveled (near or far)? Did anyone **accompany** you, or did you go alone?
2. Say a very large number. What's a number that **exceeds** the number you just said?
3. When you go shopping, do you make only **rational** decisions about what to buy, or do your emotions affect your buying decisions?
4. What's the **toughest** school assignment you've ever completed?
5. How can one **distinguish** between acquaintances and real friends?
6. Do you have any preferences about what happens to your body after you **die**?
7. As people get older, do you think illnesses and other physical problems are **inevitable**?
8. What do you think about the ancient Egyptians' idea of preserving the dead for **eternity**?
9. Who do you admire? What **aspect(s)** of that person's personality or character do you admire most? Explain.
10. If people believe they cannot do something—for example, write a poem in English— should they at least make an **attempt** to do it, or is it better if they focus their energy on something else?

D | The following are frequent collocations—words that commonly occur together. Write a sentence of your own using each collocation:

1. distinguish between

   I can't distinguish between /b/ and /v/ sounds in English. They sound the same to me.

2. aspect of

   _____

3. make an attempt

   _____

Before Listening

Using Context Clues

When you are listening, it's not unusual to miss a few things that a speaker says, even if he or she is speaking your native language. Often, using context clues—other words and phrases that surround the part you missed—can help you to follow the speaker's ideas.

A | Listen to part of a talk on an archaeological expedition and read the transcript below. Imagine that you miss two small parts of the talk.

In Abydos, Egypt, Egyptologist Salima Ikram works very carefully on an animal mummy from a burial site.

The Abydos site was really interesting because of the contrasts, but also the similarities among the mummies we found there. Beginning around 5000 years ago, Egyptian kings and queens were buried there along with food and luxury items to enjoy in the next world, and in some cases, their pets (1) . . . . she must have loved it very much because the gazelle[1] was carefully wrapped in special cloth strips, and the mummy was placed inside a special gazelle-shaped coffin. Then in another part of the site, we found (2) . . . . He was buried a couple of thousand years later, and he didn't have the valuable art and furniture that the kings and queens had, but that dog was as well preserved as any mummy and was lying at its master's feet.

[1]A **gazelle** is an animal similar to a deer.

B | Circle the topics that the speaker probably discussed in the missing parts of the talk.

1. a. a king and an animal to eat
   b. a queen and a pet animal
2. a. description of the burial place of a royal person
   b. description of the burial place of an ordinary person

C | **Discussion.** Look again at the transcript of the talk in exercise **A**. Which information near the missing sections helps you to guess what you missed? Discuss your ideas with a partner.

Listening: A Discussion about a Group Project

track 3-23 **A | Listening for Main Ideas.** Listen to a group of students discussing a group project for a class. Choose the correct answer using context clues in the three places where information is missing.

1. During the first missing part of the conversation, the students were probably discussing _____.
   a. the topic of the presentation
   b. the importance of Celtic music
   c. the role of each group member

2. During the second missing part of the conversation, the students were probably discussing _____.
   a. the fact that Tyler's notes are tough to read
   b. the time and place to practice the presentation
   c. the advantages of getting up early

3. During the third missing part of the conversation, the students were probably discussing _____.
   a. narrowing their topic
   b. making visual aids
   c. taking pictures of the group

track 3-23 **B | Listening for Details.** Listen again and fill in the missing sections of the group secretary's notes on the group's plans.

ancient culture: _____

presentation topic: _____

presentation length: _____

meeting to practice;   place: <u>study hall at the student union</u>

                        time: _____

meeting after class at: _____

After Listening

 Discussion. With a partner, discuss the questions below.

1. What are some of the advantages of doing group assignments? disadvantages?
2. Did the speakers in the listening passage seem to work well together? Explain.
3. When you work in a group, which role are you most comfortable in?

Grammar

Comparatives: *The –er, the –er*

The –er, the –er is a type of comparative that usually describes an increase or decrease of something over time.

> ***The longer*** *we wait,* ***the hungrier*** *I get.*
>
> ***The longer*** *they were married,* ***the happier*** *they were.*

We also use *the more/the less, the -er.*

> ***The more*** *it rained,* ***the higher*** *the water rose in the reservoirs.*
>
> ***The less*** *he studies,* ***the worse*** *he does on exams.*

Unlike most sentences with more than one clause, sentences with *The –er, the –er* do not require connecting words such as *and* or *while* to join the clauses.

> ***The colder*** *it gets,* ***the less*** *I want to go outside.*

The colder it gets, the less I want to go outside.

A | With a partner, use the ideas below to say sentences with *The –er, the –er.*

1. As the weather gets warmer, I see an increasing number of birds outside.
2. As I get fewer emails, I think about my friends less often.
3. As I buy more clothes, it gets harder to decide what to wear.
4. As the price of olive oil goes down, more people buy it.
5. As it rains less, farmers grow smaller crops.
6. As the size of my vocabulary increases, I can express myself better.

B | With a partner, read the information below about a fictitious civilization. Then use sentences with *The -er, the -er,* and *The more/less, the -er* to tell a story about the civilization.

- They lived in a mountainous region between 300 BC and AD 1300.
- The climate got cooler over time, so they moved their villages and animals into lower and lower elevations.
- As they got closer to the lowlands, they began to have more conflicts with another civilization that lived in the coastal region.
- As the conflicts became more frequent, the mountain civilization had less time to take care of their animals and to preserve food.
- As the food supply and the number of animals decreased, the mountain population also decreased.
- As the population decreased, the mountain people married the coastal people more often.
- Eventually, the mountain civilization disappeared.

Language Function: Interrupting and Holding the Floor

 A | Listen to the following conversation. Then practice the conversation with a partner.

rack 3-24

Joel:	And then he told me that he had some tickets to the basketball game, so I said . . .
Antonio:	If I could just add something . . .
Joel:	I'm almost done—so I said I could go to the game with him!
Antonio:	And speaking of the game, did you hear that it's been cancelled? They said that . . .
Joel:	Um . . . did you say, *cancelled*? I can't believe it!
Antonio:	It's true. The other team couldn't get here or something.

Student to Student: Interrupting and Holding the Floor

In some situations, you need to interrupt someone who is speaking to add an idea or ask a question. Here are some expressions you can use to interrupt politely.

Sorry to interrupt, but . . .   *If I could just add something . . .*   *Um . . . um . . .*

When you are speaking, you may not want to be interrupted because you want to finish your thought. Here are some expressions you can use when you want to hold the floor.

Just a second . . .   *Just one more thing . . .*   *I'm almost finished . . .*

B | Form a group with two or three other students and have a five-minute conversation about one of the topics below. Practice interrupting each other politely, to add ideas or ask questions. Try to hold the floor if you are interrupted. Feel free to take the conversation beyond the topic you begin with.

- The positive and negative aspects of the city you're living in
- The advantages and disadvantages of using English as an international language
- Ways to distinguish between a good restaurant and a bad restaurant

C | **Self-Reflection.** Discuss the questions with your group.

1. In your culture, do interruptions during conversations occur frequently or infrequently?
2. Did you feel comfortable interrupting members of your group in exercise **B**?

In this presentation, you will summarize information and work with a group to present your summary to the rest of the class.

 A | Form a group with three to five other students and follow the directions.

1. Assign each group member one or more of the roles described on page 160 of Unit 8.
2. Research an ancient civilization that was not discussed in this unit, or find out more about a specific aspect of one of the civilizations from this unit. You can research your topic online or using printed materials.

3. Prepare a presentation for the class that includes visuals to support your topic. You can use paper, the board, or PowerPoint®. (Your instructor will tell you how long the presentation should be.) *(Use the Presentation Outline and Research and Presentation Checklists on pages 217–218 of the Independent Student Handbook to help you prepare your presentation.)*
4. Plan and practice your presentation as a group.
5. Each member of the group should do some of the speaking. Follow the guidelines in the Presentation Skills box below for supporting your group members.

The ruins of a village built by the Anasazi people in the U.S. state of Colorado

---

Presentation Skills: Supporting Your Co-Presenters

One of the advantages that group presentations have over individual presentations is that when you have co-presenters, you have someone to help you through difficult moments.

When members of your group are speaking, pay careful attention to what they're saying, and notice the audience's reactions as well. If a speaker forgets a point and looks to you for help, speak up and provide the information in a supportive manner. Or if the audience seems to be confused, you might need to interrupt the speaker politely and ask if there are any questions.

In short, now is the time to be helpful, not to have your head in your notes, planning what to say when it's your turn to speak.

 B | **Discussion.** After all of the presentations are finished, discuss the questions below with a partner.

1. Were there any moments when a speaker needed help from a group member? If so, was help provided in a supportive way?
2. What have you learned in this course about doing group work that you might use again in the future?
3. Have your feelings about doing group work changed in any way during this course?

Emotions and Personality

ACADEMIC PATHWAYS
Lesson A: Listening to a Radio Interview
            Conducting a Survey
Lesson B: Listening to an Informal Conversation
            Assessing the Credibility of a News Article

Think and Discuss

1. Look at the girl in the picture. How do you think she feels?
2. What factors do you think shape a person's personality?
3. What is the attitude towards psychologists and psychotherapy in your country?

Local girls ride home-made toboggans down one of the giant sand dunes in Mui Ne, Vietnam.

Exploring the Theme:
Emotions and Personality

Look at the photos and read the information. Then discuss the questions.

1. Look at the masks in the main photo. What facial expressions do you see?
2. What percentage of people in New Zealand are thriving? in Malawi? Based on this information, would you say that happiness has more to do with wealth or with other factors? Explain.
3. What do you think the poll numbers would be for your country?

Young people wearing masks pass through a mustard field on their way to a festival in Catalonia, Spain.

How Do You Measure Happiness?

According to the **Gallup World Poll**, money does have something to do with a country's happiness, but it isn't the whole story. In the countries that scored highest in the poll, people also felt that their social and psychological needs were being met. Here's how Gallup measured happiness:

1. **Percentage thriving:** People were asked about their overall satisfaction with their daily lives, including their income. Those who are "thriving" are doing well financially.
2. **Daily experience:** People were asked how they had felt the day before on a **scale of 1–10**. Factors such as sleeping well, being free of pain, and being respected by other people make up this data.

Happiest Country in Australasia: New Zealand

Percentage thriving: 63%
Daily experience: 7.6

Happiest Country in Africa: Malawi

Percentage thriving: 25%
Daily experience: 8

A | **Meaning from Context.** Read and listen to the conversation. Notice the words in blue. These are words you will hear and use in Lesson A.

track 3-25

Fear

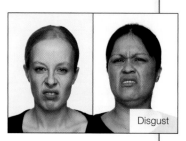

Sadness

Happiness

Disgust

Max: What's the matter? You look like you're sad.

Abigail: I'm reading a newspaper. How can I look sad?

Max: I'm just reading your facial expression. I learned that when people experience **basic** emotions, like sadness or **fear**, you can see it in their faces.

Abigail: But I'm Indonesian, and you're Canadian. Maybe we make different facial expressions to express the same emotions.

Max: Well, that's the interesting thing. Back in the 1800s, Charles Darwin **speculated** that our facial expressions, like smiling when we're happy, are a **universal** human **phenomenon**.

Abigail: So was he right? Do we all make the same facial expressions?

Max: We do. Around 40 years ago, a psychologist named Paul Ekman **confirmed** Darwin's theory. He **conducted** an experiment, and the results showed that people across cultures make the same facial expressions to express the same emotions.

Abigail: So it doesn't matter which culture we come from?

Max: Right. He also wondered whether the things that **trigger** our emotions might be universal.

Abigail: Interesting. So are the things that cause our emotions the same for everyone?

Max: The answer is—yes, and no. Certain things are universal, like a sudden movement in our field of vision triggers fear, for example.

Abigail: That makes sense. A sudden movement could signal danger, so maybe we react because of our instincts.

Max: Right, but some things don't trigger the same emotion. For example, one person could **associate** the smell of the sea with something positive, like a vacation.

Abigail: And another person might associate the smell with a sad time in their lives.

Max: Exactly!

Abigail: And I suppose that those emotional triggers might have to do with **personality** as well.

Max: You're probably right.

B | **Discussion.** Practice the conversation with a partner. Then discuss the questions below.

1. Are you surprised that facial expressions are the same across cultures? Why, or why not?
2. Which emotions do you feel are easiest to recognize? Which are most difficult? Explain.

C | Write each word in blue from exercise **A** next to its definition.

1. _____ (adj.) involving the simplest or most important aspects of something
2. _____ (v.) to connect one thing with another in your mind
3. _____ (n.) an event that is known to happen
4. _____ (v.) showed that something is definitely true
5. _____ (n.) one's whole character and nature
6. _____ (v.) to cause something quickly or automatically
7. _____ (adj.) having to do with everyone or everything
8. _____ (v.) made a guess about something
9. _____ (n.) organized and did something, like an experiment or study
10. _____ (n.) the feeling of being afraid

D | Complete each question from the Personality Test below with the correct form of a word from the box.

fear	associate	basic	triggers	phenomenon

QUIZ: Personality Test

1. Would you describe your _____ personality as shy or outgoing?
2. What is one thing that always _____ a feeling of happiness in you?
3. Do you feel _____ while preparing for something important such as an exam?
4. What feeling do you _____ with the sound of a bell ringing?
5. Is there a natural _____ such as lightning or sunsets that makes you feel sad?

E | **Critical Thinking.** Take turns asking and answering the questions from the Personality Test with a partner. Then discuss what the test might reveal (tell you) about your personalities.

F | **Discussion.** Take turns asking and answering the questions below with a partner. Explain your answers.

1. If you could **conduct** a psychology experiment, what would you want to find out about the human mind and/or people's behavior?
2. Do you think people are born with a certain **personality**, or does it develop later in life?
3. What do you think is the best way to **confirm** that your life is moving in a good direction?
4. If a friend is in a bad mood, would you **speculate** about the reason, or just ask your friend what's wrong? Explain.
5. Do you think all human emotions are **universal**, or are some of them specific to certain cultures?

Pronunciation

Are human beings born with a fear of certain things such as this snake, or do we learn from the people around us what we should fear?

Intonation for Thought Groups

You already know that in sentences, content words are usually emphasized, while function words are reduced, or receive less stress (see page 36 in Unit 2). Another pattern in English is for one content word—often the last content word in a sentence or phrase—to receive the greatest stress. That word can be called the "focus word" in the sentence. For example:

track 3-26

*What kind of **car** did you buy?*
*I bought a used **sedan.***

Longer sentences are usually divided into thought groups, which are groups of words that belong together because of their topic or grammar structure. In general, each thought group:

1. contains one focus word.
2. ends with a falling pitch and a slight pause.

Here are some examples with slashes (/) to show the thought groups.

It's better to <u>give</u>/than to <u>receive</u>.
The Johnson's <u>baby</u>/wasn't afraid of <u>snakes</u>/before that <u>day</u>.

track 3-27

In each sentence, separate the two thought groups with a slash (/). <u>Underline</u> the focus words. Then listen and check your answers.

1. Elena has a good <u>personality</u>,/but she doesn't have many <u>friends</u>.
2. We went to the store, and we bought some fruit.
3. I can't decide between the red shoes and the brown ones.
4. Do you want to fix the car yourself or take it to a mechanic?

Before Listening

Predicting Content. You are going to hear an interview about fear on a radio talk show. What aspects of fear do you think will be discussed? Discuss your ideas with a partner.

Listening: A Radio Interview

track 3-28

A | Listening for Main Ideas. Listen to an interview and write brief answers to the questions.

1. What are the two speakers' professions? _____
2. What question do they want to answer? _____
3. What is the answer to the question you identified in #2? _____
4. What kind of evidence does the man give for his answer? _____

track 3-28 **B** | **Listening for Details.** Read the statements and listen again. Circle **T** for *true* or **F** for *false*. Then change the false sentences to make them true.

1. The woman's name is Nancy Morales.   **T**   **F**
2. The man's name is Leroy Bateman.   **T**   **F**
3. The man says that the fear response protected our ancient ancestors from dangers such as hungry tigers.   **T**   **F**
4. The man's example of putting our foot on the brakes in a car is an example of a learned fear response.   **T**   **F**
5. The man says that researchers were able to teach lab monkeys to be afraid of flowers.   **T**   **F**

C | **Discussion.** Listen to the interview a third time and pay attention to the speakers' intonation. How do thought groups help you to understand the speakers' ideas? track 3-28 Discuss this question with a partner.

After Listening

A | **Summarizing.** Talk to your partner about the experiments with monkeys. What did the researchers do and what did they learn from the experiments?

B | Form a group with two or three other students. Read the list below of things that might cause fear, add one idea of your own, and then rank them from 1 (the most frightening) to 6 (the least frightening) according to the level of fear they cause. Discuss any differences of opinion.

_____ seeing a mouse, a large spider, etc.

_____ swimming in the ocean

_____ taking an important exam

_____ going alone to a social event, such as a party

_____ flying on an airplane

_____ your group's idea _____

Rhesus monkeys are sometimes used for scientific research.

Student to Student: Expressing Emotions

It can be difficult to talk about emotions, but it can also help to build friendships and let people know what you're feeling, especially when something is wrong. When talking about difficult topics, modifying your words in order to soften or minimize them can be helpful. Here are some useful words and expressions you can use.

kind of   *sort of*   *a little*   *a bit*   *just*

C | **Discussion.** Discuss the question below with your group.

In the experiments that Dr. Bateman talks about, monkeys spend their whole lives inside a scientific laboratory. What do you think are the advantages and drawbacks of using animals such as monkeys for scientific research?

Grammar

The Past Perfect Tense

The past perfect tense is formed with *had* + the past participle of a verb. We use the past perfect to talk about an event that happened before another event or time in the past.

> *The researchers showed the monkeys the videos they* **had made***.*
> (They made the videos first. Then they showed them to the monkeys.)
> *I looked for my friend in the library, but she* **had left** *already.*
> (She left before I got to the library.)

The words *already, not yet, not ever,* and *never* are often used with the past perfect to emphasize the event that happened first.

> *Before they showed the monkeys the videos, the researchers* **had never seen** *them afraid.*
> *They* **had already finished** *the study by the time Dr. Bateman was hired by the university.*

The simple past is often used instead of the past perfect in sentences with words such as *before* and *after* that make the time relationship clear.

> ***After*** *he* **saw** *the snake, he ran into the house.*
> *The researchers* **made** *the videos* **before** *they started the fear–response study.*

A | Read the pairs of sentences in the chart. Then work with a partner to write one sentence giving the same information as each pair of sentences. Use the past perfect and *when*, *before*, and *already*.

First Event	Second Event	
Her brother graduated from high school.	Sonia was born.	1. When Sonia was born, her brother had already graduated from high school.
The lecturer finished speaking.	I arrived at ten thirty.	2.
Ken and Rieko ate dinner.	I arrived at the restaurant.	3.
Kim fell asleep.	The movie ended.	4.
The children made a mess.	Their parents came home.	5.
The meeting started.	Sheila got to work at 10:00.	6.

B | Read and listen to the article. Then <u>underline</u> the uses of the past perfect verb tense.

Hand Washing Wipes Away Regrets?

If you have to make a tough decision, research suggests that you should wash your hands afterwards. The research was conducted at the University of Michigan in the U.S. by Spike W.S. Lee and Norbert Schwarz, who asked student volunteers to participate in what they thought was a consumer survey.

The students were asked to rank 10 music CDs in order of preference. Then the researchers let them choose between the fifth and the sixth CD to take home as a gift. Once the volunteers had made a decision, some students chose to evaluate a liquid hand soap by washing their hands, while others just looked at the bottle. The students who didn't wash their hands later ranked their chosen CDs higher than they had before, but students who did wash up ranked the 10 CDs in basically the same order as before.

Research shows that if you have to make a difficult decision, washing your hands afterwards can help.

After you make a decision, you want to feel like you've made the right choice.

This phenomenon is called post-decisional dissonance. "You want to feel that you made the right choice, so you justify[1] it by thinking about the positive features of your decision," Lee explained.

The researchers conducted a similar survey in which they asked people to choose a jam[2] without tasting it first. People who hadn't used an antiseptic wipe expected their chosen jam to taste better than the rejected one. Those who had used the wipe thought the jams would taste about the same.

It's as if hand washing in any form "wipes the slate[3] clean" and removes the need to confirm that we've made the right choice, Lee said.

[1]To **justify** something is to give reasons why it is right.
[2]**Jam** is a sweet food made by cooking fruit and sugar together. It is usually spread on bread.
[3]**Slate** is a stone that can be used as a chalk board. "Wiping the slate clean" means erasing any marks and starting fresh.

C | **Discussion.** With a partner, discuss the questions below.

1. Look at the places in the article where you underlined the past perfect. In each case, what was the past event that happened after the event in the past perfect?
2. Do the researchers' findings surprise you? Explain.
3. Have you ever had regrets about decisions you have made? How did you deal with your regrets?

Language Function: Discussing Past Events

A | **Critical Thinking.** The photo on the left was taken in 1975. Work with a partner. Make a list in your notebook of 8–10 things you think the couple had done before 1975 using the past perfect.

> Do you think they had children?

> Yes, I think they had raised four children.

B | Form a group with another student pair and share your list from exercise **A**. Did you have any of the same ideas? Do all of your sentences use the past perfect?

Critical Thinking Focus: Assessing the Credibility of Sources

If information is credible, it is believable. Deciding whether or not you can believe information that you hear or read is important, especially if you're going to use the information to support a claim. The list in exercise **A** below provides several factors to consider when assessing the credibility of a source.

A | **Critical Thinking.** Form a group with two to four other students. Look back at the article on page 189. Then read the list below and mark each item on a scale of 1–3 according to its impact on the credibility of the article: 1=very important; 2=somewhat important; 3=not very important.

_____ number of volunteers in the study

_____ how recent the study is

_____ degrees or titles held by the researchers

_____ existence of a control group (that did not receive the treatment)

_____ tone of the language in the article

_____ nature of the source (e.g., journal vs. Internet article; radio interview vs. lecture)

_____ association with a respected university or other institution

_____ conclusion reached by the researchers

B | **Discussion.** Share your ideas from exercise **A** with the rest of the class and discuss the questions below.

1. What information in the hand washing article made it credible?
2. What additional information could have been included in the article to make it even more credible?
3. In general, whether you're listening to a presentation or reading information, what makes you more likely to believe or not believe the information? List any new ideas you have in your notebook.

Conducting a Survey

A | Follow the instructions to conduct a psychological survey of your classmates.

1. Choose three of the following questions to include in your survey. Then write two new questions of your own.
   a. How would you rate your overall satisfaction with life on a scale of 1–10? Explain.
   b. How would you describe your personality? (outgoing, shy, thoughtful, etc.) Explain.
   c. On a scale of 1–10, how good do you expect your life to be 10 years from now? Explain.
   d. What feelings or emotions do you associate with speaking English? Explain.
   e. On a scale of 1–10, how important to you are other people's opinions of you? Explain.
2. On a piece of paper, write your questions in a chart similar to the one below.
3. When the chart is completed, stand up, and find someone in the class whom you don't usually work with. Ask and answer the survey questions you've chosen, and take notes on your classmate's answers.
4. If there is any question you don't want to answer, simply say, "Pass." The survey-taker will move on to the next question.
5. After completing the survey, stand up and look for another person you don't know very well to talk to. Repeat the procedure until you've talked to three different classmates.

Question	Name	Name	Name
a.			
b.			
c.			
d.			
e.			

B | **Discussion.** Form a group with two or three other students. Discuss the survey you conducted. What is interesting or surprising about the answers you heard? Can you make any generalizations?

> It seems like most people care a lot about other people's opinions.

Sigmund Freud

Sigmund Freud has changed the way we think about the human mind.

Before Viewing

A | **Prior Knowledge.** You are going to watch a video about Sigmund Freud. Write anything you know about him.

_____

_____

_____

B | **Using a Dictionary.** You will hear these words in the video. Write each word in the box next to its definition. Use your dictionary to help you.

drive	fled	hallmark	masterpiece	suppress	unconscious

Young Sigmund Freud and family

1. _____ (n.) the part of our mind that makes thoughts or attitudes that we are not aware of

2. _____ (v.) to not express feelings or reactions even if you may want to

3. _____ (n.) energy or determination

4. _____ (n.) the most typical quality or feature of something

5. _____ (v.) escaped from

6. _____ (n.) the best work that an artist, writer, or composer has created

While Viewing

A | Watch the video. Check if any of the information you wrote down from exercise **A** in the Before Viewing section is mentioned.

B | Read the statements below. Then watch the video again and circle **T** for *true* or **F** for *false* for each statement.

1. Sigmund Freud was born in Austria.   **T**   **F**
2. Vienna is the city that is most associated with Freud.   **T**   **F**
3. Freud created the name *psychoanalysis*.   **T**   **F**
4. Freud believed that certain people have an unconscious   **T**   **F**
   part of the mind.
5. Freud believed that dreams were a way to discover   **T**   **F**
   people's desires and fears.
6. Freud's masterpiece is called *The Interpretation of Fears*.   **T**   **F**
7. Today a lot of patients are treated using Freud's method   **T**   **F**
   of psychoanalysis.

Vienna, Austria

After Viewing

A | Read the pairs of sentences about Sigmund Freud in the chart below. Then work with a partner to write one sentence giving the same information as each pair of sentences. Use the past perfect and *after*.

First Event	Second Event	
Freud earned his medical degree.	Freud became fascinated with the human mind.	1. *Freud became fascinated with the human mind after he had earned his medical degree.*
Freud named the practice of *psychoanalysis*.	Freud wrote his masterpiece in 1899.	2.
The Nazis burned his book.	Freud turned 81 in 1938.	3.
Freud's family fled to England.	Freud died.	4.

B | **Critical Thinking.** Form a group with two or three other students and discuss the questions.

1. What do you think Freud might say about people who have dreams about the following things?

   Dreams about flying   *Dreams about falling*   *Dreams about being chased*

2. The studies in Lesson A involved studying the behavior of monkeys. Freud studied dreams and the unconscious mind of humans. Which of these studies do you think would provide more accurate information about people's fears and behaviors? Explain.

A | **Using a Dictionary.** Check (✔) the words you already know. These are words you will hear and use in Lesson B. Then write each word from the box next to its definition below. Use your dictionary to help you.

❑ anxiety (n.) ❑ attribute (n) ❑ awkward (adj.) ❑ charming (adj.) ❑ depression (n.)
❑ differ (v.) ❑ extroverted (adj.) ❑ interaction (n.) ❑ introverted (adj.) ❑ upset (adj.)

1. _____ outgoing and sociable
2. _____ communicating and spending time with other people
3. _____ somewhat unhappy or disappointed
4. _____ pleasant and attractive
5. _____ to be unlike something else
6. _____ a feeling of extreme nervousness or worry
7. _____ a quality or feature of someone or something
8. _____ a mental state marked by extreme sadness and hopelessness
9. _____ somewhat shy and reserved around other people
10. _____ uncomfortable and embarrassed

track 3-30 **B** | Read and listen to the information about personality psychology. Notice the words in blue.

Personality psychology can help us to understand different personality types.

Introverts

Modern psychology offers many models to explain personality types, but nearly all of them include two terms made popular by Carl Jung in the early 20th century: *introverted* and *extroverted*. These two personality types have very different attributes, and while almost everyone has some aspects of both types in their own personality, one type is usually stronger.

In general, introverted people prefer activities they can do alone, such as reading or playing video games. They may feel awkward in social situations, where they're worried about how they should behave. In some cases, they may even feel enough anxiety about social situations to avoid them altogether. For most people, however, having an introverted nature simply means they prefer to have less frequent social contact with smaller numbers of people.

 C | **Discussion.** With a partner, discuss the questions below.

1. Do you think you have any of the **attributes** of an introverted person? Explain.
2. Unlike fear, **anxiety** is not considered one of the basic emotions. Do you think everyone experiences **anxiety** at some time, or is it only a problem for very **introverted** people?
3. When people feel **awkward** in a social situation, what might they do or say that reveals their awkwardness? What might you do or say to make them feel more comfortable?

A | Read and listen to the information about the extroverted personality type. Notice the words in blue.

ck 3-31

Extroverts

Extroverted people differ from introverted people in several ways. Extroverted people thrive on interaction with others and feel energized at social gatherings such as large parties. Politicians, teachers, and business managers are often extroverted. They may be very charming in order to attract people to interact with, or they may be overly talkative and so outgoing that people become uncomfortable around them.

Extroverted people may become upset when they lack human contact on the job or in their social lives, and in more serious cases, feelings of being alone can lead to depression. In these cases, psychological counseling can give extroverted people insights into themselves and ways to manage their feelings.

B | **Critical Thinking.** With a partner, discuss the questions below.

1. Why do you think **extroverted** people enjoy each of the jobs mentioned in this article?
2. Do you think everyone feels **depression** at times, or is it a fairly rare mental condition?
3. At a party, what kinds of things might an **extroverted** person do in order to be **charming**?

C | **Discussion.** With your partner, discuss the questions below.

1. Based on the descriptions in this lesson, would you describe yourself as more **introverted** or more **extroverted**? What are some of your personality **attributes**?
2. How does your personality differ from that of your siblings (sisters and brothers), or if you're an only child, from the **personalities** of your close friends?
3. Have you ever felt **anxiety** about an exam or an important assignment? What did you do to calm yourself? What's the best thing students can do when they feel **anxiety** about school?

D | **Discussion.** Get together with a new partner and discuss the questions below.

1. Do you enjoy a lot of social **interaction**, or is a small amount of it enough for you?
2. Describe a **charming** person that you know. What is he or she like?
3. Describe a situation in which you felt **awkward**, or a situation in which you might feel **awkward**. What did you (or would you) do in order to deal with that feeling?
4. When people are very upset or experiencing **depression**, do you think counseling from a psychologist or psychiatrist is usually helpful, or can most people deal with such problems on their own?

Before Listening

 Critical Thinking. In the Gallup World Poll, social relationships were found to play a large part in people's happiness. Form a group with two to four other students and discuss the questions below.

1. What's the nature of each kind of relationship listed below? For example, are they close relationships or casual ones? Are they important for a short time or situation in our lives, or for a long time? What are some characteristics of each type of relationship?
2. How important is each kind of relationship in your own life? Explain.

- relationships between parents and children
- relationships with personal friends
- relationships among siblings
- relationships with coworkers
- relationships with neighbors
- relationships with classmates and teachers
- relationships within couples
- other _____

Listening: An Informal Conversation

track 3-32 **A** | **Listening for Main Ideas.** Listen to a conversation between a married couple, Leo and Reba, and answer the questions.

1. What kind of party did the couple go to? _____
2. What is the main topic of the conversation? _____
3. Do the speakers seem like introverted or extroverted people? Why? _____

   _____

4. What suggestion does the man make at the end of the conversation? _____

   _____

track 3-32 **B** | **Listening for Details.** Listen again and take notes on the conversation using your own words. What do the speakers say about each person?

Gloria	The Manager	Toby

After Listening

Presentation Skills: Role-Playing

Role-playing is a common activity in language classes because it provides semi-realistic situations for practicing speaking and listening skills. But role-plays are used in other situations as well; for example, in a psychology course, a role-play can be a way to experience someone else's viewpoint by "standing in their shoes," or to demonstrate how people's state of mind can affect a situation. Role-plays can also be used in work situations, such as to practice an important conversation you plan to have with a coworker or boss. Role-playing can also be helpful when preparing a presentation for any situation. A friend or family member can role-play an audience member by asking the types of questions you might be asked during your presentation.

When role-playing, it's important to get over any embarrassment you might feel and participate fully in the role-play in order to gain the most from it. This means acting out the role you are assigned and not laughing or saying things that are "out of character." A role-play can be an excellent learning tool, but only if the participants can put any uncomfortable feelings aside.

A | Planning a Presentation. Form a group with four other students and prepare to role-play a conversation from the party you heard about in the listening passage. Follow the directions below.

1. Assign a role to each group member.

   Leo and Reba: The couple
   Gloria: The coworker
   The manager
   Toby: The coworker

2. Make a list of the "scenes" from the party. For example, Leo and Reba arriving; Gloria greeting them and telling her story, etc. You do not need to act out the conversation after the party, only the party itself. (You may want to listen to the conversations again.)

3. Practice the role-play using your own words to act out the scenes. You do not need to write out what you're going to say, but you should speak the way your character would speak.

B | Presentation. Get together with another group who will be the audience for your role-play. Perform your role-play for the other group.

C | Discussion. After everyone has finished doing their role-plays, discuss the questions below as a group.

1. Was it easy or difficult for you to play the character you were assigned? Explain.
2. What did you learn from doing the role-play? For example, did it increase your comprehension of the listening passage? Did it lead you to think more deeply about each character's personality?

Grammar

Used To + Verb vs. Be Used To + Noun

Used To

Used to + verb is used when we're talking about past states or events that are no longer true or happening.

> I **used to** live in that house when I was a child.
>
> Sara **used to** be a manager, but she isn't a manager now.

In questions and negative sentences, we use the auxiliary verb *did*.

> **Did** you **use to** go to a different school?
>
> People **didn't use to** talk about their emotions very often.

Be Used To + Noun

Be used to means the same as *be accustomed to*. We use it to talk about things that are usual or normal to us, and to talk about habits. *Be used to* is followed by a noun or gerund phrase.

> People here **are used to** hot weather.
>
> They **'re used to** eating dinner late in the evening.

The phrase, *get used to* can be used to talk about the process of becoming accustomed to something.

> When you're at the university, you have to **get used to** studying several hours each day.

Read each sentence and add the correct form of the word *be* only where it's needed. If *be* is not needed, write Ø.

1. We _____ used to doing something with our neighbors every Saturday.
2. Thanks for offering, but I _____ not used to drinking coffee at night.
3. Did you _____ use to have much longer hair?
4. I live in a small apartment now, but I _____ used to live in a larger one.
5. When they lived in Paris, they _____ used to walk everywhere.
6. Nadia lives in Bangkok now, so she has had to _____ get used to the heat.

Language Function: Discussing Study Habits

A | Work with a partner. Read about Salim's study habits when he was a high school student.

Salim Then

When Salim was in high school, he was a poor student. Here are some reasons why:

- was unable to concentrate
- studied at a disorganized table
- didn't have a good system for note-taking
- was often confused about complex ideas and issues
- was worried and stressed out much of the time
- was less self-confident

B | Use the picture and the information in the box to talk to your partner about Salim's habits as a high school student using *used to*.

> When he was younger, Salim used to be unable to concentrate.

C | Work with a partner. Look at the picture of Salim now. Read about his study habits now as a graduate student.

Salim Now

Salim is in graduate school, and he is a good student. Here are some of the reasons why:

- avoids distractions and focuses on his work
- studies at an organized desk
- takes notes using a system that works well for him
- uses critical thinking skills to understand ideas and issues
- meets with his professors when he needs help
- manages his time well, so he can complete assignments on time

D | Use the picture and the information to talk about his habits as a graduate student using *be used to*.

> Now, Salim's used to avoiding distractions, so he can focus on his work.

E | **Self-Reflection.** List several differences between yourself as you are now and yourself as you used to be ten years ago.

F | Share some of your sentences from exercise **E** with a partner. Did you have any habits in common ten years ago, or do you have habits in common now?

Traditionally, neuroscience, or the study of the brain and nervous system, was only a branch of biology, but many modern-day psychologists have become interested in neuroscience and the connection between the brain's structures and functions, and the behavior of people. In this assignment, you will assess the credibility of a news article about neuroscience and present your ideas and assessment to the class.

 track 3-33 **A** | Read and listen to a news article.

Making Music Boosts Brain's Language Skills

Do you have trouble hearing people talk at parties? Try practicing the piano before you leave the house. That's because musicians—from karaoke singers to professional cello players—are better able to hear targeted sounds in a noisy environment.

"In the past 10 years there's been an explosion of research on music and the brain," Aniruddh Patel, the Esther J. Burnham Senior Fellow at the Neurosciences Institute in San Diego, said today at a press briefing.

Most recently, brain-imaging studies have shown that music activates many diverse parts of the brain, including a part of the brain that processes both music and language. Language is a natural aspect to consider in looking at how music affects the brain, according to Patel. Patel states that, like music, language is "universal, there's a strong learning component, and it carries complex meanings."

According to study leader Nina Kraus, director of the Auditory Neuroscience Laboratory at Northwestern University in Illinois, the brains of people with even casual musical training are better able to generate the brain wave patterns associated with specific sounds, whether musical or spoken. In other words, musicians are used to "playing" sounds in their heads, so they've trained their brains to recognize selective sound patterns, such as spoken words, even as background noise goes up.

B | **Critical Thinking.** Look back at the list of factors to consider when assessing the credibility of a source of information on page 190. Reread or listen to the article above and take brief notes in your notebook on the aspects of the article that make it more or less credible to you.

C | **Planning a Presentation.** Form a group with two or three other students and discuss the credibility of the article. Make a list of factors that make the article credible, as well as a list of factors that might make the article more credible.

D | **Presentation.** Share your group's ideas with the rest of the class, and make comparisons between your ideas and those of the groups that have already spoken. Make sure every member of your group does some of the speaking.

Overview

The *Independent Student Handbook* is a resource that you can use at different points and in different ways during this course. You may want to read the entire handbook at the beginning of the class as an introduction to the skills and strategies you will develop and practice throughout the book. Reading it at the beginning will provide you with another organizational framework for understanding the material.

Use the *Independent Student Handbook* throughout the course in the following ways:

Additional instruction: You can use the *Independent Student Handbook* to provide more instruction on a particular skill that you are practicing in the units. In addition to putting all the skills instruction in one place, the *Independent Student Handbook* includes additional suggestions and strategies. For example, if you find you're having difficulty following academic lectures, you can refer to the Listening Skills section to review signal phrases that help you to understand the speaker's flow of ideas.

Independent work: You can use the *Independent Student Handbook* to help you when you are working on your own. For example, if you want to improve your vocabulary, you can follow some of the suggestions in the Vocabulary Building section.

Source of specific tools: A third way to use the handbook is as a source of specific tools, such as outlines, graphic organizers, and checklists. For example, if you are preparing a presentation, you might want to use the research checklist as you research your topic. Then you might want to complete the presentation outline to organize your information. Finally, you might want to use the presentation checklist to help you prepare for your presentation.

Table of Contents

Improving Your Listening Skills
Formal Listening Skills   202
Improving Your Note-Taking Skills   206

Building Your Vocabulary
Independent Vocabulary Learning Tips   208
Prefixes and Suffixes   209
Dictionary Skills   209

Improving Your Speaking Skills
Everyday Communication   210
Doing Group Projects   211

Presentation Skills   211
Classroom Presentation Skills   211

Resources
Understanding and Using Visuals:
    Graphic Organizers   214
Reading Maps, Graphs, and
    Diagrams   216
Presentation Outline   217
Checklists   218
Summary of Signal Phrases   219

Formal Listening Skills

Predicting

Speakers giving formal talks or lectures usually begin by introducing themselves and then introducing their topic. Listen carefully to the introduction of the topic and try to anticipate what you will hear.

Strategies:

- Use visual information including titles on the board, on slides, or in a PowerPoint presentation.
- Think about what you already know about the topic.
- Ask questions that you think the speaker might answer.
- Listen for specific phrases.

Identifying the Topic:

Today, I'm going to talk about . . .
Our topic today is . . .
Let's look at . . .

Understanding the Structure of the Presentation

An organized speaker will use certain expressions to alert you to the important information that will follow. Notice the signal words and phrases that tell you how the presentation is organized and the relationship between the main ideas.

Introduction

A good introduction includes something like a thesis statement, which identifies the topic and gives an idea of how the lecture or presentation will be organized.

Introduction (Topic + Organization):

I'll be talking about . . .	*My topic is . . .*
There are basically two groups . . .	*There are three reasons . . .*
Several factors contribute to this . . .	*There are five steps in this process . . .*

Body

In the body of the lecture, the speaker will usually expand upon the topic presented in the introduction. The speaker will use phrases that tell you the order of events or subtopics and their relationship to each other. For example, the speaker may discuss several examples or reasons.

Following the Flow of Ideas in the Body:

The first/next/final (point) is . . .	*Another reason is . . .*
However, . . .	*As a result, . . .*
For example, . . .	

Conclusion

In a conclusion, the speaker often summarizes what has already been said and may discuss implications or suggest future developments. For example, if a speaker is talking about an environmental problem, he or she may end by suggesting what might happen if we don't solve the problem, or he or she might add his or her own opinion. Sometimes speakers ask a question in the conclusion to get the audience to think more about the topic.

Restating/Concluding:

As you can see, . . .　　　　　　　　　　*In conclusion, . . .*
In summary, . . .　　　　　　　　　　　*To sum up, . . .*

Listening for Main Ideas

It's important to distinguish between a speaker's main ideas and the supporting details. In school, a professor often will test a student's understanding of the main points more than of specific details. Often a speaker has one main idea just like a writer does, and several main points that support the main idea.

Strategies:

- Listen for a thesis statement at the end of the introduction.
- Listen for rhetorical questions, or questions that the speaker asks, and then answers. Often the answer is the thesis.
- Notice ideas that are repeated or rephrased.

Repetition/Rephrasing:

I'll say this again . . .　　　　　　　　*So again, let me repeat . . .*
What you need to know is . . .　　　　*The most important thing to know is . . .*
Let me say it in another way . . .

Listening for Details (Examples)

A speaker will often provide examples that support a main point. A good example can help you understand and remember the main point better.

Strategies:

- Listen for specific phrases that introduce an example.
- Notice if an example comes after a generalization the speaker has given, or is leading into a generalization.
- If there are several examples, decide if they all support the same idea or are different aspects of the idea.

Giving Examples:

The first example is . . .　　　　　　*Let me give you an example . . .*
Here's an example of what I mean . . .　*For example, . . .*

Listening for Details (Reasons)

Speakers often give reasons, or list causes and/or effects to support their ideas.

Strategies:

- Notice nouns that might signal causes/reasons (e.g., *factors, influences, causes, reasons*) or effects (e.g., *effects, results, outcomes, consequences*).
- Notice verbs that might signal causes/reasons (e.g., *contribute to, affect, influence, determine, produce, result in*) or effects (often these are passive, e.g., *is affected by*).
- Listen for specific phrases that introduce reasons/causes.

Giving Causes or Reasons:

The first reason is . . .   *This is due to . . .*
This is because . . .

Giving Effects or Results:

As a result . . .   *One consequence is . . .*
Consequently . . .   *Therefore, . . .*
Another effect is . . .

Understanding Meaning from Context

Speakers may use words that are unfamiliar to you, or you may not understand exactly what they've said. In these situations, you can guess at the meaning of a particular word or fill in the gaps of what you've understood by using the context or situation itself.

Strategies:

- Don't panic. You don't always understand every word of what a speaker says in your first language either.
- Use context clues to fill in the blanks. What did you understand just before or just after the missing part? What did the speaker probably say?
- Listen for words and phrases that signal a definition or explanation.

Giving Definitions:

. . . which means . . .   *In other words . . .*
What that means is . . .   *Another way to say that is . . .*
Or . . .   *That is . . .*

Recognizing a Speaker's Bias

Speakers often have an opinion about the topic they are discussing. It's important for you to understand if they are objective or subjective about the topic. Being subjective means having a bias or a strong feeling about something. Objective speakers do not express an opinion.

Strategies:

- Notice words like adjectives, adverbs, and modals that the speaker uses (e.g., *ideal, horribly, should, shouldn't*).
- Listen to the speaker's voice. Does he or she sound excited, happy, or bored?
- When presenting another point of view on the topic, is given much less time and attention by the speaker?
- Listen for words that signal opinions.

Opinions:

I think . . .   *In my opinion . . .*
Here's what I believe is happening . . .

Making Inferences

Sometimes a speaker doesn't state something directly, but instead implies it. When you draw a conclusion about something that is not directly stated, you make an inference. For example, if the speaker says he or she grew up in Spain, you might infer that he or she speaks Spanish. When you make inferences, you may be very sure about your conclusions, or you may be less sure. It's important to use information the speaker states directly to support your inferences.

Strategies:

- Note information that provides support for your inference. For example, you might note that the speaker lived in Spain.
- Note information that contradicts your inference. Which evidence is stronger—for or against your inference?
- If you're less than certain about your inference, use words to soften your language such as modals, adverbs, and quantifiers.

She probably speaks Spanish, and she <u>may</u> also prefer Spanish food. <u>Many</u> people from Spain are familiar with bull-fighting.

Summarizing or Condensing

When taking notes, you should write down only the most important ideas of the lecture. To take good notes quickly:

- Write only the key words.

  all kabuki actors men

- You don't need complete sentences.

  ~~In the~~ time of ~~William~~ Shakespeare, women ~~were generally~~ not allowed ~~to appear~~ on ~~a theater stage.~~

- Use abbreviations (short forms) and symbols when possible.

  info dr = doctor w/ = with < = less than > = more than

  b/c = because /→ = leads to causes

Recognizing Organization

When you listen to a speaker, you practice the skill of noticing that speaker's organization. As you get in the habit of recognizing the organizational structure, you can use it to structure your notes in a similar way. Review the signal words and phrases from the Improving Your Listening Skills section in this handbook.

Some basic organizational structures:

- Narrative (often used in history or literature)
- Process (almost any field, but especially in the sciences)
- Cause and Effect (history, psychology, sociology)
- Classification (any field, including art, music, literature, sciences, history)
- Problem and Solution

Using Graphic Organizers

Graphic organizers can be very useful tools if you want to rewrite your notes. Once you've identified the speaker's organizational structure, you can choose the best graphic organizer to show the ideas. See the Resources section on page 214 in this handbook for more information.

Distinguishing between Relevant and Irrelevant Information

Remember that not everything a speaker says is noteworthy. A lecturer or presenter will usually signal important information you should take notes on.

Signals for Important Information:

This is important . . .

The one thing you want to remember . . .

Let me say again . . .

Write this down . . .

Instructors and other lecturers may also signal when to stop taking notes.

Signals to Stop Taking Notes:

You don't have to write all this down . . .

You can find this in your handout . . .

This information is in your book . . .

This won't be on your test . . .

In a similar way, they may let you know when they are going to discuss something off-topic.

Understanding Sidetracks:

That reminds me . . .

This is off the subject, but . . .

On a different topic . . .

By the way . . .

As an aside . . .

Recognizing a Return to a Previous Topic

When a speaker makes a sidetrack and talks about something that is not directly related to the main topic, he or she will often signal a return to a previous topic.

Returning to a Previous Topic:

So, just to restate . . .

Back to . . .

Getting back to what we were saying . . .

To return to what we were talking about earlier . . .

OK, so to get back on topic . . .

To continue . . .

Using Notes Effectively

It's important to not only take good notes, but to use them in the most effective way.

Strategies:

- Go over your notes after class to review and to add information you might have forgotten to write down.
- Compare notes with a classmate or study group to make sure you have all the important information.
- Review your notes before the next class so you will understand and remember the new information better.

Independent Vocabulary Learning Tips

Keep a Vocabulary Journal

- If a new word is useful, write it in a special notebook. Also write a short definition (in English if possible) and the sentence or situation where you found the word (its context). Write a sentence that uses the word.
- Carry your vocabulary notebook with you at all times. Review the words whenever you have a minute.
- Choose vocabulary words that will be useful to you. Some words are rarely used.

Experiment with New Vocabulary

- Think about new vocabulary in different ways. For example, look at all the words in your vocabulary journal and make a list of only the verbs. Or list the words according to the number of syllables (one-syllable words, two-syllable words, and so on).
- Use new vocabulary to write a poem, a story, or an email message to a friend.
- Use an online dictionary to listen to the sound of new words. If possible, make a list of words that rhyme. Brainstorm words that relate to a single topic that begin with the same sound (*student, study, school, skills, strategies, studious*).

Use New Words as Often as Possible

- You will not know a new vocabulary word after hearing or reading it once. You need to remember the word several times before it enters your long-term memory.
- The way you use an English word—in which situations and with which other words—might be different from a similar word in your first language. If you use your new vocabulary often, you're more likely to discover the correct way to use it.

Use Vocabulary Organizers

- Label pictures.

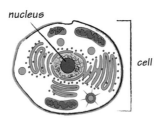

- Make word maps.

- Make personal flashcards. Write the words you want to learn on one side. Write the definition and/or an example sentence on the other.

Prefixes and Suffixes

Use prefixes and suffixes to guess the meaning of unfamiliar words and to expand your vocabulary. Prefixes usually change the meaning of a word somewhat. Suffixes usually change the part of speech. If you train yourself to look for the base meaning, or meaning of the stem of the word, you can understand more vocabulary.

Prefix	Meaning	Example
a-	completely	awake
bi-	two	bilingual, bicycle
dis-	not, negation, removal	disappear, disadvantages
pre-	before	pre-historic, predict
mis-	bad, badly, incorrectly	misunderstand, misjudge
re-	again	remove
un-	not; the opposite of	unhappy, unusual, unbelievable

The following are derivational suffixes that change the part of speech of the base word.

Suffix	New Part of Speech	Example
-able	adjective	unbelievable
-ary	noun	summary
-ent	adjective	convergent, divergent
-ful	adjective	beautiful, successful
-ed	adjective	stressed, interested
-ize	verb	summarize
-ly	adverb	carefully, completely
-ment	noun	assignment
-tion	noun	information

Dictionary Skills

The dictionary listing for a word usually provides the definition, the pronunciation, part of speech, other word forms, synonyms, examples of sentences that show the word in context, and common collocations.

Synonyms

A synonym is a word that means the same thing (e.g., *baby–infant*). Use synonyms to expand your vocabulary.

Word Families

These are the words that have the same stem or base word, but have different prefixes or suffixes.

Different Meanings of the Same Word

Many words have several meanings and several parts of speech. The example sentences in the word's dictionary entry can help you determine which meaning you need. For example, the word *plant* can be a noun or a verb.

Collocations

Dictionary entries often provide collocations, or words that are often used with the target word. For example, if you look up the word *get*, you might see *get around*, *get into*, *get there*, etc.

Everyday Communication

Summary of Useful Phrases for Everyday Communication

It's important to practice speaking English every day, with your teacher, your classmates, and anyone else you can find to practice with. This chart lists common phrases you can use in everyday communication situations. The phrases are listed in this chart from more formal to less formal.

Getting Clarification

Could you explain what the professor said?
What did the professor mean by that?
Did you catch what the professor said about that?
Did you understand that?

Expressing Thanks and Appreciation

Thank you so much for . . .
Thank you for . . .
I really appreciate your . . .
Thanks for. . .

Agreeing

That's my opinion also.
I think so, too.
I totally agree.
You're right about that.
Right!

Responding to Thanks

You're very welcome.
You're welcome.
No problem.
Any time.

Disagreeing

I'm afraid I have to disagree.
I see your point, but . . .
I see what you mean, but . . .
I'm not so sure about that.
I disagree.
No way.

Refusing

Thank you, but (I have other plans/I'm busy tonight/I'd rather not/etc.).
I wish I could, but (I don't have a car/I have a class at that time/etc.).
I'm sorry, I can't.
Maybe some other time.

Inviting

Would you like to get a cup of coffee/go have lunch?
Do you have time before your next class?
Are you doing anything now/after class?
What are you doing now?

Voicing a Small Problem

Actually, that's a problem for me because . . .
I hate to say it, but . . .
It's no big deal, but . .

Showing Surprise

That's unbelievable/incredible.
You're kidding!
Wow!
Really?
Seriously?

Congratulating

That sounds great!
Congratulations!
I'm so happy for you.
Well done!
Good for you!
Way to go!

Making Suggestions

I recommend/suggest . . .
Why don't I/you/we . . .
Let's . . .

Expressing Sympathy

Oh, no, I'm sorry to hear that.
That's really too bad.

Asking for Repetition	**Making Suggestions**
I'm sorry?	*We could . . .*
I didn't catch what you said.	*Why don't you . . . ?*
What's that?	*I recommend . . .*
I missed that.	*I suggest that you . . .*
	Let's . . .

Staying Neutral	**Asking Sensitive Questions**
Either one is fine with me.	*I hope this isn't too personal, but . . . ?*
I don't really have a preference.	*Do you mind if I ask . . . ?*
I can understand both points of view.	*Would you mind telling me . . . ?*
I think you both make good points.	*Can I ask . . . ?*

Doing Group Projects

You will often have to work with a group on activities and projects. It can be helpful to assign group members certain roles. You should try to switch roles every time you do a new activity. Here is a description of some common roles used in group activities and projects:

Group Leader—Makes sure the assignment is done correctly and all group members participate. Ask questions: *What do you think? Does anyone have another idea?*

Secretary—Takes notes on the group's ideas (including a plan for sharing the work).

Manager—During the planning and practice phases, the manager makes sure the presentation can be given within the time limit. If possible, practice the presentation from beginning to end, and time it.

Expert—Understands the topic well; invites and answers audience questions after the presentation. Make a list of possible questions ahead of time to be prepared.

Coach—Reminds group members to perform their assigned roles in the group work.

Note that group members have one of these roles in addition to their contribution to the presentation content and delivery.

Classroom Presentation Skills

Library Research

If you can go to a public library or school library, start there. You don't have to read whole books. Parts of books, magazines, newspapers, and even videos are all possible sources of information. A librarian can help you find both print and online sources of information.

Online Research

The Internet is an easy source of a lot of information, but it has to be looked at carefully. Many Web sites are commercial and may have incomplete, inaccurate, or biased information.

Finding reliable sources

Strategies:

- Your sources of information need to be reliable. Think about the author and the publisher. Ask yourself, *What is their point of view? Can I trust this information?*

- Your sources need to be well-respected. For example, an article from *The Lancet* (a journal of medical news) will probably be more respected than an article from a popular magazine.

- Start with Web sites with *.edu* or *.org* endings. Those are educational or non-commercial Web sites. Some *.com* Web sites also have good information, for example www.nationalgeographic.com or www.britannica.com.

Finding information that is appropriate for your topic

Strategies:

- Look for up-to-date information, especially in fields that change often such as technology or business. For Internet sources, look for recent updates to the Web sites.

- Most of the time, you'll need to find more than one source of information. Find sources that are long enough to contain some good information, but not so long that you won't have time to read them.

- Think about the source's audience. If it's written for computer programmers, for example, you might not be able to understand it. If it's written for university students who need to buy a new computer, it's more likely to be understandable.

Speaking Clearly and Comprehensibly

It's important that your audience understands what you are saying for your presentation to be effective.

Strategies:

- Practice your presentation many times before at least one other person, and ask him or her for feedback.

- Make sure you know the correct pronunciation of every word—especially the ones you will say more than once. Look them up online, or ask your instructor for the correct pronunciation.

- Try to use thought groups. Keep these words together: long subjects, verbs and objects, clauses, prepositional phrases. Remember to pause slightly at all punctuation and between thought groups.

- Speak loudly enough so everyone can hear.

- Stop occasionally to ask your audience if they can hear you and follow what you are saying.

Demonstrating Knowledge of Content

You should know more about your subject than you actually say in your presentation. Your audience may have questions, or you may need to explain something in more detail than you planned. Knowing a lot about your subject will allow you to present well and feel more confident.

Strategies:

- Practice your presentation several times.
- Don't read your notes.
- Say more than is on your visuals.
- Tell your audience what the visuals mean.

> **Phrases to Talk about Visuals:**
>
> *This graph/diagram shows/explains . . .*
> *The line/box represents . . .*
> *The main point is that . . .*
> *You can see . . .*

Engaging the Audience

Presenting is an important skill. If your audience isn't interested in what you have to say, then your message is lost.

Strategies:

- Introduce yourself.
- Make eye contact. Look around at different people in the audience.
- Use good posture. *Posture* means how you hold your body. When you speak in front of the class, you should stand up straight on both feet. Hold your hands together in front of your waist if you aren't holding notes. This shows that you are confident and well prepared.
- Pause to check understanding. When you present ideas, it's important to find out if your audience understands you. Look at the faces of people in the audience. Do they look confused? Use the expressions from the chart below to check understanding.

> **Phrases to Check for Understanding:**
>
> *Do you know what I mean?*
> *Is that clear?*
> *Does that make sense?*
> *Do you have any questions?*
> *Do you understand?*

Understanding and Using Visuals: Graphic Organizers

T-Chart

Purpose: Compare or contrast two things, or list aspects of two things

Why the Giant's Causeway Was Built	How the Giant's Causeway Formed
According to the legend...	*According to geologists...*

Venn Diagram

Purpose: Show differences and similarities between two things, sometimes three

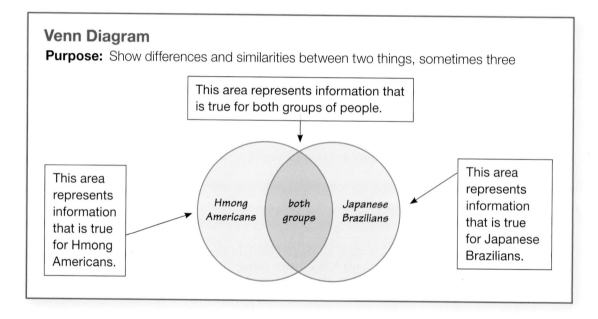

This area represents information that is true for both groups of people.

This area represents information that is true for Hmong Americans.

Hmong Americans — both groups — Japanese Brazilians

This area represents information that is true for Japanese Brazilians.

Grid

Purpose: Organize information about several things

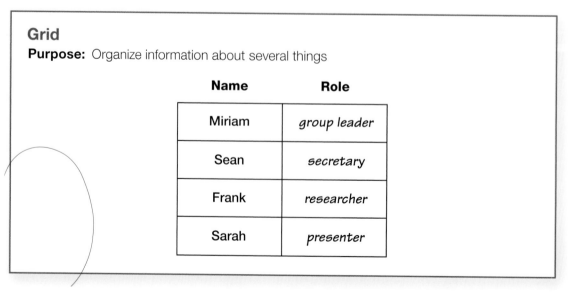

Name	Role
Miriam	*group leader*
Sean	*secretary*
Frank	*researcher*
Sarah	*presenter*

Flow Chart

Purpose: Show the stages in a process, or show a cause-and-effect chain (Flow charts have many different shapes.)

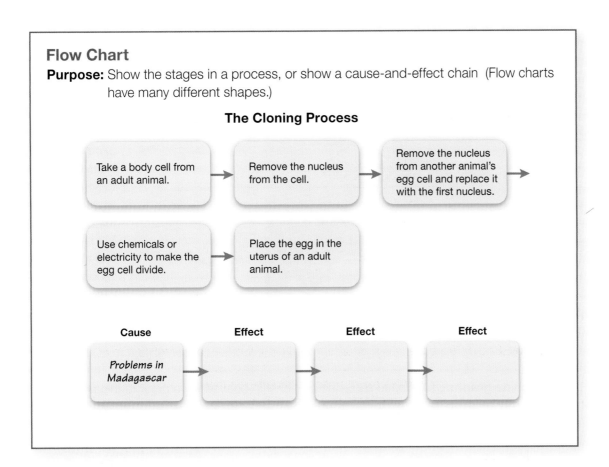

The Cloning Process

| Take a body cell from an adult animal. | → | Remove the nucleus from the cell. | → | Remove the nucleus from another animal's egg cell and replace it with the first nucleus. | → |

| Use chemicals or electricity to make the egg cell divide. | → | Place the egg in the uterus of an adult animal. |

| **Cause** | | **Effect** | | **Effect** | | **Effect** |

| *Problems in Madagascar* | → | | → | | → | |

Timeline

Purpose: Show the order of events and when they happened in time. Timelines start with the oldest point on the left. Timelines are frequently used to show important events in someone's life or in a larger historical context.

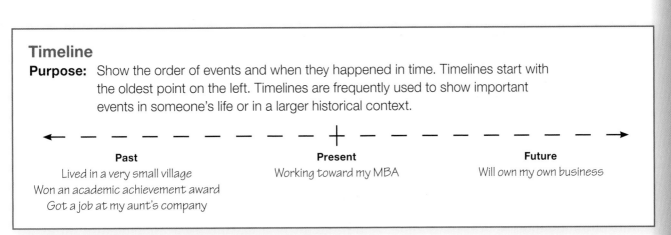

Past
Lived in a very small village
Won an academic achievement award
Got a job at my aunt's company

Present
Working toward my MBA

Future
Will own my own business

Understanding and Using Visuals: Maps, Charts, Graphs, and Diagrams

Maps are used to show geographical information.

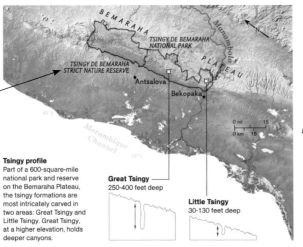

The **labels** on a map show important places mentioned in a reading or listening passage.

The **key** or **legend** explains specific information about the map. This legend shows the location of Madagascar and the Tsingy de Bemaraha National Park.

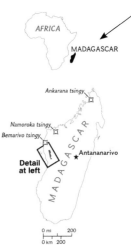

Tsingy profile
Part of a 600-square-mile national park and reserve on the Bemaraha Plateau, the tsingy formations are most intricately carved in two areas: Great Tsingy and Little Tsingy. Great Tsingy, at a higher elevation, holds deeper canyons.

Great Tsingy
250-400 feet deep

Little Tsingy
30-130 feet deep

Bar and **line graphs** use axes to show the relationship between two or more things.

Bar graphs compare amounts and numbers.

Migrant Population

- Australia/Oceania 5.0 million
- North America 44.5 million
- Europe 64.1 million
- Africa 17.1 million
- Asia 53.3 million
- Latin America/ Caribbean 6.6 million

Percentage of regional population

15.2 13.5 8.8 1.9 1.4 1.2

Line graphs show a change over time.

The **y axis** shows the percentage of foreign immigrants in Germany.

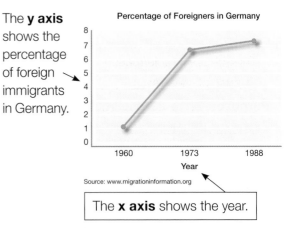

Percentage of Foreigners in Germany

Year

Source: www.migrationinformation.org

The **x axis** shows the year.

Pie charts show percents of a whole, or something that is made up of several parts.

Fossil Fuel Use by Sector

This section shows that the Energy Supply sector uses the most fossil fuels.

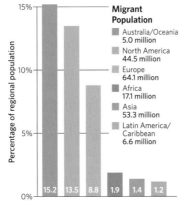

Waste and Wastewater 3%

Energy Supply 26%

Transportation 13%

Forestry 17%

Industry 19%

Agriculture 14%

Residential and Commercial Buildings 8%

Diagrams are a helpful way to show how a process or system works.

The earth's atmosphere

Heat

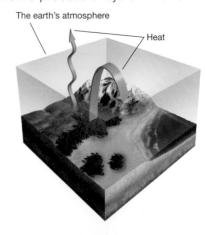

Presentation Outline

When you are planning a presentation, you may find it helpful to use an outline. If it is a group presentation, the outline can provide an easy way to divide the content. For example, someone could do the introduction, another student the first main idea in the body, and so on.

1. **Introduction**

   Topic: _____

   _____

   Hook/attention getter: _____

   _____

   Thesis statement: _____

   _____

2. **Body**

   First step/example/reason: _____

   Supporting details: _____

   _____

   _____

   Second step/example/reason: _____

   Supporting details: _____

   _____

   _____

   Third step/example/reason: _____

   Supporting details: _____

   _____

   _____

3. **Conclusion**

   Major points to summarize: _____

   _____

   Any implications/suggestions/predictions: _____

   _____

   Closing comment/summary: _____

   _____

Research Checklist

☐ Do I have three to five sources for information in general—and especially for information I'm using without a specific citation?

☐ Am I correctly citing information when it comes from just one or two sources?

☐ Have I noted all sources properly, including page numbers?

☐ When I am not citing a source directly, am I using adequate paraphrasing? (a combination of synonyms, different word forms and/or different grammatical structure)

☐ Are my sources reliable?

Presentation Checklist

☐ Have I practiced several times?

☐ Did I get feedback from a peer?

☐ Have I timed the presentation?

☐ Do I introduce myself?

☐ Do I maintain eye contact?

☐ Do I explain my visuals?

☐ Do I pause sometimes and check for understanding?

☐ Do I use correct pronunciation?

☐ Am I using appropriate volume so that everyone can hear?

☐ Do I have good posture?

Pair and Group-Work Checklist

☐ Do I make eye contact with others?

☐ Do I pay attention when someone else is talking?

☐ Do I make encouraging sounds or comments?

☐ Do I ask for clarification when I don't understand something?

☐ Do I check for understanding?

☐ Do I clarify what I mean?

☐ Do I express agreement and disagreement politely?

☐ Do I make suggestions when helpful?

☐ Do I participate as much as my classmates?

☐ Do I ask my classmates for their ideas?

Summary of Signal Phrases

Identifying the Topic:
Today, I'm going to talk about . . .
Our topic today is . . .
Let's look at . . .

Introduction (Topic + Organization):
I'll be talking about . . .
My topic is . . .
There are basically two groups . . .
There are three reasons . . .
Several factors contribute to this . . .
There are five steps in this process . . .

Following the Flow of Ideas:
The first/next/final (point) is . . .
Another reason is . . .
However, . . .
As a result, . . .
For example, . . .

Restating/Concluding:
As you can see, . . .
In conclusion, . . .
In summary, . . .
To sum up, . . .

Repetition/Rephrasing:
I'll say this again . . .
So again, let me repeat . . .
What you need to know is . . .
The most important thing to know is . . .
Let me say it in another way . . .

Giving Examples:
The first example is . . .
Let me give you an example . . .
Here's an example of what I mean . . .

Giving Causes or Reasons:
The first reason is . . .
This is due to . . .
This is because . . .

Giving Effects or Results:
As a result . . .
One consequence is . . .
Consequently . . .
Therefore, . . .
Another effect is . . .

Giving Definitions:
. . . which means . . .
In other words . . .
What that means is . . .
Another way to say that is . . .
Or . . .
That is . . .

Opinions:
I think . . .
In my opinion . . .
Here's what I believe is happening . . .

Signal to Stop Taking Notes:
You don't have to write all this down . . .
This information is in your book . . .
You can find this in your handout . . .
This won't be on your test . . .

Returning to a Previous Topic:
So, just to restate . . .
Back to . . .
Getting back to what we were saying . . .
To return to what we were talking about earlier . . .
OK, so to get back on topic . . .

Understanding Sidetracks
That reminds me . . .
By the way . . .
This is off the subject, but . . .
As an aside . . .
On a different topic . . .

Checking Understanding
Is that clear?
Did you get that?
Do you follow?

VOCABULARY INDEX

ability 14
abroad 44
accompany* .174
accurate 115
adopt 164
adult* 24
advance 134
ancestors 54
anxiety 194
appealing 164
aspect* 174
assertive 14
assess 85
assimilate 54
associate 184
attempt 174
attitude 54
attract 34
attribute* 194
awkward 194

balance 74
basic 184
basis 74
battle 164
behavior 4
burn 134

campaign 134
cancer 144
capture 104
cash 94
celebration 164
challenge* 24
characteristic 4
charity 94
charming 194
colony 24
community* 44
compromise 74
concept* 94
conclude* 14
conduct* 184
confirm* 184
consist* 154
constantly* 74
contemporary 115
conventional* 134
cooperate 84
crack 64
crucial* 144

deep 64
defend 24
defense 164
depend 24

deplete 124
depression 194
design* 134
device* 154
die 174
differ 194
discrimination .54
dissolve 64
distance 134
distinguish 174
diverse 84
drop 94

earn 85
edge 74
effective 85
emigrate* 44
empirical* 144
encourage 14
endure 164
enormous 124
enterprise 84
entrepreneur .85
equal 14
era 124
erode 64
essential 124
eternity 174
ethnic 54
eventually* 114
exceed* 174
external* 104
extract* 124
extraordinary 154
extroverted 194

fascinating 34
fear 184
feature* 74
female 4
feminine 4
form 64
formula* 114
fundamental* .94

gap 14
gain 115
gender* 4
generally 4
generation 54

hereditary 154

imitate 34
immigrant* 44
inevitable* 174
influence 104

inhibit* 144
insect 34
insight* 104
instinct 34
interaction 194
introverted 194
invade 164
investigate* 14

knowledge 14

lack 64
level 14

male 4
manufacture 134
masculine 4
mate 24
mechanism* 154
mention 115
minority 54
muscle 154

native 44
negative* 44

observation 104
obtain* 34
option* 74
original 44
otherwise 114
outcome* 94
owner 84

payment 94
peak 124
permanent 44
personality 184
phenomenon* 184
poem 104
political 104
positive 54
possibly 14
poverty 85
predator 24
previous* 114
print 114
priority* 124
promising 144
protect 64
publish* 104

radical* 154
raise 104
rare 64
rate 94
rational* 174

rebellious 164
refine* 134
reflect 104
remedy 144
reproduction .24
resemble 34
responsible 94
restore* 144
retain 54
reverse* 4
role* 4
ruins 164

scent 34
sector* 134
settle 54
severe 154
sharp 64
shelter 34
shift* 124
solution 134
speculate 184
stone 64
substitute* 124
sufficient* 74
surface 74
surround 164
symptom 144
synthetic 144

temporary* 44
tend 154
territory 24
threat 74
tough 174
transfer* 94
transmit* 154
trend* 44
trick 34
trigger* 184

universal 184
upset 194

variety 124
virus 144

wealth 84
weigh 24
whereas 115

*These words are on the Academic Word List (AWL). The AWL is a list of the 570 highest-frequency academic word families that regularly appear in academic texts. The list was compiled by researcher Averil Coxhead based on her analysis of a 3.5 million word corpus (Coxhead, 2000).

Critical Thinking

analyzing information, 1, 2–3, 21, 22–23, 41, 42–43, 47, 53, 55, 61, 62–63, 81, 82–83, 97, 101, 102–103, 107, 121, 122–123, 132–133, 135, 138, 141, 142–143, 161, 162–163, 181, 182–183, 190, 196
    for cause and effect, 67, 72
    for relevance, 27, 31, 120, 207
applying information from notes, 117
arguing a point of view, 133
assessing credibility of sources, 190, 200
brainstorming, 20, 33, 59, 75, 79, 98, 131, 150, 157
comparing ideas with a partner, 15
contrasting information about people, 151
creating questions about a video, 113
debating, 20
deducing meaning from context, 4, 14, 24, 26, 34, 44, 64, 65, 74, 94, 104, 114, 115, 132, 134, 144, 154, 174, 184, 204
demonstrating comprehension from listening, 87
developing materials for a promotional plan, 140
drawing conclusions, 170
evaluating claims, 150, 151, 153
evaluating reasons, 15
expressing and explaining opinions, 7, 13, 15, 32, 71, 87, 93, 196
identifying information, 30, 173
identifying the speaker's purpose, 86
interpreting statistics, 90
making group plan for research study, 40
making group presentations, 40, 60, 160, 180, 211
making inferences, 126, 127, 157
organizing presentations
    group presentations, 180
    organizing ideas, 40
about real conditionals, 149
relating content to personal experience, 150, 185, 193
relating information to personal experience, 1, 12
restating information from notes, 147
surveying a partner about personality, 195
synthesizing information, 65
telling a partner about a text, 109
understanding and using visuals/graphic organizers, 9, 11, 51, 56, 59, 67, 73, 124, 131, 196, 206, 214–215
    for building vocabulary, 208
    identifying information, 173
    interpreting graphs, 52
    interpreting maps, 2–3, 42–43, 164
    understanding and using flow charts, 215
    understanding timelines, 102–103, 171, 215
    using charts, 28, 33, 44, 51, 56, 67, 71, 73, 90, 130, 131, 157, 164, 188, 191, 196, 214
    using T-charts, 73, 131, 157, 214
    using Venn diagrams, 55, 214

understanding viewpoint and bias, 126, 127, 132–133
using context clues, 176
using new information in a discussion, 150
using new vocabulary, 25, 35, 55
using simple past vs. present perfect tense, 109–110

Grammar

adjectives
    comparisons with *as. . .as,* 90–91, 93
    with *enough, not enough* and *too,* 48–49
adverbs, comparisons with as. . .as, 90–91, 93
clauses
    adjective clauses, 30, 32
    adverb clauses with future time, 138
collocations, 175, 209
comparatives: *The -er, the -er,* 178
comparisons with *as. . .as,* 90–91, 93
critical thinking, 30, 138, 168
expressions for talking about rules and expectations, 8
future time with adverb clauses, 138
for making suggestions, 38
nouns
    comparisons with *as. . .as,* 90–91, 93
    with *enough, not enough* and *too,* 49
    specific and general, quantifiers with, 158
prefixes, 209
pronouns
    indefinite, 9–10
    in reported speech, 128
    usage, 10
quantifiers with specific and general nouns, 158
questions
    indirect, 98
    negative, 118–119
quoted speech, 128
reported speech, 128–129
so + adjective + *that,* 78, 79
suffixes, 209
time expressions in reported speech, 129
transition words, 29
used to + verb *vs. be used to* + noun, 198–199
verbs
    objects of verbs, 38
    past continuous tense, 58, 68–69, 73
    past perfect tense, 188–189
    past real unconditional, 168, 169
    real conditional, 148–149, 153
    in reported speech, 128
    simple past tense with past continuous tense, 68–69, 73
    simple past tense vs. present perfect tense, 109–110, 112
    transitive, 38

Language Function. *See also* Grammar; Pronunciation; Speaking

asking for reasons, 50

asking negative questions, 119

critical thinking, 8, 130, 150, 170, 190

discussing conclusions, 170

discussing health, 149–150

discussing past events, 190

discussing study habits, 198

explaining a process, 29

inclusive language, 18

interrupting and holding the floor, 179

making judgments about the future, 139

making sidetracks and returning to a topic, 106, 108–109, 207

making suggestions, 38, 159

reporting what someone has said, 129

responding to suggestions, 79

talking about historical events, 69

telling a personal history, 58

using indirect questions, 99

using numbers and statistics, 88

Listening

to articles, 86, 189, 194, 195

asking questions while listening, 146

to class question and answer session, 96–97

to club meeting, 126

collaboration after, 17, 27, 117

for context clues, 176

to conversations, 16–17, 26–27, 36–37, 66, 77, 94, 110, 136–137, 146, 147, 148, 156–157, 179, 196

critical thinking, 7, 27, 47, 67, 86, 87, 97, 107, 117, 126, 127, 196

deducing meaning from context, 26, 204

to descriptions, 76

for details, 7, 17, 26, 37, 47, 56, 77, 87, 117, 127, 147, 156, 177, 187, 196, 203–204

determining relevance of information, 207

discussion after, 176, 187, 195

discussion before, 16, 56

to discussions, 177

in class discussion session, 116–117

about a group project, 177

to documentaries, 67

for emphasis on key words, 36

to fast speech, 57

to guest speakers, 87

identifying the speaker's purpose, 86

to lectures, 7, 46–47, 106, 167

for main ideas, 7, 16, 26, 37, 46–47, 77, 87, 106, 116, 126, 156, 167, 177, 186, 196

making inferences, 126, 127, 157, 205

note-taking while, 6, 29, 67, 107, 117, 120, 206–207

predicting content, 46, 186, 202

prior knowledge and, 6, 56, 136, 154, 167

to radio interview, 186–187

recognizing a return to a previous topic, 207

recognizing a speaker's bias, 205

role-playing and, 197

self-reflection and, 37, 156, 167

sidetracks, 106, 108–109, 207

to statistics, 88

for stress patterns before suffixes, 28

structure of a presentation, 202–203, 206

summarizing after, 187, 206

tuning out distractions, 66, 67

using graphic organizers, 56, 67, 196

charts, 28, 67

using notes effectively, 207

viewing diagrams, 66

to vocabulary, 4, 14, 24, 34, 44, 54, 64, 74

Presentations

appropriate volume for, 131

checklists for, 218

collaboration for, 40, 60, 160, 180, 211

supporting co-presenters, 180

demonstrating knowledge of content, 213

engaging the audience, 213

evaluating claims, 150–151

finding reliable sources, 212

informal, 131

looking up while speaking, 159

making eye contact, 79

about a name, 11

outline for, 217

planning, 197, 200

practicing and timing, 100

preparing notes for, 11

reporting to class, 31, 51, 91, 140, 150

research for

finding information appropriate for topic, 212

library, 211

online, 80, 100, 212

role-playing, 159, 197

signal phrases for, 219

speaking clearly and comprehensibly, 212

storytelling, 59

summary presentations, 120

using reported speech, 130
using specific details, 40
visuals/graphic organizers for, 11, 60
  explaining timelines, 171
  using T-charts, 131

Pronunciation

can/can't, 17
contractions, 96
fast speech, 57, 137
intonation
  for choices and lists, 76–77
  for questions, 116
  for thought groups, 186
linking vowels with /y/ and /w/ sounds, 156, 157
reduced /h/ in pronouns, 137
stress patterns before suffixes, 28
voiding and syllable length, 166

Resources

checklists for presentations, 218
visuals/graphic organizers, 206, 214–215
  for building vocabulary, 208
  charts, 28, 214, 215, 216
  diagrams, 216
  flow charts, 215
  graphs, 216
  grids, 214
  maps, 216
  T-charts, 214
  timelines, 215
  Venn diagrams, 214

Speaking. *See also* Language function; Presentations; Pronunciation

asking and answering questions, 25, 48–49, 58, 70, 73, 85, 89,
  105, 145, 146, 149, 155, 158, 175, 185
  asking questions while listening, 147
  asking sensitive questions, 59
asking for repetition, 31
brainstorming, 20, 33, 75, 79, 98, 131, 150
collaboration, 39, 40, 51, 73, 111, 150
conducting a survey, 191
conversations, 37, 38, 39, 77, 95, 118, 129, 145, 148, 166, 170,
  179
critical thinking, 31, 71, 130, 151
debating, 20
discussion, 1, 2–3, 5, 8, 9, 10, 11, 13, 15, 18, 19, 21, 29, 30, 31,
  32, 37, 41, 45, 47, 49, 51, 53, 55, 56, 57, 61, 65, 67, 69,
  77, 79, 80, 81, 82–83, 84, 85, 86, 89, 90, 91, 93, 94, 98,

99, 101, 102–103, 107, 110, 111, 113, 114, 115, 116, 117,
  118, 119, 121, 122–123, 125, 127, 130, 132, 133, 135,
  136, 137, 139, 140, 141, 142–143, 146, 148, 149, 150,
  153, 157, 161, 162–163, 167, 170, 171, 176, 177, 181,
  182–183, 184, 187, 189, 190, 191, 194, 195, 197, 198
ending a conversation, 159
evaluating claims, 151
explaining causes and effects, 71
explaining processes, 93, 147
expressing emotions, 187
fast speech, 57
greeting a friend, 17
group summaries, 160
interviewing, 50
making comparisons, 91
making judgments about the future, 127
numbers, 88
persuading group members, 119
questions, 77
reduced words, 137
reporting to class, 5
role-playing, 98, 129, 133, 148, 159, 197
self-reflection, 77, 171, 179
sentences, 69, 91, 178
showing interest in what speaker is saying, 98
softening assertions, 139
staying neutral, 119
storytelling, 73, 178
talking about rules and expectations, 8, 19
useful phrases for everyday communication, 210–211
visuals/graphic organizers, 9, 11, 51, 59, 131

Test-Taking Skills

categorizing, 164
checking off correct answers, 37, 53, 64, 84, 85, 106, 164, 172
circling correct answers, 10, 16, 53, 64, 65, 67, 77, 156, 167, 172
fill in blanks, 17, 18, 25, 26, 35, 38, 39, 54, 66, 73, 84, 85, 88,
  95, 97, 104, 105, 112, 113, 125, 137, 145, 155, 165, 177,
  185, 198
giving reasons, 15
labeling, 27
matching, 8, 15, 24, 32, 44, 66, 72, 75, 92, 124, 126, 134, 144,
  152, 153, 155, 164, 172, 175, 185, 192, 194
multiple choice, 16, 26, 37, 66, 87, 92, 107, 167
note-taking, 97
numbering steps, 93
ordering items, 124
ranking items, 31, 187, 190
sentence completion, 19, 30, 49, 53, 58, 64, 75, 153, 154, 158,
  168, 173

short answer questions, 16, 33, 45, 68, 77, 87, 96, 97, 111, 147, 153, 196

true/false questions, 17, 25, 93, 110, 113, 127, 132, 154, 157, 193

underlining correct responses, 28, 67

Topics

Emotions and Personality, 181–200

Fascinating Planet, 61–80

Gender and Society, 1–20

Human Migration, 41–60

The Legacy of Ancient Civilizations, 161–180

Making a Living, Making a Difference, 81–100

After Oil, 121–140

Reproducing Life, 21–40

Traditional and Modern Medicine, 141–160

A World of Words, 101–120

Viewing

The Business of Cranberries, 92–93

Canadian Oil Sands, 132–133

collaboration after, 33, 73

critical thinking, 12, 13, 32, 53, 72, 93, 113, 132–133, 153, 173, 193

for details, 13

dictionary use, 72, 152, 192

discussion after, 93, 113, 133, 173

The Giant's Causeway, 72–73

Lost Temple of the Mayans, 172–173

meaning from context, 132

note-taking, 13, 33, 73

for numbers, 73

photos, 2–3, 22–23, 45, 74, 82–83, 91, 102–103, 122–123, 139, 142–143, 162–163, 165, 169, 181, 182–183

predicting content, 152

prior knowledge, 92, 172, 192

role-playing after, 133

self-reflection, 32

Sigmund Freud, 192–193

Sleepy Hollow, 112–113

Turkish Germany, 52–53

Turtle Excluder, 32–33

understanding main idea ideas, 33

visuals/graphic organizers
    charts, 33, 71, 73
    diagrams, 66
    graphs, 52
    maps, 2–3, 74, 164
    timelines, 171

Wild Health, 152–153

Wodaabe, 12–13

Vocabulary

building vocabulary, 4, 14, 24, 34, 44, 54, 64, 84, 85, 94, 114, 115, 124, 134, 164, 194
    experimenting with new vocabulary for, 208
    graphic organizers for, 208
    using new words for, 208
    vocabulary journal for, 208

critical thinking, 15, 25, 35, 55, 65, 75, 132, 185, 195

dictionary use, 12, 32, 35, 44, 64, 72, 84, 85, 92, 94, 114, 115, 152, 164, 192, 194, 209

discussion, 184, 185, 194

to give reasons, 15

graphic organizers, 55, 208

meaning from context, 4, 14, 24, 34, 44, 64, 65, 74, 94, 104, 114, 115, 132, 134, 144, 154, 174, 184

note-taking, 55

prefixes, 209

self-reflection, 54

suffixes, 28, 209

using vocabulary, 5, 15, 25, 35, 45, 55, 65, 75, 85, 95, 105, 115, 125, 135, 145, 155, 165, 175, 185, 195

Writing

brainstorming, 59, 157, 159

collaboration, 39, 40, 117, 140

collocations in, 175, 209

conversations, 39, 159

details for a story, 59

group plan for research study, 40

letters, 33

lists, 78, 152, 159

notes
    for slides, 47
    for speaking, 11

note-taking, 6, 9, 13, 20, 27, 29, 33, 45, 51, 55, 67, 73, 97, 107, 108, 117, 120, 206–207

numbers in words, 88

organizing ideas, 120

promotional campaign, 140

questionnaires, 50

questions, 117

sentences, 48, 78, 93, 138, 145, 169, 192

visuals/graphic organizers, 59
    charts, 33, 44, 51, 56, 67, 73, 157, 164, 188, 191, 196

PHOTOS (continued)

89: AP Photo/Mary Ann Chastain, 91: Chris Hill/National Geographic Image Collection, 91: Justin Guarigila/National Geographic Image Collection, 91: Aaron Huey/National Geographic Image Collection, 91: Michael & Patricia Fogden/Minden Pictures/Getty Images, 91: AP Photo/Mary Ann Chastain, 92: Rich Reid/National Geographic Image Collection, 92: Chris Johns/National Geographic Image Collection, 93: Bill Curtsinger/National Geographic Image Collection, 93: Sean Sherstone/iStockphoto.com, 95: Jonas Bendiksen/National Geographic Image Collection, 96: Annie Griffiths/National Geographic Image Collection, 97: Roger Leo/PhotoLibrary, 99: Noah Seelam/AFP/Getty Images, 99: Amy White & Al Petteway/National Geographic Image Collection, 99: Michael Melford/National Geographic Image Collection, 99: Shehzad Noorani/PhotoLibrary, 100: James P. Blair/National Geographic Image Collection, 100: Per-Anders Pettersson/Getty Images News/Getty Images, 100: Maria Stenzel/National Geographic Image Collection, 101: Kate Thompson/National Geographic Image Collection, 102–103: Chris Hill/National Geographic Image Collection, 102: Erich Lessing/Art Resource, NY, 102: Sam Abell/National Geographic Image Collection, 102: INTERFOTO/Alamy, 104: Michael S. Yamashita/National Geographic Image Collection, 104: Getty Images/Photos.com/Jupiter Images, 104: Snark/Art Resource, NY, 106: Michael S. Yamashita/National Geographic Image Collection, 107: trufero/Shutterstock.com, 108: Gilbert M. Grosvenor/National Geographic Stock, 108: SAM ABELL/National Geographic Image Collection, 109: Pali Rao/iStockphoto, 111: Bates Littlehales/National Geographic Image Collection, 112: Fotolistic, 2010/Shutterstock.com, 112: Library of Congress, 113: Paula Stephens/Shutterstock.com, 114: Bob Krist/National Geographic Image Collection, 114: Diana Lundin/iStockphoto, 115: Krista Rossow/National Geographic Image Collection, 115: Guy Cali/PhotoLibrary, 116: Michael S. Yamashita/National Geographic Image Collection, 117: Michael Newman/PhotoEdit, 118: Cotton Coulson/National Geographic Image Collection, 119: Tino Soriano/National Geographic Image Collection, 120: O. Louis Mazzatenta/National Geographic Image Collection, 120: Ira Block/National Geographic Image Collection, 121: Sarah Leen/National Geographic Image Collection, 122–123: Sarah Leen/National Geographic Image Collection, 123: Sarah Leen/National Geographic Image Collection, 123: Greg Dale/National Geographic Image Collection, 125: Joel Sartore/National Geographic Image Collection, 126: AP Photo, 127: James P. Blair/National Geographic Image Collection, 128: Joel Sartore/National Geographic Image Collection, 129: Mikhail/Shutterstock, 131: Andrew Penner/iStockphoto.com, 132: Carr Clifton/Minden Pictures, 132: Peter Essick/National Geographic Image Collection, 133: Peter Essick/National Geographic Image Collection, 134: Michael Klinec/Alamy, 135: Sarah Leen/National Geographic Image Collection, 136: Robert Clark/National Geographic Image Collection, 137: Robert Clark/National Geographic Image Collection, 139: Michael Melford/National Geographic Image Collection, 139: Mattias Klum/National Geographic Image Collection, 139: Eric Gevaert/Shutterstock.com, 139: James A. Sugar/National Geographic Image Collection, 141: Lynn Johnson/National Geographic Image Collection, 142-143: Abranowitzham/National Geographic Image Collection, 142: Avava, 2010/Shutterstock.com, 142: Reika/Shutterstock.com, 142: kzww/Shutterstock.com, 142: Mark Thiessen/National Geographic Image Collection, 142: Lynn Johnson/National Geographic Image Collection, 144: Lynn Johnson/National Geographic Image Collection, 144: Lynn Johnson/National Geographic Image Collection, 144: Cyril Ruoso/JH EDITORIAL/MINDEN PICTURES, 146: Jupiter Images/Getty Images, Robert S. Clark/National Geographic Image Collection, 147: Sam Abell/National Geographic Image Collection, 148: Ira Block/National Geographic Image Collection, 149: w49/ZUMA Press/Newscom, 150: Eric Nathan/Alamy, 151: Monkey Business Images/Shutterstock, 151: kali9/iStockphoto.com, 151: Dmitriy Shironosov, 2010/Shutterstock.com, 151: Palmer Kane LLC/Shutterstock.com, 152: Winfried Wisniewski/FOTO NATURA/National Geographic Image Collection, 152: Ian Nichols/National Geographic Image Collection, 153: Paul Damien/National Geographic Image Collection, 153: Steve Winter/National Geographic Image Collection, 154: Karen Kasmauski/National Geographic Image Collection, 155: Ted V. Tamburo/National Geographic Image Collection, 157: Mark Thiessen/National Geographic Image Collection, 159: craftvision/iStockphoto.com, 159: Richard Nowitz/National Geographic Image Collection, 159: arteretum/Shutterstock.com, 161: Kenneth Garrett/National Geographic Image Collection, 162–163: Gordon Wiltsie/National Geographic Image Collection, 162: Jim Richardson/National Geographic Image Collection, 162: Steve Mccurry/National Geographic Image Collection, 162: Richard Barnes/National Geographic Image Collection, 165: Joe Mcnally/National Geographic Image Collection, 165: Jim Richardson/National Geographic Image Collection, 165: Jim Richardson/National Geographic Image Collection, 167: Jim Richardson/National Geographic Image Collection, 168: Robert Clark/National Geographic Image Collection, 169: Robert Clark/National Geographic Image Collection, 170: Robert Clark/National Geographic Image Collection, 171: Bikeriderlondon, 2010/Shutterstock.com, 172: Joe Scherschel/National Geographic Image Collection, 172: Kenneth Garrett/National Geographic Image Collection, 173: Kenneth Garrett/National Geographic Image Collection, 173: W.E. Garrett/National Geographic Image Collection, 174: shalunts/Shutterstock, 174: Richard Barnes/National Geographic Image Collection, 174: Richard Barnes/National Geographic Image Collection, 176: Richard Barnes/National Geographic Image Collection, 178: Dean Conger/National Geographic Image Collection, 179: Ira Block/National Geographic Image Collection, 180: Steve Bower/Shutterstock, 180–181: Kris Leboutillier/National Geographic Image Collection, 182–183: Tino Soriano/National Geographic Image Collection, 183: Brian J. Skerry/National Geographic Image Collection, 183: John Warburton-Lee Photography/Alamy, 184: Cary Wolinsky/National Geographic Image Collection, 184: Cary Wolinsky/National Geographic Image Collection, 184: Cary Wolinsky/National Geographic Image Collection, 184: Cary Wolinsky/National Geographic Image Collection, 184: Cary Wolinsky/National Geographic Image Collection, 184: Cary Wolinsky/National Geographic Image Collection, 184: Cary Wolinsky/National Geographic Image Collection, 186: Cary Wolinsky/National Geographic Image Collection, 187: Raymond Gehman/National Geographic Image Collection, 189: Joel Sartore/National Geographic Image Collection, 189: Joel Sartore/National Geographic Image Collection, 190: James P. Blair/National Geographic Image Collection, 192: UPPA/Photoshot, 192: Keystone/Hulton Archive/Getty Images, 192: Bruce Ayres/Stone/Getty Images, 193: Andre Goncalves/Shutterstock.com, 194: Zagorodnaya/Shutterstock.com, 195: istockphoto.com, 196: Olga Lyubkina/Shutterstock.com, 200: Jozef Sedmak, 2010/Shutterstock.com.

MAP AND ILLUSTRATION

2–3: National Geographic Maps; 7: National Geographic Maps; 12: National Geographic Maps; 23: National Geographic Maps; 32: National Geographic Maps; 42–43: National Geographic Maps; 46: Mapping Specialists, Ltd. Madison, WI USA; 52: National Geographic Maps; 63: National Geographic Maps; 66: Fernando Baptista/Sean McNaughton/National Geographic Image Collection; 72: Mapping Specialists, Ltd. Madison, WI USA; 73: Mark Snyder for American Aritsits Rep., Inc; 74: National Geographic Maps; 76: National Geographic Maps; 89: National Geographic Maps; 112: Mapping Specialist, Ltd, Madision, WI, USA; 132: National Geographic Maps; 164: National Geographic Maps; 169: National Geographic Maps; 170: National Geographic Maps.